Chief

My Journey Thru Iraq at the Peak of War

SCOTT H. DEARDUFF

Mary

Thanks for being a patriotic American. Your support of our men and women of the Armed Forces.

Scott Dearduff
Red Tail Chief

Fourth Edition

ISBN: 1484181379
ISBN-13:978-1484181379

DEDICATION

This book is dedicated to the men and women of the 332d Air Expeditionary Wing, Balad Air Base Iraq who served and sacrificed from July 2006 – July 2007.

And

To those 13 Airmen who made the ultimate sacrifice on the battlefields of Iraq from July 2006 – July 2007
May we never forget?

Finally

To my family, who stood by me while I served yet another combat tour in Iraq. They held down the home front while I served forward…but certainly they had the tougher role to complete.

CONTENTS

ACKNOWLEDGMENTS

I would like to thank several people who helped me complete this labor of love. During a four month period of time immediately following my retirement from the U.S. Air Force, I decided to meet the challenge of writing this book. The effort took several hours out of each day that should have been spent with my wife and kids who had been without me for more than 1200 days since the terrorist attacks on America in September 2011. Once again they stood by me as I took on this mission to document this year in Iraq as part of the 332d Air Expeditionary Wing, the modern day Tuskegee Airmen. Special thanks for my puppy dog Bella who walked with me every day as I formulated the chapters and sat by my feet each day as I put them on paper. She was faithful and supportive, never questioning my intentions.

Others who helped contribute to this effort include, Don Dewsnap, Lynn Brennard, David Ellis, Phil Rand, and General Robin Rand. Special thanks to Dianne Dearduff for her dedicated work on the cover of this book.

Finally, a specific thanks to my wife who is the best part of my life. She was with me through every step of this process, from the actual events, to the long talks about what happened, to the close scrutiny we placed on the actual words in each chapter. Her support made this effort worth every moment spent putting it together.

INTRODUCTION

On 21 October, 2011, the President of the United States declared that the military operations in Iraq were over and all of the remaining 40,000 US military members would be out of the country by 31 December, 2011. For most Americans this was a historic announcement, and brought joy to the general public around the world. Finally, the war in Iraq would be over and the people of the United States would be satisfied, only now waiting to get the troops home from Afghanistan. But it wasn't that easy? The war in Iraq was not really over.

Most of the American casualties during the Iraq war happened after the announcement in 2003 that combat operations were over. Nobody knew then how the Insurgency would rise and drag us into one of the longest wars in our nation's history. Few Americans know the whole truth about the war in Iraq and what happened behind the scenes, because the media decided what they reported. There were hundreds, maybe thousands of personal stories that impacted the lives of the Iraqi people, none of which the general public ever heard about. I plan to tell a portion of that story and hope many of my brothers and sisters in arms will do the same in the years to come.

The toll of war: 4,424 American military members killed in action as of 2016. For their families, friends and units, this war is not over and never will be. For 32,226 Americans who were wounded in action, and for countless thousands who have hidden wounds, this war is also not over and likely never will be. More than 500 Americans suffered injuries resulting in amputations, which does not count amputations of toes and fingers. For them, life will always be different, and the challenges will never stop. For many this was may never be over.

The story in this book is a true account of my life and mission as the Command Chief Master Sergeant for the 332d

Air Expeditionary Wing, Balad Air Base in Iraq from July 2006 through July 2007. The Command Chief position is the senior enlisted position in a wing organization and reports directly to the Wing Commander, normally a general officer. The scope of responsibility for this position included leadership for more than 8,000 Airmen serving in more than 50 locations. The selection process for this position was tough, but certainly worth the trouble to be given this opportunity. To serve in this critical leadership position gave me a unique perspective during the war. Although I served other combat tours before and after, this one was the most impactful of my professional life.

I prepared myself for this battle over the first 20 years of my career, and vowed when I got the chance to impact a war, I planned to win…at all costs. The only thing I did not expect from this war was the personal emotional roller coaster I would experience following the tragic loss of life suffered by our wing. I knew war came with tragedy, but to lose so many close to me, friends, family and comrades, was devastating.

The stories in this book reflect a true personal accounting of my year in Iraq from 4 July 2006 through 4 July 2007. Records reflect the worst 12 months of Operation Iraqi Freedom were June 2006 to Jun 2007. Statistically, 11 of our 12 months on this tour were completed during the worst period of the war (the peak of war). The names and places used in this book are true. If a name was omitted, that was done intentionally to avoid any humiliation to the person involved. The book contains no classified information or any information relevant to an enemy of the United States.

What this book does include are the stories of some great American Airmen who served beyond the call of duty. It includes the personal stories of 13 Airmen who were killed in action from our unit during the year, along with the stories of some of the wounded in action. It also includes the story of an American Soldier serving in the 82d Airborne Division, a family friend, who made the ultimate sacrifice for his nation. It's a first-hand personal accounting compiled from my notes taken throughout the year. I have also combined my personal recollection with interviews and accounts from fellow Airmen who served in the wing. Everything in this book is based on my own personal perspective and some details may differ from other warriors who were there. None of the details were altered purposely, and any dispute of the facts will simply be considered a difference of opinion.

This story is also about me--a determined warrior Airman, conflicted between love of family and love of nation. The tour and these stories found within came on the heels of previous deployments into Iraq at Baghdad International Airport in the fall of 2003 and in southern Iraq at Tallil Air Base near Nasiriya through May of 2004. I was called to take this duty on and did so voluntarily, because I am a warrior, and this was my war.

This book and my story are about the global war on terrorism (GWOT)—it was my war to fight and win. It was about making sure the GWOT remained an away game so my family, and the families of those I know and love, could go about their lives living free of worry that a terrorist organization could come into their hometown and create modern terror. It was about ensuring the freedom we enjoy as Americans in the greatest country in the world.

Don't be mistaken, it's not my own personal war to wage alone, for there have been literally hundreds of thousands of men and women, military, civilian and contractors who have served in this war. There were forces from across the world, representing foreign nations in large and small parts. Too many gave the last full measure of life on the battlefields of Iraq. Never forget that it's their war, and a war that will impact their families for many years to come.

Basically, this was about my desire to serve in combat where I could lead Airmen and serve with a leader I highly respected. I could not escape the daily feeling that I had more to give, more to accomplish on the battlefield, and it just kept drawing me back.

Proving oneself as a combat leader is something many of us in the US military strive to do. It's a proving ground, but not a training ground. There is a fine line between who goes and who does not. Throughout the entire Operation Iraqi Freedom there were only six Airmen who served yearlong tours as the 332d Air Expeditionary Wing Command Chief in Iraq.

The history of the 332d comes from the famed Tuskegee Airmen of World War II fame. The wing banner was carried forward from the great legacy of those Tuskegee Airmen who fought oppression in our own country and they fought valiantly against worldwide terror. They were the first all-black pilots and maintainers who were formed in Tuskegee Alabama as a test program when blacks were not considered qualified to fly aircraft. Not only did they prove they could maintain and fly planes, but they took the famed P-51 Mustang and accumulated an incredible record of performance. Among their many claims to fame was the flawless record of escorting bombers on long runs over the combat battlefields.

The 332d Wing lineage which began in 1942 was reactivated in Kuwait in 1998 and subsequently moved to Iraq in 2003. The original location of the wing headquarters was at Tallil Air Base located near the town of An Nasiriya. In May 2004 the wing headquarters was moved to Balad Air Base located 60 miles north of Baghdad. Balad air Base was the former home of the Iraqi Air Force Academy and had much better infrastructure for the wing to use. Balad Air Base had a long history of being attacked by local insurgents dating to the early days when the former regime took the land to form the base from local farmers without permission. Those locals would not be any happier that Americans were now using the base and the amount of noise from aircraft would increase.

Although the wing's mission was a little different than in World War II, the result needed to be the same. We needed to fight a determined enemy who wanted to terrorize others around the world. The move to Balad Air Base increased the wing's ability to respond to any corner of the country within minimal time. The central location of the base also provided a great location to house convoy teams that were moving north and south and required lodging and supplies. The decision to use Balad Air Base proved to be a highly effective decision.

During the period of this story, our daily missions included escorting convoys on the ground, tracking insurgent fighters, and responding to reports of hostile activities. In this book you will read some bits and pieces of the missions and gain an understanding of the critical nature of the US Air Force in modern warfare. You will come to know stories not told by the news media.

There was no enemy in the air. However, the wing and its Airmen were charged with hundreds of flying missions each month with specific objectives to accomplish. Behind the flying operation, there were many Airmen who maintained aircraft, fueled the jets, provided Intelligence support, weather data, life support, and an entire host of medical and mission support functions. The 332d wing was filled with professional Airmen across the spectrum of operations, including active duty, Air National Guard and the Air Force Reserves. Air Force units were deployed in teams ranging from the 13-person security forces squad to entire maintenance and operations squadrons with more than 200 people assigned. Most Airmen served 120-day deployments once they arrived in country. Typically only the senior leaders were assigned to 365-day deployments.

We flew C-130 and C-17 cargo aircraft, HH-60 Pavehawk helicopters for rescue missions, F-16 and A-10 fighter jets and even the Predator, unmanned aerial vehicles for Intelligence, Surveillance and Reconnaissance.

Unlike most previous conflicts, the Air Force was tasked to support Army and Marine forces directly through the "In-Lieu of" (ILO) tasking process. In Lieu of became the term of the day but would later come under scrutiny and be changed. It simply meant Airmen and Sailors were called upon to support missions traditionally handled by the Army and Marines in combat. In some areas, we already had the trained Air Force Specialties to handle the task. Those Airmen attended "Just in Time" training to get ready for the specific missions they would perform. In other areas, we had to send Airmen to training courses to provide the combat skills necessary. Prior to the Iraq war and the tasking of USAF Airmen for ILO missions, only select career fields trained on combat skills. With the onset of ILO taskings, every Airman needed to complete combat skills training and were subject to participating in ground combat missions outside of the controlled environment of a forward base. Airmen assigned to ILO missions served on 179-day deployments. This was a cultural change for the Air Force and it had support through the chain of command.

As you read this book you will notice many of the casualties discussed are from the ILO taskings. This is not a reflection on the capabilities of the US Air Force, but more a true indicator of how dangerous the missions were that Airmen performed outside the wire (outside the confines of the protected bases and forward operating locations).

A huge part of my story includes the time and energy spent with the ILO forces. These Airmen held incredible bonds with the Soldiers and Marines they supported. It was important for me to show my willingness to take on the same missions they did, and never ask them to do anything I was not willing to do myself. Over time I started calling this leadership philosophy "walking the mile."

Lastly, this book is about a hidden enemy many of us have and are dealing with. Post-Traumatic Stress and the disorder many are suffering from is a real thing. It's not some catch phrase people use to get help from the Veteran's

Administration when they separate or retire. It's a problem many have, and yet they don't recognize the symptoms. PTSD will negatively affect society for many years to come. I have spent many hours and days talking with, listening to and helping my fellow Soldiers, Sailors, Airmen and Marines deal with their own PTSD and hope to have brought comfort to them.

Writing this book was very therapeutic. It will never take away the constant feeling of looking over my shoulder and wondering who is coming up behind me. It will not change my reaction to loud noises. Life is different for us following combat action in Iraq as we try to blend into a normal society. An entire generation of combat warriors will come back home and look for their chance to integrate back into society.

Chief

Dearduff

1
BACK TO IRAQ

31 July 2004

We rolled into town on a gorgeous Arizona summer afternoon, the temperature hovering around 110 degrees. My executive assistant was waiting for us at the gate and she had meticulously handled all the details of our arrival. Immediately we found Luke Air Force Base a friendly place.

My assignment to this position was achieved earlier in my career than expected. Many fortunate events led to this point, including several combat deployments as a Security Forces Chief Master Sergeant. The family knew this would be different from any other assignment we had been to, and there was no way we could anticipate all we were about to encounter.

Later in the evening the new boss arrived to greet us and go out for a casual dinner and enjoy some "get to know each other" conversation. His wife Kim was out of town, as she was spending time with their daughter and son-in-law preparing for the birth of their first grandchild. Brigadier General select Robin Rand was a kind human being who immediately made us feel welcome and at ease. We also took easily to him.

Even though we had only spoken on the phone, talking with the General seemed like we had known each other for years. From the day he called to offer the position it was easy to tell he was a special leader. He asked to speak to Mags on the phone before we discussed what the future held. I listened in and heard him ask her, "Are you ready to come to Luke?" That statement showed that he cared about family and wanted her to be a critical part of the team. This assignment would be a great learning opportunity and I was excited about the possibilities in front of us.

We dined at a local restaurant that served authentic Mexican food. A man with a guitar approached and asked if we would like a song played for us. Wow, another great welcome to Arizona, our own private musician for dinner. We agreed, he played, and then promptly stuck out his hand and said, "Five dollars!" I said, "Five dollars for one song, you must be kidding, how about another one." To which he replied, "Another five dollars." General Rand said, "You had better just pay him and be done before this gets real expensive." It was obvious he had a sense of humor.

We enjoyed hearing about his expectations for our tour at Luke AFB and his personal philosophies about leadership. I wanted to hear about his previous tour at Kunsan Air Base in Korea where he was the wing commander since I had never been stationed in Korea. But General Rand knew I had just returned from a combat tour in Iraq, and he was more interested in hearing about my experience.

As the night ended the General said, "Chief, I hope that my next assignment allows me to serve and lead in Iraq. And if I am given that honor, it would be great to have you with me." We all hesitated momentarily and I pondered what he had just said. My response to my new commander on day one; "Of course I will, General, I love serving in combat."

The look on Mags' face was piercing me as the words came out. As we arrived back at the base she asked, "Are you serious? You want to go back again? How many times do you think you can tempt fate and come back home alive?"

I said, "Well, if General Rand is assigned as the wing commander at Balad, I am very serious and I would love the opportunity to serve with him in combat. But the likelihood of that happening is slim to none. He has just completed a tour as a wing commander, is now filling his second tour as a wing commander, and nobody, well almost nobody, would be given a third wing command opportunity in a row, especially not one serving directly in combat. That would be too much stress on any one person, and would certainly not be an expectation placed on any leader by the Air Force."

Mags did not like it, but I knew she would support me for any mission, combat or otherwise, just as she had in the past. In the back of her mind, she knew I was going back to Iraq. She knew being in combat is where my leadership thrived and where I felt professionally fulfilled. She also knew I considered the war in Iraq as "my war" to fight and win. She knew there was more to accomplish and I would do whatever it took to contribute to the best of my ability.

She was quiet for the remainder of the evening. Mags and I focused on the opportunity we had directly in front of us, to serve with General and Kim Rand. We were ready for this new level of responsibility, and looked forward to the challenges it would bring.

10 April 2006:

Rumors were swirling around the building that something was going on inside General Rand's office. I figured it was about his next command assignment so I let myself in to see what the commotion was about. When his phone call was complete, the General said, "Chief, I got the call and I have been asked to lead Airmen in combat at Balad this summer. I know you said you would go with me, but I am not going to hold you to it, I know you have been there and proven yourself, and you don't need to go back."

I stood silently for a moment. I said, "General, I told you I would go, and anything less than keeping my promise to you would be unacceptable." Over this past 20 months we had grown very close through some difficult times. The pressure of critical incidents brought us close under the stress of life and death situations; we were nearly blood brothers already and had not set foot on the field of battle.

He said, "Chief, really, you can skip this one and find me a suitable chief to go in your place." I said to the General, "Sir, there is nobody who knows you better and is more willing to go and serve beside you. And besides it would be my highest honor to be your wingman for this next year."

I knew this would be hard on Mags. I knew the stress of being a family with someone in combat would come back at her extremely hard. But this was my calling; it's what I needed to do. I knew deep down inside I had not fulfilled all of my personal goals for leading in combat, and there was much I had left to give. Telling Mags and the kids would be the hardest part, but they needed to know immediately and begin preparing for the next disruption of our family.

Her initial reaction to my announcement was exactly what I expected it to be. She was upset, and rightfully so. How many times is she supposed to accept that I was going back to combat. There were stressful days around the house and many conversations on the subject. Finally, after a few days and many thoughts, I found the right words to explain my desire to return to Iraq and complete my mission. This had nothing to do with wanting to leave the family or the comforts of home, this was simply a warrior needing to be at war. She accepted my need and pledged her full and faithful support for what I was about to do. I felt relieved and appreciated her support. It was time to get back to Iraq.

2 July 2006:

We entered a holding pattern at 10,000 feet above ground level circling the airfield. This was a normal pattern when entering a combat airfield, but especially at Balad Air Base which regularly came under attack during both daylight and darkness. On this particular day our C-12 transport plane, carrying General Rand, me and Lieutenant Matt Robinson, the General's son in law, was placed in the holding pattern because the airfield had just come under attack from indirect fire just outside base perimeter to the northeast. We had no idea if the attack was successful, caused any injuries or damage, but we knew one thing; this was not going to be an easy one-year tour, and the enemy would get a vote in how it went. We were not even on the ground to complete our 48 hours of turnover with the outgoing leadership team and we were already under attack.

Thoughts began racing through my head about my wife and kids. I was frozen in time, wondering what they would do if something happened to me during this tour. Where would they go, what would their future hold? My thoughts would not leave my wife. What would she do alone? I met Mags in 1982 when we were both stationed in the Netherlands. Two kids from different parts of the country had joined the Air Force, neither wanting to be assigned overseas, but both ending up at the same duty location at nearly the same time, and working closely together. It seemed like fate would have a hand in our future.

I came from a family of six, Catholic by practice, and sports-oriented. The second child of the four kids, I was the odd one out. I had no plans to attend college, and a not-likely baseball future left me with few options. At the suggestion of my father, I joined the Air Force to start a career, or at least learn a little about life and make a man out of myself before it was too late.

Mags was quite different. A very active member of the Marine Corps Junior ROTC program through high school, she had every intention to join the Marines following high school and become a police officer. When she found out they would not let her fulfill that dream she found the Air Force recruiter. At the time the Air Force was accepting females into the Security Police career field on the Law Enforcement side, so she was hooked.

I was in place at Soesterberg Air Base on her first day on camp, and I tried my hardest to get her attention. Initially she wanted nothing to do with me and thought I was overbearing. This feisty young lady with an Irish temper and Philly attitude, thought I was overbearing?

Somehow I had to gain the full attention of this woman, because the attraction was too strong. It took some time, and some convincing that I was right for her, and I even had to pass the test of talking with her Irish parents on the phone before she would take me seriously. As you can imagine, I was a little intimidated. But here I was some 24 years later having my full thoughts turning toward the woman I fell in love with back in 1982. I could not help wondering what would become of her life if I were killed in action and she received a knock on the door.

Reality snapped me back to the present as we suddenly descended and the captain told us to buckle up, as it would be a fast approach and there was no time for loitering. We landed on the massive air field and a sigh of relief came over us and we looked at each other without saying a word. We both knew this was the beginning of a difficult year, but we wanted it no matter the cost.

I reflected on a conversation I had with the General's wife Kim at the airport before our departure, during a final embrace. Over the previous two years we had formed a great relationship and there was a strong bond of trust between us. She knows I would be with the General at every turn. She whispered softly into my ear, "Chief, take care of him for me and bring him home." I held her close and assured her we would be safe and we would be coming home together.

As the C-12 completed its taxi into the parking spot, we noticed a small crowd gathered to greet us. Not expecting this, we quickly lost track of each other. Being separated was not an issue since we knew each other so well. I could complete his sentences, and he always knew my train of thought…to a fault, because we were so comfortable knowing what each other was thinking that we would often move out without checking with the other beforehand.

On this occasion the General was whisked away to get his initial briefing from the outgoing General on the mission and operational matters for the wing. Chief Layton Clark was my predecessor and already a friend from previous assignments. He had a different plan already set up for me and we immediately moved out. He quickly made me realize the importance of building strong relationships around this large base with a military and civilian population of more than 16,000. He introduced me to key leaders and showed me where they worked, so in the days to come I could visit and form my own relationships with them.

Our last stop of the day was with my new Army counterpart, a hard core command sergeant major with a very strong personality. Command Sergeant Major (CSM) Dave Wood welcomed me into his unit and handed me his traditional welcome cigar. He directed me to join him in having a stogy to end this long combat day.

I thanked him, but held onto the cigar as I would not be lighting up with him tonight. At first he took offense. Then, after a short conversation, he realized that I was a man of my own convictions and I was going to stand my ground. He and Chief Clark enjoyed cigars and we all talked about the great things going on around the base. Most of the stories were about the fantastic contribution of the Airmen assigned to the 332d Air Expeditionary Wing.

The strength of their relationship was obvious. I was hopeful I could forge the same one over time. I was proud of Chief Clark, Brigadier General Frank Gorenc and their leadership team. They poured their hearts and souls into the mission and they were leaving us in a great position to succeed considering the challenges in front of us.

As the night came to a close I had a good feeling about fulfilling the mission. I felt proud to be taking over from Chief Clark and holding up my promise to maintain the high standards they had worked so hard to establish. We drove back to the living compound where my quarters were located. Along the way he showed me his personal challenge coin which represented him well. He gave me the last box so I could have some time to design my own and get them ordered. I was grateful for his forethought.

Challenge coins had really grown in popularity in the US Military in recent years. A command chief was authorized to purchase coins and present them to deserving warriors who earned recognition. There would likely be many deserving people throughout the year who earned this level of recognition, so I knew we had to get on it right away.

The living compound for senior leaders was known as Red Tail Village. There were twelve individual trailers located inside the village. The compound was surrounded by 12-foot-high concrete barriers used to protect us from rockets and mortars. It would provide a private setting during the few hours of retreat we could fit into each day.

Once inside my quarters I stopped, took a long breath and let out a laugh. Chief Clark looked at me and laughed because he knew what I was thinking. Both of us had served as Security Force Chiefs during previous deployments and the best we ever got was a smaller ratio of men in our tent than the others. Seeing my own private space with my own bathroom for the year was a little surprising.

When he turned on the television and showed me there were 4 American channels, including an all-sports channel; I was speechless. During previous overseas assignments the Armed Forces Network kept me in tuned with my favorite sports teams and the big games. Now, even in the heart of combat, I could retreat to my quarters and watch a game from home, an escape during this coming year.

We spent a few hours talking about what would lie ahead for me over the next twelve months, and what we needed to accomplish in the remaining hours. Sleep was not a priority and we would only get four hours tonight before attending our first gathering at 0600.

The next day and a half was event filled and the time flew by as he explained my new responsibilities in this wing. He introduced me to so many people that I eventually lost track. Chief Clark assured me I would have time to established relationships with all of them. He said they would be calling in the days and weeks to follow.

4 July 2006:

Morning came quickly and it was time for the 332d Air Expeditionary Wing Change of Command Ceremony.

The wing took its heraldry from the mighty 332nd Fighter Group from World War II, the legendary Tuskegee Airmen. These Airmen were the first unit of all black aviators, specifically chosen to form at Tuskegee Field in Alabama. In addition to learning to fly, they also had to prove to the nation that blacks were just as capable as whites of being successful aviators. The Tuskegee Airmen gained fame for never losing a bomber in combat while escorting them over the battlefields of Europe. They famously painted the tail flash on their P-51 Mustangs bright red, earning the nickname, "Red Tails" during combat in World War II. We were the recipients of their legacy...the modern day Tuskegee Airmen, and we were proud to be the Red Tails. All of the senior leaders in the wing adopted calls signs for radio communications starting with Red Tail 1, assigned to the commanding general. The command chief master sergeant call sign was "Red Tail Chief."

Arriving at the 332d AEW headquarters building before the ceremony, a young noncommissioned officer (NCO) walked into my office and introduced himself as Staff Sergeant Jackson. He told me he was happy to be my executive assistant, but he was not sure what I needed from him. Rather than sit him down and start talking, I said, "Let's go for a ride, Sergeant Jackson, and get to know each other." We jumped into the truck and started to drive around. In addition to getting to know him, I also wanted to have him as a guide in case I got lost around the massive base.

"Sergeant Jackson, what is your first name?" I asked. He looked at me with a wry smile and said, "Its Michael, Chief." I glanced his way and said, "Are you serious? Michael Jackson?" He said, "Yes, Chief, it's my name. My parents had a sense of humor and were really into music." We both sat silent for a minute, then he said; "I have a wife and two kids so we decided to get a dog and now we are the Jackson 5!" I knew I was going to like this guy right away; his sense of humor and mine were similar.

Michael asked me if I was going to have a battle cry like Chief Clark did. I knew from first-hand experience that a combat unit needed an identity and I was responsible to ensure we had one everyone could believe in. Developing a proper battle cry was easy, but needed some thought. The battle cry would help bring the unit together in tough times.

I put considerable thought into it and created a battle cry which incorporated the legacy of the Tuskegee Airmen with the mission statement we were given by our higher headquarters. Our mission statement was "Combat Airpower for America, Right here, Right now." I decided we would have a battle cry that all Airmen could relate to, regardless of their squadron affiliation or chosen career field. It started with me shouting, "Tuskegee Airmen" and the crowd responding with "The Legend Continues." I would then shout, "Right Here," and the final response was "Right Now."

Our battle cry would prove to be powerful in many ways and often rally the forces on tough days. Writing it down in my notebook was the first order of business. Knowing my schedule would take me many places throughout the year, I realized how important it would be to always have a notebook handy. I planned to introduce it to the General and the commanders and their chief master sergeants at the very first meeting following the change of command.

The commanding General for all Air Forces in the Central Command Region was a highly decorated and renowned three-star General with a great history in combat operations. Lieutenant General Gary North was a battle hardened commander with a great deal of experience in this region and he was now at Balad to officiate the ceremony. He led with passion and a commitment far beyond anything a normal person could conceive, often working more than 20 hours a day to complete his mission.

After the ceremony General North pulled me aside and said, "Chief, you should count your blessings that I let you take this command chief position." I quickly thanked him and said I was honored to have the opportunity to help lead the 332d and I would give him my best effort." I wanted to be in this combat wing and he fully understood. He looked at me with his serious look and I knew he was counting on me to do my part and lead Airmen successfully.

I was immediately introduced to the senior enlisted leader assigned to Multi-National Forces Iraq, Command Sergeant Major Jeff Mellinger. He was responsible to the Commanding General for Iraq. CSM Mellinger had a reputation for being a strong combat leader. I was completely comfortable around him from the first introduction. We spent the next several hours meeting Airmen in all areas and my learning immediately began.

I did not know my way around the base. I had not met any of the Airmen we would encounter and had not learned all of their particular missions…but that would not deter me from being a leader. I stepped in and provided on-the-spot guidance and corrective action as the situation dictated and he appeared to be very pleased.

CSM Mellinger was all business and did not spend much time talking about his personal life during this first encounter. I did learn from his assistant NCO he was the only remaining draftee from the Vietnam era. He told me CSM Mellinger was now in his 35th year of continuous active service to the nation. Pausing, I realized I was standing next to someone very special and I had better pay attention to his every word. We bonded quickly.

As we made our way around the base to visit work centers, he shared leadership gems with me. As we drove between the first stops we talked about some of the issues he encountered around the AOR (area of responsibility) and wanted me to be aware of. After he mentioned some of them, I said; "It appears we have much to fix." He looked at me with a stern face and said, "Are we perfect? No, but that's why we have well trained supervisors who understand their role." He had me hooked, and it was very apparent we shared similar philosophies.

After the last stop of the day we sat for a few minutes to wrap up what had transpired. He told me how impressed he was with the Airmen he had encountered and he held great confidence and high expectations for those he came across. As we said goodbye he looked at me one last time and said, "I'm not sure, if we turned the clock back 20 years that we would be qualified to stand in their formations." This was his way of complimenting the force of today and all they are capable of. I could not have agreed more. We parted, but I looked forward to dealing with this leader again.

I'm not sure where the hours went but before I knew it the sun was gone. I noticed a strange smoke cloud covered the night sky. I also noticed that General Rand and I had been on separate paths all day and it was time to catch up and calibrate our way ahead. We chatted briefly back at the headquarters building and you could tell he was ready for this mission. I knew the General well at this point and could tell his heart and soul were already engrained with what we were about to face.

I retreated to the sanctity of my quarters and settled in for a quick four hours of sleep before the first meeting of the next day. I had not unpacked my gear.

The General and I met to collect our thoughts before we gathered the rest of the staff. I also knew he would be ready to fly his first combat sortie in the F-16 and take it to the enemy. He had many years of experience flying this fabulous fighter and we both knew that flying combat missions was the highest calling for a fighter pilot. I reminded him since I could not be in the back seat of his aircraft to watch his back while he was flying, he should be extra careful to bring his ass home from each mission so I did not fail in mine. He reminded me he was a skilled aviator and in the words of the original Tuskegee Airmen that he would "straighten up and fly right."

We spent the next few days forming our team, sharing our philosophy, and learning the strengths and weaknesses of all key leaders in the organization. I planned to spend many days and nights going out into the work centers, control centers, on the flight line, and into the air traffic control tower to see where these great modern-day Tuskegee Airmen were working and how well they were completing the mission. I was really looking forward to walking a few miles in their shoes

At the end of each night there was a small gathering on the roof of the headquarters building. It was referred to as the Tactical Observation Deck or TOD for short. The TOD provided a great vantage point to watch the nightly display of airpower as planes took off from the adjacent airfield. Standing or sitting on the TOD it was easy to feel proud of all that was going on around Balad. It provided a place to watch F-16s take off under full after-burner; helicopters fly overhead, tactical and strategic planes landing and Airmen moving about with great precision. It also provided a place to find the comfort and solitude shared between the brotherhood of warriors serving by your side. The TOD would become a critical place for all of us to help maintain our focus.

The initial days contained a full slate of meetings and greetings with key leaders around the base. Late one afternoon Michael came in to explain to me what the schedule looked like for the coming days. He told me that on Friday nights it had become traditional for the wing staff to attend a movie being played at the base theater to entertain all the forces assigned to Balad. He said the theater was capable of seating 700 people and was part of the Iraqi Air Force Academy which formerly resided at Balad Air Base. He told me it was never a problem to get seats, but the real treat was sitting in the balcony and watching from the "best seats in the house."

Michael mentioned he had two seats for the show that evening and wanted to know if I would go watch with him. I told Michael I was not much for watching movies in the combat zone, but I would make an exception as long as the movie was a good one. We shared an affinity for comedies and even had some of the same favorite actors. We laughed together, and I could tell he was happy about my decision to go.

Sitting in the theater balcony gave me a bird's-eye view of how many people came here to escape the reality of combat on Friday nights. There was popcorn and more. It truly felt like a movie theater and provided a nice venue for Michael and I to get to know each other. As the movie progressed, I found myself getting more and more comfortable. Then I realized I had not had much sleep in the past week since leaving home, and my body was starting to fade. Michael looked at me and said, "Chief, did you hear that? Shake and Bake." I had missed it from dozing off and did not catch what he meant. Shortly thereafter the characters in the movie looked at each other and said, "Shake and Bake" as they bumped fists. Now I got it; Michael wanted us to be like these guys in the movie, and this was a great beginning. As we walked out of the theater two hours later I told Michael I appreciated him convincing me to take time out for this movie and I thought we would make a good team. He looked at me and said, "Shake and Bake!"

Suddenly, I was brought back to reality by the sound of the base alert signal and the firing of a .50 caliber automatic machine gun engaging an incoming mortar round. Moments later, I could hear the chatter on the radio that a round had impacted the base and it was right near the aircraft on the strategic parking ramp. I knew I had to go and see how things were, and how the Airmen working on and around those aircraft were doing.

I geared up in my battle gear, including my helmet, flak vest, hearing protection along with my safety glasses and headed to the point of impact to made contact with Security Force Defenders who were collecting information from the scene. Arriving at the point of impact with the Defenders it was great to see them all wearing their battle gear as they checked for injured personnel or damage to aircraft. It was apparent this attack had been a close one that shook many in the area. I could not understand why most of the Airmen were not wearing their battle gear.

Moving to the first bunker where Airmen had taken cover there were many scared faces, many worried minds, and some who needed additional reassurance the attack was over. I reminded them to remain under cover and wait for the all clear until notified otherwise. Soon the situation was over and everyone came out from their positions of cover. Fortunately the damage from this attack was minimal and there were no injuries. But it was a quick reminder that we were in combat and life was not going to be about watching movies and eating popcorn.

As I returned to Red Tail Village hoping to retreat to my quarters and finally get things unpacked, the General called me on the radio and asked me to stop by his trailer for a de-briefing. Once inside I noticed he and two colonels were sitting with him discussing the day's events, and the plan for the week ahead. They each took turns blasting me for running to the scene of the last rocket attack and scolded me to take cover the next time.

I looked at the two colonels and told them I could not do that. I saw the General smiling because he knew what was coming. I told them "As long as we have Airmen out there under fire that is where I will be." I reminded them I was a 22-year Defender whose nature was to be a first responder when there was trouble. They laughed, but they knew I was very serious and would continue to respond to emergencies when they occurred. Soon it was off to my quarters for another short night of sleep.

Monday morning rolled around and it was time to attend my first meeting of the senior enlisted members serving at Balad. The U.S. Army had responsibility for the support on base so this was CSM Wood's meeting. He greeted me and seated me at the head table right next to him. Sitting at the front of the room and seeing the joint nature of this meeting provided a great perspective. The flow of the meeting was impressive and there was always food in the room so these enlisted leaders could accomplish two goals at once.

When everyone completed their updates on things happening around the base, CSM Wood looked at me and asked if I had anything to add. I kept my comments brief and complimentary, but since I was still new on the base there was not much to add. I told them how much I looked forward to serving out this year with them. I promised I would bring updates from the Air Force at future meetings.

When I finished, CSM Wood looked at me and said, "I need a minute with you when we are done here." Then he told the entire room of more than 50 enlisted leaders that our base would be visited this week by the Secretary of Defense (SECDEF). He said there would be more details to follow, but everyone should be ready to send young warriors to attend a town hall with the SECDEF. The meeting was complete and he dismissed them. Stepping off to the side he said to me, "I need you to take on this town hall with the SECDEF because this is not something in my comfort zone." I asked him what the duty would entail. He said, "You have to have them in the room 2 hours prior to his arrival and then keep them entertained until he arrives." I told him I could manage and would not have a problem keeping them happy while they waited.

11 July 2006:

Time for the event came quickly and the crowd assembled in a large recreation room. For nearly two hours I found ways to entertain the forces. It felt like I was running a comedy show and they all seemed to appreciate the flow. It sure beat sitting around and being quiet while they were sweating in the searing heat waiting for the SECDEF to arrive. My plan was to get off the stage before he came into the room, but we were surprised by a quick entrance. I was center stage when he walked in so I turned to the audience and announced, "Ladies and Gentlemen, the Secretary of Defense!" The entire crowd jumped to their feet and just as we had rehearsed, they cheered so loud it hurt my ears. Mr. Donald Rumsfeld walked across the stage and shook my hand before I could depart. I moved off to the side of the stage and found CSM Wood. His smile was telling.

General Rand and I began traveling to our forward operating bases (FOBs) to visit Airmen. Even though we had unit commanders and chiefs at those locations, they were our responsibility, and we planned to visit every operating locations across the country. There would be many missions in helicopters in the days ahead. Flying low across the battlefield was dangerous but necessary...there was always the threat of small arms and RPG fire.

July was over quickly. The General had flown a dozen combat sorties, each time returning successfully to the ground after making a direct impact on the battlefield. Spending the entire month behind the scenes learning all aspects of the mission left me little time to reflect on the family and it started to eat at me as each day went by.

My absence from their lives was filled by the strong presence of my wife, who cared with compassion beyond belief. I talked about her and how proud I was of all she did while I was away on combat tours, and I talked about how much she did for the other families of Airmen who were deployed, even though she was a deployed spouse herself. I talked about her being the most selfless person one could know and that I wished I would have told her so before I left.

I realized early on in this tour that my fate was not in my hands. There were going to be many dangerous situations and my safety and survival were not guaranteed.

Family photo taken at Luke AFB before departing for the tour in
Iraq. L-R Sean, Brianna, Scott, Mags, Amber & Matt

Meeting Secretary of Defense Donald Rumsfeld in July 2006 as he
addressed a large audience of joint forces.

Meeting Command Sergeant Major Jeff Mellinger following the
Change of Command ceremony.

Red Tail Village, our living compound for the year, surrounded by 12
foot high concrete walls.

2
THE SOUNDING OF TAPS

One of the first things I noticed after arriving at Balad was the great cooperation between the US Army units and the US Air Force. I had a similar experience in previous combat tours, but was not expecting anything to the level it had reached here at Balad. CSM Wood was a key player in this teamwork and he along with his Commanding General, Brigadier General Rebecca Halstead, worked hard to show their appreciation for everyone on the base.

CSM Wood's office called and set up a time for General Halstead to come over and present her personal coin to some Airmen deserving of recognition, a great chance to expand this relationship. The group chiefs provided the names of five Airmen from their group who met a tough set of criteria to earn General Halstead's recognition.

We set up a gathering on the air traffic control tower. It provided a great view of the airfield and had a large enough area to hold a large formation in a safe location. I met General Halstead and CSM Wood at the bottom of the tower and escorted them up the stairs, all eleven floors. The elevator did not work, so visiting the tower was always good for a little extra physical training. They did not seem to mind and we laughed as we climbed.

Over the next hour General Halstead went through and made presentations to each Airman. We had a supervisor standing with them to explain to her what each had done and why they deserved special recognition. The supervisors did a fantastic job of speaking with her and CSM Wood, so this was a huge success. It would go a long way in solidifying an already great relationship.

As we completed this event and went back down the stairs, I thanked the US Army leadership team and asked if they would accept one of my personal coins as a small token of my appreciation for their care and concern for our Airmen. I truly appreciated their efforts and pledged to keep the relationship strong.

Later in the day I went out and found some Airmen working in the vehicle maintenance shop. The hardened aircraft shelter was full of trucks large and small. Inside were four Airmen hard at work making sure everything was being fixed and put back into service as quickly as they could. I asked them all to stop for a few minutes so we could talk. As they gathered around the table we sat and began introductions. These Airmen were covered in engine oil, grease and enough dirt to disguise the actual color of their coveralls.

The discussions went on for a while and then one of them mentioned the need to get back to work. Some of the vehicles they had on line needed to be done and out the door tonight. I thanked them for allowing me to spend some time with them and shared a personal promise they were helping me fulfill.

Back in 2004 when I was hired to become a command chief, I called my dad to share the news. Once I explained to him what the command chief's role was, he said, "So you are the guy who goes around and visits people, checking on them to make sure they have what they need?" I told him I was that guy, among other things. He said, "Good, do me a favor. Go by the motor pool." I waited a second, and then asked, "OK, but why?" He laughed and said, "When I served in the Air Force all those years ago, nobody ever came by and visited the motor pool." I took his comments to heart and after telling him we no longer called it the motor pool, I assured him I would make it a point to meet his expectation.

Before departing I thanked these Airmen again for helping me keep my promise to my dad. I told them I would be back again to stick my head under the hood and turn some wrenches with them to keep our vehicle fleet moving. We parted ways and I headed off for another very personal situation for me. I needed to pay my first solo visit to the Air Force Theater Hospital.

General Rand and I completed a tour of the hospital with General North and the outgoing leadership team on the night after our arrival, but there was so much going on that I did not have to face my fear of being around the wounded. Now was the time. Being around the ill and wounded was something critical to my leadership role. I needed to get comfortable being around the hospital no matter the cost.

The legend of the Air Force hospital at Balad was growing by the day as they gained worldwide fame for the ability to save lives against the toughest of odds. I knew if there was some way I could contribute to the medical mission it would help me overcome my hesitation about being around the blood and guts in traumatic times. I looked forward to meeting the medical professionals and learn what they were doing to earn their reputation for saving lives. By this time in the war, the Balad hospital boasted a 96% survival rate of all those patients who made it into the facility alive. They were creating and re-writing medical procedures each and every day because of the magnitude of the injuries they treated. This was truly history in the making.

My first visit to the hospital proved eventful. I entered the emergency department (ED) with Chief John Gebhardt, the Medical Group Chief. He showed me the way they bring patients in and move them through this maze of tents, portable buildings, sandbags, folding chairs and tables.

We stood back and watched as a trauma situation came in by helicopter, six patients in all. Like a well-oiled pit crew from a racing team, a group of medics arrived from all parts of the hospital, each representing a separate discipline. They stood by waiting for the trauma team to demand action, and they would spring forward, handle the business and move back into position.

As blood was drawn from the patients, a young laboratory technician sprinted away to analyze the blood work and ensure the right type was set for any pending procedures. The X-ray technician wheeled the portable machine into place, took the shot, and sprinted off with the board to have it analyzed by a surgeon waiting in the next hallway. The pharmacist stood waiting on the call for medications, handing them off or sending a runner for something new. They had everything you could think of and were quick to respond.

Watching this event was truly like watching a well-orchestrated play with many moving parts. At one point I noticed someone climb upon one of the gurneys and begin what looked like a very delicate procedure. I asked the chief what was going on. He calmly said, "She is performing a tracheotomy." So I watched from a safe distance and asked quietly, "Is she a doctor or a nurse?" He laughed, turned to me and said, "She is an enlisted combat medic and she is a 22 year old senior Airman. He went on to tell me this was the sixth or seventh one of these she has done this month."

I stood in awe of the capabilities of the entire medical staff. Doctors, nurses and medics worked in a cohesive orchestra of motion, all designed to quickly treat the patient and move them along to the surgical ward. I was amazed at the level of responsibility we placed on 20-year-old medical technicians.

The work continued, and after a short four minutes, the first patient was wheeled off to the operating room. Within ten minutes of his arrival, a team of surgeons went to work attempting to save his life. An American was injured on the battlefield and the Tuskegee Medics would not rest until he was saved.

Chief Gebhardt moved us along to visit other parts of the hospital. He described each one in great detail and ensured I knew their significance to the care and treatment of the wounded. We visited wards and watched as nurses performed the most delicate level of care on burn victims whose skin was gone, and needed gentle cleaning each hour to keep from getting infected. We watched as medics and nurses held the hands of Soldiers and Marines whose faces were covered in bandages, with tubes sticking out from several areas. We watched the compassion of those nurses move throughout the room effortlessly. I could feel the love and care they were sharing.

After an hour we ended up back at the operating room where several procedures were under way. Chief Gebhardt told me to look through the window and see what was going on. This would be a great challenge for me, as I was not prepared to see into the surgical procedure and witness what would likely cause me some pain. As I neared the window I could tell there was much going on inside this operating room, so I looked in.

What I saw were six people huddled around one person who was stretched in several directions. I watched intently, trying to figure out what was going on, until finally I had to ask. The chief said calmly, "What you have going on here are three simultaneous surgeries. The team on the left is working to restore a vessel in the arm of the patient so he does not have to lose the arm. The team on the right is working on the lower leg, trying to save blood flow so there will not be an amputation. And the last team, the one at the top of the table, well they are performing brain surgery to relieve some of the pressure on the brain from the blast injury."

Frozen in my footsteps, I was once again speechless. Before I could grasp what I had seen, we were walking back to my truck, and I could not help thinking about what had transpired in front of my eyes. Miracles, I thought, true modern miracles of medicine.

What I had just witnessed renewed my assurance about my fate should I become injured. In years past I had wondered what would happen to me if I had a battlefield injury. I wondered what my chances of survival would be or if it would be too late and they would not be able to save me, leaving my beautiful wife and kids behind. But now I knew what many before and many after would find out. Our medical teams were so dedicated, so talented, and so willing to do whatever it took to preserve life for those wounded on the battle field. All we had to do was survive long enough to get back to this hospital. From there my chances were very high for survival.

A major difference from previous wars could be seen in the increase in combat lifesaving abilities of those on the battle field. From the front lines, a complex system of helicopters would be dispatched to pick up the wounded and get them to the nearest medical facility. If the wounds were serious enough, the wounded would be further transported to the Level 3 trauma center at Balad. Within mere hours of arrival, triage, surgery, and recovery, the severely wounded found themselves on a C-17 transport plane to Germany and part beyond. The medical evacuation system contributed immensely to the survival rates for combat wounded.

I headed back to my quarters to reflect on this long day. My thoughts quickly drifted back home. Focusing on the visit to the hospital, I imagined my wife sitting outside the operating room and wondering what I would be like if I survived. I could hear my kids trying to make jokes to relieve some of the stress from the room, and it brought a smile to my face. I could hear others around them saying it was going to be OK, he's the chief, and he will be fine.

21 August 2006:

The early wakeup call came and I could hear something strange in the voice on the other end of the line. It was a controller from the Balad Command Post. His words were loud and clear. "Chief, All Red Tails are directed to report to the command post." I had no idea what was wrong, but knew this was no drill. Quickly getting into uniform, I exited the camp for the headquarters building.

The worst thoughts began passing through my mind as I drove quickly to the building, realizing I had not shaven or prepared my uniform for the day. It did not matter at times like this, but it crossed my mind, maybe as a way to subconsciously avert thinking about the situation at hand.

Our new Vice Wing Command, Colonel Gary Renfrow had recently arrived and we quickly grew close. He caught me in the hallway and shared the tragic news. He said General Rand was on his way after just landing from a combat sortie and once he arrived we would brief the staff.

Once all key players were in place, General Rand walked in and shared the horrific news, something none of us wanted to hear. It was the worst news possible. It came from one of our units assigned in Baghdad performing the In Lieu Of (ILO) missions with the US Army. It seemed a patrol was hit by an Improvised Explosive Device (IED), and there was one casualty, a master sergeant who was an Explosive Ordnance Disposal (EOD) specialist deployed in from Alaska. He was a key member of a weapons intelligence team trained to gather information in the quest to defeat the insurgents who were using IEDs to kill Americans.

Colonel Renfrow took charge of the leadership team and they went into action inside the battle staff room. General Rand gathered the details he needed to make the formal notification to General North at the headquarters for US Air Forces Central Command. He ordered all outbound email and phone traffic restricted until further notice. At times like this we had to control information. Locking down communication channels was the only option.

Details of the incident became clear as the hours passed. We learned more about this particular Airman, who was highly experienced in the EOD field and a well-trained battlefield warrior. Master Sergeant Brad Clemons was killed instantly during the attack. Even with all protective equipment in place and the best available armored vehicle, he had no chance of survival from this brutal attack.

His death was hard to grasp and it felt like someone just kicked me in the gut and I wanted to puke. I did not want to accept the tragedy of an Airman being taken from our ranks. Our first taste of the harsh reality of combat. Something inside me knew it would not be out last.

During the course of the next several hours, I watched as people came and went from the battle staff, each giving input or gathering data. All of the military services go to great lengths to ensure the family of Americans killed in action is properly notified by a well-qualified team, including a chaplain, a commander and a personnel officer to answer any and all questions. With today's communication capabilities we didn't want word getting to the family through informal channels.

The family dynamics of this situation brought a new level of emotion to many of us in the room. Sergeant Clemons was a dedicated husband and father. Learning that Mrs. Clemons was pregnant with another child drove the pain even deeper. Certainly there would be extra caution taken by the notification team to ensure her health and safety upon hearing the terrible news. I reflected on this family back in Alaska, and wondered what it was going to be like for her following the knock on her door. For a brief moment I reflected on my own family. I wondered what they would have to go through, just as she was about to experience. The lowest of lows. The worst of all tragic news.

We prepared to visit the EOD flight at Balad and share our condolences for this loss. The EOD community was a very tight knit group who all trained together, worked and lived together, and because of the nature of their duties, often suffered together. I knew this would not be an easy encounter, so I began to prepare my thoughts. Deciding what to say was not easy. What was the appropriate response if they asked tough questions?

It was a short ride to their compound, but it seemed to last a long time. The air was thick with black smoke from the burn pit, making for an eerie sight in the middle of this otherwise sunny day. The smell from the burn pit was horrible on a regular day, but today it seemed worse. The garbage burning in the pit was overwhelming given the situation. On a regular basis, gasoline was poured onto the items and burned, as the only means to get rid of the massive amount of waste being produced by the large base population. The smells coming out of the smoke today seemed to add an extra layer of stench to the day which already stunk in our minds. The heat and humidity were higher than normal, so each of us had sweat stains coming through the fabric of the desert camouflage uniforms we were wearing. We smelled absolutely horrible.

The faces of the EOD brothers in the compound revealed exactly what we would expect from a team following the loss of their brother. There had been tears in their red eyes, but they were wiped away before we entered. There was an obvious feeling of great loss in the room, but certain resilience came through loud and clear by their actions. The pain on their faces was obvious as they mourned together. Yet somehow, it seemed they remained ready for any task sent their way.

We offered condolences to each member of the team face to face, hand to hand. Within minutes we sensed their need to be left alone so they could begin preparations for the memorial service to honor Sergeant Clemons. Our presence in the room was distracting them from what they wanted to focus on. As we departed, I walked over to the officer in charge and simply said, "I'm sorry for your loss." His eyes and handshakes told me they knew my words were sincere, not just a rote condolence. I prayed I would not have to use those words again.

Back at the battle staff room everyone was in high gear, taking care of the action necessary to properly send a battlefield casualty home to his family. I overheard someone in the room say they were working the official documentation for the transfer of the body during his journey home. Those words stuck in my mind for the next 24 hours; I kept hearing the statement over and over. The day seemed to go on forever, and although I knew there were many things getting accomplished, I felt like there was still more I could have been doing.

General Rand and I departed for the hospital so he could present a purple heart to an Air Force convoy operations driver who was hit by an IED earlier in the day. A small crowd assembled near Staff Sergeant Lee Lipperts from Kirtland Air Force Base as General Rand made the presentation. Sergeant Lipperts right arm was badly injured, but he stood and made it through the ceremony. Once everyone had the chance to shake his hand and thank him for his service, we both needed this day to end. We departed the hospital and headed for Red Tail Village. We were exhausted.

24August 2006:

The memorial service for Master Sergeant Brad Clemons was about to take place in a hot and muggy recreation center tent converted to look like a large chapel. In the combat zone we made do with what we had. Most buildings and tents were used for multiple purposes and this was no exception. Once inside, the crowd filled every seat in the tent and there were people standing in the back and on both sides.

The room was quiet as many sat and made silent peace with their own mortality. As we were escorted into the front row, I glanced around and saw many eyes in the crowd were swollen with tears, and I knew most of these Airmen had no personal recollection of the fallen, nor had they ever encountered him in their travels. But this was a family, a group of Americans brought together by a common purpose in this war, with a common goal, and the loss of one family member was a loss for all.

It was a very sobering time for me, sitting there listening to the preacher talk about life's meaning and how none of us controls our final calling, nor the time it will come. He reminded us to be smart in what we do, but to live life to the fullest as this warrior had done. I caught myself wondering how this chaplain knew so much about Sergeant Clemons because I had no idea how much time and effort they put into making memorial services meaningful.

Brad Clemons deserved to be honored by all who came to pay their respect. The chaplain and his staff worked diligently to make every detail of the ceremony go well. The prayers were read with exacting perfection. Comments from EOD warriors who worked with Sergeant Clemons shared hard hitting details about his dedication to serving our nation. They talked of his leadership and his love of family. They also talked about his love of the EOD career field. It was easy to sense the level of pain shown on their faces. You could hear it in their voices.

Near the conclusion of the ceremony, the base Honor Guard formed in the rear of the tent and prepared to complete a very moving flag folding ceremony. This was something normally only seen at the grave site as the casket is lowered into the ground, but had been adapted to add meaning to the combat zone memorial. Warriors assigned to combat were not able to travel back home to attend the formal military burial so this was more than appropriate. As they finished folding the flag and placing it at the foot of the battlefield cross, the tent was silent. Outside a rifle party was formed and fired three volleys from their M-16 rifles. The rapport from those rifles rippled through the air and chilled me to the bone. A trumpeter played Taps. The entire room saluted in a slow and honorable motion. Tears flowed in every row of the tent.

There is no mistaking the sound of Taps, and it brings a lump into the throat each time I hear it. I thought to myself, "What is Taps really all about?" As a veteran of more than 20 years of service I should have known the words to Taps and the meaning behind those words. Hearing it during this ceremony reminded me how solemn the song really was.

The ceremony was officially over but nobody moved. There was one more way to pay respects to Sergeant Clemons. General Rand led the procession from the first row, followed by the other General officers sitting to his right. They approached the display of boots, a rifle, a helmet and dog tags, commonly known as the Battlefield Cross. General Rand rendered a slow salute before reaching forward to hold Sergeant Clemons' dog tags which hung from the rifle. He prayed for Sergeant Clemons and his family, then stepped back and rendered a final salute. He walked out of the tent and was followed in sequence by all of the senior officers in attendance. When the last officer was complete it was my turn to pay respects. Like those before me, I took the time to say a quick prayer and salute this warrior Airman.

General Rand and I met at the back of the tent to observe this procession of everyone in attendance. It was a fitting tribute to Sergeant Clemons for his dedicated and faithful service to our nation. He whispered to me "Chief, if there is a next time, I want you and I to render our final salute together as a leadership team." I acknowledged him and remained silent as we watched in awe. I knew his inclusive leadership style was unbreakable. He always wanted his command chief standing next to him, in good times and bad. It would be my honor to accompany him and he knew it.

Driving away from the ceremony, I reflected on my wife and what she must be doing today. I thought about how much pain it would bring her hearing we lost an Airman from our unit. I planned to call her later in the evening and try to reassure her I was OK and dealing with this tragedy to the best of my ability.

I decided to continue driving around the base for a while, knowing full well nothing I would do today would be as meaningful as attending the memorial ceremony. It was locked into my memory and would motivate me to work as hard as humanly possible to serve everyone in the wing. I found a new level of motivation to work harder for every American I came across, regardless of their affiliation, military or civilian.

Arriving back at my quarters I needed some rest, but knew I also wanted to call home. I wanted to share everything I knew about Sergeant Clemons and tell her about his service leading up to his tragic ending. She listened intently and was more than understanding and provided me with a sense of calm. She kept the reality of war in line with common sense and tried her best to make me realize how little control any one person could have over the fate of every Airman, even though she knew I wanted the responsibility.

Regardless of their location or career field, every Airman deployed to Iraq during this year was my responsibility and nobody was going to change my thought process. It would be impossible to protect them all at all times, but I took the obligation to heart. This call ended with a positive note, and I promised I would take her words to heart as the demands of leading in combat continued.

I spent the next hour lying on my bed inside my quarters. It seemed like a great time to reflect on what had taken place in the past few days by reading all of the personal notes inside my notebook. Looking at the entry concerning the memorial, I turned to the last page of my notebook and began a list of Fallen Airmen.

The list would be a constant reminder of the service and sacrifice of Airmen who fought and died in combat. It would become part of the daily routine, something I checked at the beginning and end of each day. I never wanted to forget their sacrifice. My hand was shaking as the pen hit the paper to make the first entry on the page.

Master Sergeant Brad Clemons, killed in action 21 August 2006.

Chief Dearduff spending time with the vehicle maintenance team at Balad.

Command Sergeant Major Dave Wood returning from a combat mission.

Brigadier General Rebecca Halstead (center) and Command Sergeant Major Dave Wood (far left) complete coin presentations to deserving Airmen while overlooking the airfield.

Master Sergeant Brad Clemons during his pre-deployment training. Master Sergeant Clemons, killed in action, 21 August 2006.

3

A MEMORIAL VISION BEGINS

Traveling extensively throughout the country to visit Airmen and Soldiers would become the weekly routine. It took a real toll on our bodies and minds but was worth the effort. Many days we worked 20 straight hours from the alarming sound of the early morning indirect fire attack, to the calm that came over the camp and the base following the last attack of the night. Many days we would rise to the chaotic noise and sounds of people thrashing about to take cover in concrete bunkers while the sirens whistled and the Counter Rocket and Mortar (CRAM) defensive guns sent outbound rounds to defeat the threat.

Night fell while I was driving around the base perimeter. Driving down the road near the flight line I found myself within 100 meters of the perimeter fence, with no protective measures between us and most of the street lights out. The enemy operated in the area immediately outside the fence and it felt like I was under constant surveillance from something hiding in the dark.

Passing the Balad hospital I thought I could hear the warning siren going off, but could not be sure. Sometimes it would sound in one area but not all as the system was so sophisticated it could tell where the mortars were coming in and not alarm or disturb the remainder of the base. Pulling my vehicle over to the side I rolled down the window to figure out where it was coming from as I put my battle gear on in order to engage in the situation and help with anyone who was wounded.

Suddenly, "Boom" from my left, and then "Boom" from my right, it seemed I was right in the middle of several mortar rounds fired from just outside the fence line. I looked ahead and saw the hospital and knew the first round was close, and they needed to be checked on right away. I headed their way being careful to listen for any additional warning sirens while I maneuvered my truck down the road, remaining alert for movement of injured people.

Reaching the parking lot at the hospital I noticed some movement to the side and told everyone to stay down for two minutes as we had been trained to do. Sure enough a third round hit on the back side of the hospital just outside the Casualty Staging Facility (CASF) where the patients were prepared for transport. I ran through the door in full gear to make sure our amazing medics and the patients they cared for were OK.

The nursing staff and medics were all on the floor taking cover and one of them looked at me and said "Where did you come from?" They were astonished I was on scene so soon, and wondered how I could have known to respond there. I told them I was driving by when the attack started and they were my first priority to check for casualties. They assured me all was well inside, but the explosion sounded like it hit just outside of the building near their vehicle staging area.

Departing the CASF I reminded them to remain under cover and report the status of all patients to the command post. Rounding the corner near the buses several people were already on scene taking in the damage. They reported no casualties because everyone moved swiftly when they heard the first warning siren.

If time permitted, I would have stopped to say a prayer of thanks for this alarm wing system. Certainly it had saved many lives by providing adequate warning for all those assigned to Balad Air Base. Prior to implementation of the alarm warning system, several Airmen and Soldiers were killed by incoming rounds and several more received life-altering injuries because they did not have prior warning of the incoming rounds. We were lucky this time, but I did not want to count our blessings too soon. I continued to check around the facility and would not draw an easy breath until I knew everyone was safe.

Defenders notified the command post they were on scene and taking all appropriate actions. Once I knew everyone was safe, I decided to retreat to my quarters.

3 September 2006:

Before departing Balad on a C-130 to visit the 407th Air Expeditionary Group at Tallil Air Base in Southern Iraq news came in about a mortar round hitting the Air Force living compound, injuring one Airman. The report said he was stabilized, but would remain in the hospital and asked if General Rand would present his Purple Heart Medal once we arrived. Our original plan was to attend their "Combat Dining In," so the awarding of a Purple Heart certainly took precedence.

Shortly after arrival at Tallil, we headed for the hospital where the Airman was being monitored for his wounds and a small crowd came with us. The General was introduced to the Airman and he made another remarkable speech about serving in harm's way and as much as we try, sometimes the enemy gets a vote. It was something I had heard him say before, but on this occasion it seemed most appropriate.

We had some time to walk around and meet with Airmen before the Dining In. Walking by the chapel provided the opportunity to see the Fallen Airman Memorial built in 2004. We diverted to see the memorial and one of the chiefs began to explain its history. I knew the entire story, but hesitated to stop him. Standing there reviewing the names on those plates brought a solemn feeling which made me realize the level of sacrifice already made in Iraq. When he was finished, we discussed the original plan which called for the memorial to be moved to Balad Air Base for placement at the wing headquarters. Their stunned look told me they were concerned about my intent to take this monument back to Balad. I thanked them for taking good care of it and continuing the tradition started years before.

As we walked away, an idea sprung into my head and something had to be done. There was no way we would move this memorial from Tallil which became an integral part of their location. The vision was clear…a new memorial would be built at Balad so every Airman in the wing could have a place to honor the fallen.

We made our way to the tent area where the Dining In would take place and knew something was wrong immediately. I looked at the group chief and asked him if he had forgotten the direction for conducting an event of this nature in the combat zone. He looked puzzled, and my anger level grew rapidly.

The Dining In was a complete disaster. The unit leadership allowed things to get out of hand and Airmen were acting foolish, causing everyone else to feel complete embarrassment over their actions. By the half-way point in the evening, it was obvious they had lost control of the crowd and this event was not going well. At the intermission, I told General Rand we should depart and tell them something came up and we had to get back to Balad. I wanted to stop the whole event and send everyone to their tents or back to work. The General told me even though we would be right to do so, he wanted to continue on with the event, but we would not hang around afterwards.

It angered me that a unit commander and chief could take such a cavalier attitude in combat and have an event that lacked discipline and put people's lives at risk. My concern for the discipline of this unit over their remaining four months grew deeper by the minute. There was no assurance they would remain mission focused. It seemed the enemy attack from earlier in the day escaped their memories while they partied uncontrollably.

The next morning we had breakfast with some senior NCOs before departing. At one point a master sergeant stood up and asked the General an unbelievable question in an inappropriate tone. He asked, "What are you doing about these attacks on the base? My Airmen are scared to death." Before I could pounce on him, the General let him have it.

He stated very direct; "I'm not going to apologize for you being in combat. But you did not appear very scared last night when you were shooting each other with squirt guns and tossing water balloons!" Then he said; "Why don't you take some of that energy and put some sand bags around the outside of your tents to protect your Airmen from these attacks. If someone had done it last week, the rocket attack would not have injured anyone, the projectile would have been stopped by a three-foot-high wall of bags. A wall nobody put up because they were busy filling water balloons."

We departed quickly and made our way to the flight line for departure. The commander asked if we would like to see other stuff while we waited for confirmation of the plane's arrival. We both answered with a very firm, "No." We had seen more than enough and needed to depart before things got worse. As we loaded inside the plane, the General looked at me and said, "Chief, we have some work to do down here, so get on it." I told him I understood and would engage quickly and effectively. The General did not need to say any more, I knew how serious he was.

Sitting on the C-130 for the long hot flight gave me time to sketch my idea for the design of the Fallen Airman Memorial into a crude sketch. This project would require some expertise from more talented people. My immediate plan was to get with Chief Steve Kembel from the Civil Engineering Unit and see what he could come up with or if he had someone in the unit who could design and build a fitting memorial. This was high on my priority and the goal was established to finish it before another Airman was killed in action.

Returning back to Balad always brought a sense of calm and a feeling of being home. I knew it would never truly be home, but at least I had a bed with my own pillow and the comforts I brought from our home to make it feel like mine. I found solace in my quarters, escaping from the horrors of combat for a few hours. Alone with my thoughts.

12 September 2006:

The time was flying by. Our daily routines kept us so busy I hardly knew what day or time it was. For some reason this day started off slow and I figured it was time to get some administrative work caught up. As I walked down the hallway of the headquarters building I came across General Rand who was preparing to depart for a combat sortie. I asked him if there was anything new or unusual about this particular mission and he smiled. He turned and looked at me and said, "I'm flying with Trojan today." Major Troy "Trojan" Gilbert had just arrived at Balad and both the General and I knew him well from Luke Air Force Base. I told the General I had an idea, and would meet him down at the squadron.

As luck would have it, a young Airman from the Public Affairs team, a trained photographer, was sitting in his office with nothing on his schedule for the next several hours. We headed off to the squadron where the General and Trojan would be preparing to fly. As we arrived, I told Airman First Class Chad Kellum I wanted him to capture everything as it happened, and to focus on Major Gilbert. I thought it would be a nice gift to give him a collage of photos from his first flight.

We spent the next 2 hours taking photos of them all the way until they actually took off. Once they were airborne, Airman Kellum and I headed back to the headquarters for the rest of our day. He informed me he would prepare the photos and share them with me once he sorted them out. I thanked him for the effort and we parted ways.

27 September 2006:

The following Friday took us north to Kirkuk Air Base. We had a change of command ceremony to attend, and there was a new group chief on board I wanted to meet. Landing on Kirkuk was always a tense situation as the local insurgency liked to shoot small arms at aircraft once they came into view. On this day we landed without incident and taxied into place.

The new leadership team met us along with the outgoing commander. After brief introductions, the officers headed for the headquarters building and chiefs headed out. Chief Ed Schellhase had arrived from the Iowa Air National Guard. He impressed me right away with his leadership of the team in these early days of his tour. He told me we had some time to kill before the first event and we could go anywhere to visit with Airmen.

I said, "Great Chief. Last time I was at Kirkuk we failed to visit the EOD flight, so let's go see how they are doing. We don't need to give them a warning we are coming, let's just stop by and see what's going on."

He looked happy and off we went. Driving around the end of the flight line and onto the aircraft parking side of the base we took the time to get to know each other. He told me about his background as a communications specialist and he considered it the highest honor to deploy into combat and lead Airmen at Kirkuk. He said that he already knew enough about me from his predecessor. I laughed and told him we would get along just fine and that I already liked his style.

We traveled about 20 minutes when it occurred to me something was wrong. He had a worried look on his face and was trying to disguise it. Finally, I said, "Chief, is there something wrong?" He pulled the truck over and came to a stop. He looked at me and said, "You may not believe this, but I have no idea where the EOD shop is because I have not been there yet. I was hoping as we drove by you would say something and we would just stop."

We laughed together for a solid minute. Then I said, "Well, my friend, then we have a problem, because I don't know where it is either." Again we laughed. Finally he grabbed his radio and asked for the location. By the time we got it all figured out enough time had passed and we needed to head to our next event. We never did make it to the EOD shop on this trip.

After a long day of events, lunch with Airmen and the change of command ceremony, we headed for the flight line and our pending departure back to Balad. Chief Schellhase and I laughed again about how the day started. I thanked him for a great visit and assured him we were confident in his leadership skills and I looked forward to seeing him again soon.

2 October 2006:

One of the most demanding missions of the wing, the Police Training Team (PTT), put Security Force Defenders directly in harm's way daily. This was necessary in 2006 since the entire Iraqi Police Force disbanded during the initial stages of OIF. The violence taking place on the streets of Baghdad at this time was nasty and constant. Our Defenders would routinely accompany the IP to the scene of a bomb blast and conduct an investigation of the scene; and then help clean up the broken, burnt, and dismembered bodies. Some in this unit would repeat this response and cleanup operation throughout their yearlong tour, dealing with hundreds of dead bodies from the local populace. It was an arduous duty and one you would not wish upon your worst enemy. Yet, every member of this team volunteered for this duty in lieu of something easier.

We arrived in Baghdad on a US Army Blackhawk helicopter that flew us in from Balad on a path we call "just above the rooftops." It was eye-opening to see the poverty of this city's people, and to smell the stench of waste from a disorganized culture unable to dispose of their waste. Trash was piled in open fields at the corner of each block, as if they created their own landfill.

We came upon the camp where the Defenders of this PTT were bedded down with the Army inside the controlled portion of Baghdad International Airport. They were close enough they could hear the gunfire from local citizens, and efficiently close to the entry control points they would use each day to go outside the wire and perform their mission.

The commander of this PTT was full of life, energy and enthusiasm for the mission and his people. He proudly briefed us on all they had accomplished since arriving on the mission, and he bragged about how they had avoided trouble while working the most dangerous streets in the world. The PTT mission was clearly one of the toughest we had taken on from the Army. These young Defenders mounted up in armored vehicles every day and went to local Iraqi Police stations to conduct training on police operations. They dealt with the danger of being outside the wire, but inside of a compound where the Iraqi Police Officers were known to be potentially dangerous to our forces. They could not let their guard down at any time, there was danger around every corner and every Iraqi ally was also a potential enemy.

We went around and met Airmen who had just completed a mission on this day, hearing their stories and looking deep into their eyes to see the fire contained inside. We attended a patrol briefing for an upcoming mission outside the wire. There stood a 30-year-old NCO instructing his team on critical details for the mission of the day and how they would handle emergency actions in case of an incident.

He was calm, yet his confidence permeated into the squad of 13 Defenders who averaged less than 24 years of age. Most of them were on their first enlistment, and had less than two years of military experience, but each knew more than their years would suggest. They each sounded off with pride as their names were called, and each recited bits of information critical during emergencies.

"Shout, Show, and Shoot" was the response from a 19-year-old assigned to the M-2 .50 caliber machine gun. This was the standard rules of engagement for a vehicle fast approaching the convoy as they maneuvered through the town. The confidence in his voice left you knowing he could and would execute his duties if called upon. We also observed a great sense of team pride and unity.

As the briefing ended and they prepared for departure, they asked General Rand if he would like to address the team. He spoke to them as I had seen him speak to a unit of fighter pilots about to enter battle. His encouragement of their actions was reassuring, and seemed to spark them up even more for the mission. I was proud of him and immediately told him so once we cleared the briefing tent. He said to me, "Chief, those Airmen are so young, but they are so well trained and prepared I am just flat out impressed." His statement made me proud of the enlisted corps who often struggle for this kind of recognition. This was building up to be a great day, and I had more pride than ever in the Tuskegee Airmen.

After lunch we walked into the compound where the teams rallied before breaking wire. They completed a series of walk-through actions on contact. They walked through procedures for an IED, and finally they exercised actions for a downed gunner. A downed gunner was a common form of casualty in Iraq, as the insurgents figured out our gunners were vulnerable to gunfire and IED blasts. Accepting gunner duty was reserved for only the bravest Airmen, those filled with courage and a sense of sacrifice. It was the toughest and most vulnerable spot you could take on a squad.

This squad was led by a sergeant who impressed us with courageous leadership in the face of direct contact with the enemy daily. The General and I watched their preparations with great admiration, thinking how tough this must be for a 19-year-old fresh out of high school on his first combat deployment.

Our final stop on this visit was to the armory and vehicle staging area. This area was maintained well considering the extreme field conditions; it was managed like it was inside of some multi-million dollar building on a protected base. There was pride in how they controlled their weapons and ammunition, night vision goggles, and the other tools their teams needed.

We met the support team, and could tell how they put their heart and soul they put into their effort. They told us it was their job to make sure everything was right so the guys going outside the wire were not put in unnecessary danger.

We met with one particular Airman who was performing some details while the rest of his team was off for the day, cleaning and preparing for the next day. He approached and greeted us happily, taking only a momentary break from his work, then jumping right back in with both of his dirty hands. His name was Airman Chavis and his smile and enthusiasm were contagious. On the ride back from the area, his commander assured us he was a great young man, a caring and giving friend and mentor to many other Airmen. Mostly, he was a courageous Airman who had volunteered to become his team's gunner from day one.

The day ended and we headed back to Balad. Flying low over the terrain, it was easy to see the intensity of the firefight going on in the streets below us. The flash of tracer rounds going across the road, knowing some of our comrades were in this fight, and not knowing the outcome, was gut-wrenching. We could not hear the sounds of the bullets ripping the air because of the heavy noise from the Blackhawk's rotors turning against the heavy winds, but we could sense the intensity of the situation. It was eerily like watching it on a movie screen sitting directly below our position. Our flight landed safely at Balad and we headed for our respective quarters.

Daily flying schedules were filled with F-16 sorties lasting more than 5 hours each. C-130 transport aircraft carried loads of critical supplies to the forward operating locations across the country along with thousands of Soldiers, Sailors, Marines and Airmen needing to move about to complete their missions. Every time a C-130 moved cargo to the Forward Operating Bases, it equated to several ground convoys being eliminated, saving lives. My daily routine of reviewing my notebook continued and it always started and ended by reading the list of Fallen Airmen. It still included just one name, Brad Clemons.

General Rand pins a Purple Heart Medal on an Airmen who was injured during a rocket attack at Tallil Air Base.

The original Fallen Airmen Memorial at Tallil Air Base, built in 2004.

Major Troy Gilbert preparing for his initial combat sortie in Iraq.

Chief Dearduff traveling in an HH-60 Blackhawk helicopter.

4
A BROTHER TAKEN

11 October 2006:

During the previous 100 days we experienced a multitude of mortar and rocket attacks on the base, but none where consecutive rounds struck the base. This morning started with five rounds landing on the base in rapid succession. It rocked the H6 housing area where all of our Airmen lived. The radio waves were filled with the actions of the Defenders moving about to locate injured people or damaged facilities. I dressed quickly in my full combat gear and headed for the areas where the reports were coming from. Could this be our worst day? Did some of those rounds hit populated areas or some of the aircraft? I had to respond and needed to know how we were doing. My new assistant had arrived and taken Michael's place. Since his arrival there had not been many multiple attacks and he had not often seen me respond to the sound of rockets and mortars landing around the base. I'm certain Staff Sergeant Frankie J. Lizcano would get accustomed to me quickly based on my actions today.

For the next hour there were reports coming in from all sectors of the base, including damage to facilities.

Fortunately there were no injury reports coming in, meaning we escaped tragedy again. It felt great knowing we would not have casualties from this insurgent attack. Arriving at the headquarters building the phone rang immediately. The command post notified me there was a Soldier injured during the attack. They stated he was jogging down one of the main roads and was hit by shrapnel from one of the mortars. The Soldier was hit in the face and eyes and he was now being treated in the Balad hospital. I felt bad for the Soldier, but knew if he had heard the warning sirens or the other rounds landing around the base, he could have taken cover and avoided this injury. I knew he was likely jogging with headphones on and never heard anything before being hit.

My email was filled with concerns from chiefs around Balad. They were hearing about injuries and wanted an update. I put together some notes and told them what I knew and offered for them to meet with me at the command post for a more detailed briefing on the damage. Minutes later, a group of the chiefs arrived with several first sergeants. They received a full update from the command post on the damage to facilities and the one reported injury to the Soldier.

The briefer said following the mortar attack, a joint effort between the Air Force and the Army, accounted for the capture of 14 insurgents who were responsible for the attack. An Air Force Predator, Unmanned Aerial Vehicle spotted a group of insurgents in the area where the attack initiated. They were able to confirm this group was carrying mortar tubes and relayed the information through command channels to an Army Quick Reaction Force (QRF) in the area. The QRF responded and captured the insurgents with the evidence in their hands. The end result was possible because we were becoming more effective as a joint force in the fight against the insurgency.

When the briefing was complete, I asked the chiefs and first sergeants to go back to their units and ensure people knew the truth and ensure rumors were not being spread that could put Airmen into panic mode. We did not need misinformation floating around the base.

Over the next three days we received information during our daily operations briefings indicating insurgent activity was getting worse by the day. Although we were in the period of Ramadan and expected a lull in the action, it seemed the Sunni and Shia sectarian violence was increasing. They shared a deep hatred for each other and the attacks kept coming. Deaths among Iraqi citizens was on the rise, and often times Americans were killed along with them. There was not much we could do about two religious groups who held so much anger toward each other, especially when we could not tell them apart. This situation was getting tougher by the day and everyone in our wing's leadership team knew it.

The General and I made our way around the base to meet with various groups of Airmen. Normally when we met with groups for lunch, the topics of conversation were about the bigger picture of what was going on around Iraq. But this week the conversation was only about Balad and why there were so many attacks. You could sense the concern around the tables as we ate lunch with a group of senior NCOs. They wanted to know what they could be doing to help with the attacks or at least to calm others inside their units.

General Rand handled their questions like he always did. Straight and to the point with factual information and no guesswork. He told them it was important to keep focused on the mission they were assigned. Each and every Airman needed to be good at what they were doing so our aircraft could be ready to respond and fly every combat sortie we were asked to fly. He reminded them that while the Army had the largest load of outside the wire missions to complete, we also had Airmen outside the wire facing the enemy each day. He told them about the efforts of our OSI agents to identify and find insurgents in the local area, in hopes they could stop the attacks on the base. His words were comforting to everyone in the room, and with this reassurance, I felt good about their actions once they went back to their units. People need to hear from leaders.

14 October 2006:

The morning started like many before it when the message came across the giant voice system —"Incoming, Incoming, Incoming." The standard operating procedure was for everyone to take immediate cover on the ground and head to a bunker after two minutes or when the situation permitted. But this one was unusual, having come across the way it did…even the warning signal was different.

Immediately following the attack Defenders headed to the scene for damage assessment. Their mission included this dangerous action, placing themselves directly in harm's way on a regular basis. They were ready to fight for the base if need be. I geared up, and without taking the time to tie my boots, ran out the door heading to the scene of what turned out to be hostile ground fire coming into the base.

The radio was full of reports about small arms fire coming in near the hospital, a vulnerable area the insurgents often targeted. Being near the perimeter and not being a hardened facility, the hospital was highly susceptible to attack. The chance of injury was high for the doctors, nurses, medics and patients inside. By the time I arrived our Defenders had repelled the attack from a small team of insurgents who were now gone from the area.

I headed to the hospital to check on them, fearing something bad may have happened. Inside, I found a team of medical professionals going about their business tending to the patients, despite the attack. When I approached the head nurse in the ER, he told me they were so wrapped up in caring for the patients that taking cover never crossed their minds. I just simply said, "Well I'm glad you are all doing OK, and keep doing what you are doing, we need these guys fixed up."

I made my way into the Intensive Care Unit (ICU) to find the nursing staff hard at work preparing several patients for a medical evacuation flight to Germany later in the evening.

It was a surreal sight, all of these people working and concentrating on the task at hand and not being distracted by the attack outside. I guessed it had a lot to do with their confidence in the Defenders and their faith that nothing bad would happen to those who care for everyone else. My respect for the medics continued to rise. I would learn to spend more and more time with them for inspiration and, in a strange way, to get some personal stress relief from hearing their stories and talking about the pain of their day.

As I walked out of the facility my thoughts turned toward home and I wondered what my wife would be doing in just a few days on her birthday. I knew she would rather be there in the hospital working with these patients and helping the cause, than be at home without me, trying to celebrate a birthday.

Returning to the headquarters building I was hopeful the rest of the day would be uneventful, filled with boring meetings and routine paperwork.

The call came across the radio at 1600 hours. It was the sound we never wanted to hear: "Recall, all Red Tails report to the Command Post." I knew this was not a good situation, one of those moments there was no preparing for.

I headed in with my notebook and tried to focus on what we had to deal with and not to let it get personal. As the briefer began, he said, "We have taken a casualty in Baghdad and it was a Defender." I took a deep breath, trying to block out the possibilities coming to my mind, knowing so many of them from past tours, and hoping somehow I would not know this Airman, although that would not make it any easier.

He went on, "The Airman is assigned to the Police Training Team in Baghdad…" and my mind flashed to our last visit. Would this be one of the Airmen we had met, talked with or had lunch with?

Continuing, the briefer said, "Airman LeeBernard Chavis was the gunner on the squad that was patrolling the streets of the Rashid district and he was taken out by a single sniper round, killing him instantly."

My heart stopped momentarily and I knew this must be Chavis, the one we had met and whom the commander called "brave" during our last visit, for being the first to volunteer as the gunner for his team. It took me several minutes to get my mind back on track with the briefer and take in all the data, this hurt physically. It was another huge kick in the gut.

We broke up shortly after and went about the tasks for providing recovery from the incident. Colonel Renfrow and I departed the conference room and went to meet with General Rand at the life support section where he had just completed another combat sortie. He knew by the looks on our faces we were about to share bad news, and he immediately went into business mode. Colonel Renfrow briefed him on the loss of Airman Chavis and hardly a word was said between us, we just headed for the vehicles and back to the headquarters.

We considered going to Baghdad to be with the unit, but realized the last thing the unit needed was to host us during this time, so we called them to check in. The commander relayed his teams were hurting, but they would be OK. He talked about how much impact this single Airman had made on the rest of his team and how he was the one who always gave up things for others, being especially gracious to fellow Airmen who needed things he had. He told of a situation where a new Airman arrived at the home unit and did not have a car. Rather than give him a ride, Chavis gave him his car and went out to find another one.

After talking with the Police Training Team commander, we decided we should send a leadership team from Balad to go spend the night with the unit and take care of any needs they had while they recovered. This was a young team who would experience many emotions throughout the night and the extra support would be helpful during their grieving.

When Colonel Larry Jackson, Commander of the 732d Air Expeditionary Group, and Chief Master Sergeant Hank Morgan arrived they found what you would expect. Airmen from Chavis' team were sitting around the compound and they were filled with great sadness among the silence. Some kicked the dirt and shouted at the moon while others sat silently shedding small tears from the corner of their eyes. Each mourned in his own way and each respected the other as they grieved.

Making his way around the compound, Colonel Jackson came across two Airmen sitting on the ground looking especially distraught. He approached and asked how they were doing, expecting the normal response for the situation, but getting something completely different. The older of the two Airmen looked at the leadership team and said, "Sir, I have a question for you. What now? What do we do next?" It was a question posed often following tragedy and one often answered poorly.

Being a seasoned combat veteran himself and courageous leader, Colonel Jackson looked squarely into the eyes of the Defender and said, "I'll tell you what now. Tonight, we honor Airman Chavis by remembering his service and mourning his sacrifice and keeping in mind the family he leaves behind and the ultimate sacrifice he made. What's next is tomorrow we mount back up and go out to patrol those same streets where Airman Chavis was killed today. If it was important enough for him to give his life for today, it's important enough for you and me to go back out there and try again tomorrow."

A short silence followed the answer. Then, the Airman stood up, grabbed the colonel in a tight hand grip and said, "Thanks sir, that's what I needed to hear." The colonel saluted and moved on, picking up several other Airmen along the way to get them back on their feet. This inspirational moment would carry big weight with the Defender team over the coming weeks as they continued the mission but mourned their loss.

Sitting back at Balad and not being a part of this memorable conversation, I felt helpless for the moment to provide any comfort to those Defenders. I needed something to do with my energy, so it was time to check on the construction of the memorial. The design was complete and the materials selected, but I had not visited the shop to see how much had been accomplished. Chief Kembel invited me over for a quick review to ensure they had the vision on the right track. What I found was an incredible concept being worked on by a talented young engineer. Neil Ketchum was an Airman First Class, and serving on his first combat deployment. Airman Ketchum knew what we wanted, and he was working hard to make it perfect. I was pleased with the progress and my confidence grew.

18 October 2006:

General Rand and I traveled to Baghdad to attend the memorial service along with Chavis' team. The ceremony started with a chapel full of Defenders and members of the Military Police Company of the U.S. Army responsible for the training mission. Several Army senior enlisted leaders and senior officers were in attendance, showing their great support of the Airmen on this mission and a ton of mutual respect to our service.

This would be the first Defender memorial for me during this conflict, and I was hoping it would be my last. The songs and psalms were perfectly relayed by those charged with the responsibility. The chaplain shared the right words to honor a warrior Airman who had made the ultimate sacrifice, and the commander stood tall and spoke on behalf of this great young man. It was inspiring and would impact my life from here on out.

Following the formal portion of the memorial, the first sergeant approached the front of the chapel and began the final roll call of his team. "Sergeant Martinez." "Here first sergeant." "Sergeant Davis." "Here first sergeant"… and on until the last name would be called. "Airman Chavis." but no response came. "Airman First Class Chavis," still no response. Finally, "Airman First Class LeeBernard Chavis," and when no response was heard, a sharp volley of rounds were fired just outside the chapel by a firing party.

The crack of those rounds was followed quickly by the sounding of Taps. The crowd rose to their feet and stood firmly at attention while the song played honoring our warrior. For those in attendance who had not shown any outward emotion to this point, the moment came for their reactions. Nearly everyone in the room was choked up and tearing, some more than others.

A strange silence came over the chapel as people were told the ceremony was over and they could depart. Nobody seemed to move and everyone seemed focused on the front of the chapel. General Rand and I moved forward to render our final salute. As we saluted in unison, we both withdrew a personal challenge coin from our pocket and placed them beside each other at the foot of the memorial statue erected for this ceremony. We laid our coins on the battlefield cross, stood for a final salute and exited to the back of the room.

As we turned around we expected to see the crowd leaving. Instead we saw an outpouring of brotherly love and battle field honor displayed by each and every person in the room, some 300 in all. They stood in place until their row was ready, then went forward and repeated the actions we had done at the beginning. Not all would have coins to drop, but seeing those fellow Airmen and Soldiers render a final salute was like watching them say goodbye to him in person. It was truly a spiritual time for all of us.

Outside of the chapel small groups were forming and there were many different reactions. The full spectrum of emotions could be seen in the dim light around the compound.

Some in the crowd shared recollections of good times and bad with Airman Chavis. Shortly after the chapel was emptied, Sergeant Martinez called his team together and asked us to join him. He was a 30-year-old Technical Sergeant with ten years of service, and had just lost one of his men. He wanted to address the squad in a small group and share his thoughts.

[What follows are the exact words shared by Sergeant Martinez]

"I have been able to provide my squad members with an answer for everything and make them feel better when they are feeling down or have problems. When we arrived at the combat surgical hospital on Saturday, I was at a loss for words and it gave me a horrible helpless feeling because for the first time I could not make it okay, I could not fix what had happened. I have tried to keep it together as much as I can; and I know my squad and I will be fine when we start working again, but I am hurting quite a bit now. I promised myself I would bring everyone back home safely. I feel I have broken that promise to Chavis and his family. Airman Chavis told me before coming to this squad that he was glad he was here working for me, he knew he would get that deserving chance to start over and not be judged by what's happened in the past. He had a way of communicating with people in an informal manner and making light of any situation...he had one of those contagious smiles. I remember being at the traffic station, jumping in his vehicle while SSgt Luker was out gathering numbers or at the rooftop and mess with his Blue Force Tracker (BFT). He would always tell me to stop playing with it because his

Team Leader would yell at him for letting me mess with it. Before we started missions, I would go in the tents, and it seemed like every time I would go in there I had an early task or I needed bodies for a tasking, so Chavis would see me in the tent and tell me to get out since he was the lowest ranking, he was always the first to go. I knew better than to try and joke around with him in the early mornings before a mission, he was very grouchy and I did not want to mess with him. I think, in the end we saw eye to eye though. It's not about the job we're tasked with, but the people you're surrounded with while doing it. I had this surreal feeling that nothing could happen to my squad as long as we did everything by the book. I can no longer promise my squad that no one else will get hurt because that may be out of my control, but I guarantee you I will do everything I can to ensure the right thing is done if anything else happens. I would expect the same in return from any of you. Every single person in Squad One did what was supposed to be done when this occurred. I want to thank you all for doing the right thing, making my job a lot easier. I keep playing that scenario in my head, but I don't think there was anything that could have been done any different. Sometimes doing the right thing doesn't keep the people you love from getting hurt and that is just a reality that sucks; but that's the way things are. I have said this before, if I cannot be with my wife back home, then I want to be out here with my squad members. I care deeply for every single one of you and maybe get too close at times, that is why it's so hard for me to let go of Chavis. Last Saturday, a brother was taken from us, and with that, a part of me is gone as well. I am deeply hurt by the loss of Airman Chavis. He will always have a place in our hearts and will be sorely missed. May he rest in peace."

When Sergeant Martinez was done, we spoke privately with him before departing so he could be alone with his team. He was in pain but it was clear he would carry on the mission and take care of his team. He was a genuine leader who just experienced the worst of all leadership moments, yet he stood ready to continue on another day.

We boarded the helicopter and flew back to Balad without much conversation. Our hearts were heavy over the loss of this Airman. My thoughts drifted back home as the name of another Fallen Airman was added to the list in my notebook. Several days after the memorial, General Rand spoke with Mrs. Chavis by phone. At the end of the call, Mrs. Chavis said, "Tell your Airmen I am praying for them."

My notebook now contained two names of Fallen Airmen. The last name added was Airman First Class LeeBernard Chavis, killed in action, 14 October 2006.

Visiting with one of the Security Force Defender teams performing the Iraqi Police Training Team mission in Baghdad.

Chiefs Morgan and Dearduff preparing to travel out to see Airmen of the 732d Air Expeditionary Group with Colonel Larry Jackson (right).

Airman First Class Leebernard Chavis, killed in action, 14 October 2006.

The battle field cross displayed during the memorial service for Airman Chavis.

5

ALWAYS IN THE BACK SEAT

31 October 2006:

The past two weeks went on record as the worst period of casualties so far during Operation Iraqi Freedom. The sectarian violence was at an all-time high between the Sunni and Shia tribes. More Iraqi people were being killed each day, and there appeared to be no good answer. Casualty numbers among American and coalition forces grew by the week, and it was taking a toll on the national resolve back home.

The 332d Air Expeditionary Wing engaged the enemy on a daily basis, providing direct support for the Army ground forces as they tried to get a handle on the insurgency. Most days were filled with heavy clouds and steady rain. The weather conditions around the country made our job of supporting the ground forces even tougher than normal. Our surveillance aircraft could not provide all of the reconnaissance and intelligence information needed for ground force commanders due to the limited visibility.

Airmen who arrived in September were settled in and performing well considering the weather conditions and strains of meeting all the mission demands. Attacks on the base came regularly, keeping everyone on edge as they went about their daily routines. Every week we conducted a "Right Start" briefing, for newly arriving Airmen, it seemed the enemy sent indirect fire rounds into the base, just to help us get their attention. Some people claimed I arranged the attacks while I was briefing them on the expectations for each person during an attack. While I could not take credit for the timing, it sure helped get the point across about wearing protective gear and taking protective measures under attack when an actual attack happened during the briefing. After the second time it happened, I began to wonder how much information the insurgents may have, and more importantly, how they were getting it.

The month ended with a promotion and recognition ceremony in the Town Hall. Although we were all deployed away from our home units, we still felt it was important to recognize milestones within an Airman's career. A few chiefs expressed their concern about our ceremony being a distraction from the mission and suggested we cancel them. The General and I felt different, and decided we would continue the ceremony, and expected their full support.

19 November 2006:

Our normal travel routine on Friday would be changed this week so we could make a special trip to Camp Buering in Kuwait on Sunday. We wanted to meet with the new Police Training Team Defenders who had just arrived for their in country training prior to assuming the mission.

Our C-12 landed and we were greeted by the leadership team of the Kuwait wing. Among them was a good friend of mine, Chief Thomas Narofsky. He and I had previously served as command chiefs in another command, and it was great to see his familiar face. We had some free time before heading to Camp Buering, so they treated us to some dinner at their main DFAC. We found the food somehow seemed different and you could see the smiles on the faces of our team.

Inside of a private tent we sat and dined. There was great laughter among the team. At one point I picked up a glass from the table. I poured my iced tea from the paper cup I was using into the glass and stared at it for a minute. One of the other chiefs looked at me and asked, "What's wrong with your tea?" I continued to stare and said, "Nothing wrong with the tea, it's just fine. But I just realized, this is the first time I've had a drink from an actual glass since July!" Somehow the tea tasted better being in a glass versus a paper or plastic cup, and we all laughed out loud. I wondered how many people back home had gone months at a time without such a simple luxury and if they would appreciate this like I did?

We landed a short time later at Camp Buering and met with the new PTT. I knew the chief master sergeant and several members of the team from previous assignments. After a short introduction, the General spoke to the entire crowd. When he was finished, Colonel Jackson also spoke to them and made sure they understood the serious nature of the mission they were here to perform. When both of them were complete, it was my turn. I wanted these Defenders to know we would do everything in our power to provide them with equipment and support for the tough mission, but it would require their utmost attention to detail in executing everything they did. I also asked them to ensure they looked to the left and right and did everything they could to protect their battle buddies. It was a quick opportunity to let them know we cared, and we hoped they got the message.

We boarded our C-12 and headed back to Balad for another short night of sleep before heading off to another location.

20 November 2006:

Monday morning came quickly and we arrived at the terminal for the U.S. Army Sherpa flying operations long before dawn on this brisk November morning. The air was filled with smoke and brought back memories of sitting around a campfire in the early morning before going fishing in the lake. However, I always snapped back to reality at the sight of Soldiers sitting around waiting for a ride to their next location.

The Sherpa was often used in lieu of a helicopter because of its long haul capability and its larger passenger compartment. One of the oddities of the Sherpa was the need for exact weight and balance during takeoffs and landings. Each passenger had to stand on a large meat locker style scale, holding all of his battle gear and any bags he would be taking, so he could be positioned inside the plane for best balance.

A large contingent of Tuskegee Airmen would be going with us to scout out a new location where we would stand up a fighter unit in a few months. It was a large, open airfield in the western part of Iraq, but offered many challenges to the tactical operations of the fighter unit.

Today's crew included people we rarely traveled with. There were battle tested leaders like Chief Brian Janroy, our maintenance group superintendent, and a real expert at setting up aircraft maintenance locations. Colonel David "Doc" Ellis, the Director of Staff, a Colonel with F-16 background and one hell of a sense of humor was along on this trip. He was also considered an expert at setting up squadrons, and he was always good to have around.

Among the others was Major "Trojan" Gilbert, someone I grew to know and appreciate while we were both at Luke AFB and the 56th Fighter Wing. We formed an unusual bond not often experienced between junior officers and senior enlisted. Something about him made it easy and

I really appreciated his friendship and our many discussions. He was General Rand's flying executive officer at Luke before coming to Iraq. This was the first time he and I would mission out while deployed to combat, even though he showed great enthusiasm for taking on new missions to see how our Airmen were performing. Unfortunately before this day, our schedules never matched to allow us to travel together. His extremely positive energy and amazing personality affected everyone he came in contact with.

On this particular morning, I flashed back to the night he arrived in September. Sitting in my office in the quiet of the night, I could hear an exchange between the door guard and a familiar voice. Suddenly his voice got nearer and he came around the corner with great enthusiasm, exclaiming, "Chief, it's great to see you."

I came from around the desk and gave him a warm welcoming battle hug and asked where he had been. I knew he had arrived the day before and here he was now, coming to see his chief some 28 hours later. I figured he would have a great excuse for this long delay.

He explained that after he arrived and got himself settled in, he wanted to take a short nap and get ready for the mission at hand. The only problem was he never slept on the trip over, and spent three full days talking to people on planes and in terminals about how excited he was to be going to combat. So, when he took a short nap to get some rest, it turned into a 14-hour sleep, followed by a quick bite to eat and another 4 hours of sleep. We laughed.

I completely understood the time he needed to get over the exhaustion of the trip. We began to catch up. I asked him how the basketball team was doing and he quickly replied, "They're great chief, I just talked with them." I referred to his kids as the basketball team, my way of remembering he had five children, enough to field his own team. Among them were the twin girls who were only seven months old. I asked about his wife Ginger and how she was doing with him coming to combat. He told me how strong she was and how proud he was of her. We knew Ginger from Luke as well, and had spent time around them. I knew she was tough all around, but I still worried about her and the children during Trojan's combat tour.

When we finally boarded the Sherpa and took off at low altitude and slow speed there was angst on the faces of some of my fellow passengers. They wondered why we remained so low in altitude and at slow speeds, we would make for an easy target for any insurgent on the ground. I experienced the same feeling on a previous flight and asked the question to the crew. They explained how their tactics kept the enemy from seeing us coming, and therefore would not be able to get a good aim at we flew overhead...didn't make perfect sense, but their record of not being shot down was solid, so we trusted them and moved on. The flight took more than an hour, mostly across a large body of water covering a great portion of western Iraq. It seemed strange to fly so low over water, and I think I even saw some of them starting to get seasick from being so close to the water.

Once on the ground at Al Asad Air Base, we were greeted by a small team of Airmen and many Marines who were from the lead unit on the base. They knew the presence of Airmen would mean an immediate increase in the quality of life for the base, since the Air Force always improved living, working and dining conditions in the field environment. Strangely enough, the senior Marines were cautious about showing us too much and they explained they did not want us making it too nice for the young Marines, creating an expectation that would be hard to live up to. They showed us facilities, ramp space, taxiways and living quarters all designed to enhance our ability to fly the A-10 in combat.

Once the tour was complete, we had the chance to sit and meet with the 40 Airmen who were assigned here doing aerial port operations, vehicle maintenance, and just a few other airfield-related jobs. They were happy to see their wing commander and chief, and it seemed they felt better about their care and feeding out here in the vast desert environment. They told us about how rough the conditions were and how they overcame some very basic needs all on their own without help from another unit. The General directed staff members to find resources and provide these Airmen with basic necessities immediately.

I often found the farther we got from our main operating locations, and the tougher the conditions were, the more resilient our Airmen became. We walked into their makeshift gym and found a weight bar made out of an old iron pole. They welded some old wheels onto it for pumping iron and keeping in shape. It showed the creativity and flexibility of these dedicated Airmen.

The tour was wrapping up and we prepared for the trip home. As we waited for the crew to get fuel on board, the sun began to set off in the distance. Someone broke out a camera and told everyone we should take some photos for our memory books. Not liking my photo being taken, I stayed in the back. Then someone decided we should all take a group photo and I was urged forward to join the group.

As we finished the group photo, Major Gilbert grabbed me and suggested we take a picture before take-off. We walked over and stood in front of the Sherpa, the sun setting behind us, and yet something was wrong. I looked down and saw he only had a 9mm handgun in his possession and not a long rifle of any kind. I told the major: "You cannot have a combat picture without a rifle, because that pistol is not going to scare off any insurgents." I handed him my rifle and we got ready for the photo. Suddenly I noticed there was no magazine in the weapon, and told the major to cover it with his hand, so nobody could tell he was not fully armed. It may have been from the long day and the travel, but we both found this extremely funny and we laughed, nearly splitting our sides, as he stood there trying to look tough with his hand covering the empty magazine well.

The flight back to Balad was not as uneventful as the flight out to Al Asad. About 30 minutes into the flight, the crew notified us we were taking on enemy fire from the ground and to brace ourselves for evasive actions. I started running a checklist in my mind of the immediate actions if we were forced to land or were shot down. There would be little time to regroup once on the ground, I wanted to be prepared. I looked around and accounted for the number of rifles on board. I figured those with rifles would take up positions to provide 360 degrees of coverage around our team. I would ensure the General and the other officers stayed close, and would protect them with my rifle as a last line of defense. Thinking through each step of my process, I wondered if anyone would be bothered by my assertiveness in taking charge once we landed. At the moment I did not care, and knew that General Rand would have placed me in charge of the tactical operations on the ground because of my experience.

After several minutes of evasive maneuvers by the crew, the ground fire diminished and we resumed a normal flight path and headed straight for Balad. When we landed you could tell there were some worried people. They were very glad to be back on solid ground. We each spoke briefly outside the aircraft and then we all parted ways. I went about my business of catching up from the day gone by and ended by paying my routine visit to the hospital, where I could unwind and laugh with the medics. I brought a box of blankets donated from patriotic Americans back home through a project called Operation Linus.

My intent going in was to take them to the ward and give them out to the wounded as we often had. But on this night the wards were empty, and rather than place this box of blankets into the storage room, I decided to take a different approach. I walked into the ED and gathered the staff on duty. After a minute of small talk I asked them, "Have any of you ever received a blanket while you have been on this tour?" I knew what they would say all the blankets go to the wounded and they never get considered.

There was a moment of silence with lots of stares around the room. I knew they would be uncomfortable taking them, so this one was on me.

I said, "OK, let me say this again. Who has not received a blanket while they have been here serving on this tour, working miracles for our wounded?" They smiled and most raised their hands. I said "Good. Now please come over here and get one of these great blankets." I was nearly knocked over as they dug into the box and pulled them out. The smiles on their faces told the story. I had to take some photos of them enjoying the moment. They insisted we get a group photo while they held their blankets and I just laughed. It was a hospital visit I would not soon forget. It felt like my presence brought a sense of calm to the night. The trauma bays were quiet.

We retreated to the break area of the ED where they kept the coffee pot. One of the enlisted medics told me they noticed whenever I came around at night, the ED would remain "Quiet", and no traumas would come in. But you could not use the "Q" word...doing so would jinx the crew for the night.

Although it was late in the evening, we had a cup of coffee from the break room and sat on their old beat-up couch and chair tucked neatly into the back of an old smelly tent. We talked about why they liked this old couch and I wondered how it could be comfortable. They told me it was far more comfortable than standing on their feet in the ED working trauma situations, so it was really comfortable. I departed around 0200 hours and made my way back to my quarters, without a trauma in sight, my work here complete. Tripping over the full length couch sitting inside my room seemed like a sign.

As part of the Thanksgiving week activities planned around the base, someone decided it would be a good idea to have a traditional chiefs versus colonel's softball game. Although we did not have proper equipment for a softball game, we made a substitution and acquired some whiffle ball equipment from family back home and we held a game. The chiefs and colonels came out in our Air Force PT uniform and put on a show for the 50 or so Airmen who needed some free entertainment. It was a nice break for all of us to relax and take part in a traditional American game.

That night I found an email from Mags telling me about the day and what she and the kids had been up to. It was the best way to end my mission day, reading about their day and giving them a report on mine. Tonight would be a longer message than normal, as I wanted to tell them many things, including the story about Major Gilbert and I laughing during our photo at the flight line. I also wanted to hear what they would be doing for Thanksgiving.

It seems there would never be time for any of us to rest. On Wednesday we headed for Baghdad International Airport to spend time with the Airmen from the 447th Air Expeditionary Group at Baghdad who were responsible for the passenger terminal. We enjoyed hearing their stories before bedding down for a short night of rest.

In the morning we had a chance to visit some of the Airmen working as ILO forces inside the confinement facility at Camp Cropper. This was a horrific duty, but had to be done. We found the Airmen who performed this mission to be highly motivated and extremely resilient. Visiting with this unit and seeing all they were tasked with, most of which was highly classified, helped me gain even more perspective on how tough this war was becoming on all of us. They certainly performed one of the toughest, and most non-traditional missions of Operation Iraqi Freedom.

Following the visit with the Airmen of Camp Cropper, we headed for a visit with the Police Training Team at Camp Liberty. It would be our first chance to see them in action on the mission. After viewing their operations around the compound, a team met with us in the DFAC as they prepared to depart. It was a light moment where we got to see some of their personality come through. The General, Colonel Ellis, and I all sat at separate tables so we could spend time talking with members from different squads within the team. We laughed, but all the while, I knew it was highly possible these very Airmen could be killed within a short time of finishing their meal and heading out. I listened, but my mind was racing fast through the possibilities that existed. I studied their faces, and remembered their names.

It was Thanksgiving Day and there was much more to accomplish. We headed back to Balad and found there were so many things going on. The General had to break away and host the Secretary of the Navy. Fortunately for me, I was excused and headed for the gym to get in a hard workout before having to eat more turkey and stuffing. The only other moment of solitude that day were the 15 minutes spent on the phone talking with my family; and when there are four of them to chat with, 15 minutes goes by real fast. Before I knew it, the day was gone, we had ingested lots of turkey roll and stuffing, and it was time for a long four-hour sleep.

The days following Thanksgiving went by fast. I spent time with all of the units around Balad, who often felt left out when they saw us traveling to the remote sites to be with those Airmen. It seemed to us like we were always around, but they wanted our time and attention, so we had to make a concentrated effort to give them dedicated time.

Friday was spent with Chief Maxson and the Airmen of the Mission Support Group. We stopped at the Fire Department, a place I always liked to visit because they were hard working, behind the scenes warriors who were ready to go at a moment's notice. The firefighters' energy permeated onto us when we visited. It was also reassuring to see how well we operated the fire department as a joint operation with the US Army. The Army provided a crew of Soldiers who were trained in battlefield first response. Every time I visited the station I felt the bond between our Soldiers and Airmen, and it made me proud.

25 November 2006:

Saturday was dedicated to the warriors of the 732d Air Expeditionary Group, the ILO Airmen, who were located on Balad. They performed a variety of missions traditionally handled by the Army. Chief Morgan and I spent the day going around unit to unit and spending time with them. It was amazing to see the spirit of these Airmen along with the pride they took in the task at hand, even in the mail room, a very non-traditional role for Airmen. They were very proud of the mission they undertook and knew each day their effort helped link the deployed forces with the people back home who meant the most to them.

After a long day of meeting with warriors, Chief Morgan asked if we could grab a bite to eat at DFAC #1. DFAC #1 provided a sense of anonymity for us since it was in an area predominantly occupied by Soldiers. We could stop in and have a great conversation and some peace and quiet while we ate.

Once inside, and before getting in line, I noticed two pilots standing together getting ready to get some food. As I walked toward them to say hello, I quickly recognized Major Gilbert, and knew there was a good reason we had come to DFAC #1. I had not seen him since the Sherpa ride to Al Asad the previous week, and wondered what he had been up to. Immediately I asked him how the basketball team was doing. He laughed with his normal laugh, smiled and said, "You know they are good, Chief." Then he told me about Boston and some recent soccer action he had been told of. He said Ginger and the rest of the family were fine. He asked about my family while we stood in line waiting to be served. Moving from the food line, he told me he was about to sit with his wingman for the night and have a pre-flight meal. Chief Morgan and I decided to sit at a table near them but to give them space to talk about their mission ahead.

After 30 minutes it appeared the pilots were done and heading toward the squadron. They approached our table and we stood to send them off. Trojan asked why we were out so late on Saturday night. I told him we spent the day with Airmen from the 732d Air Expeditionary Group and were catching a late dinner before heading in for the night. He told me he still wanted to travel out to some forward locations and see those Airmen, and I assured him we would make it happen. Then I looked at him and asked, "Major, what's the chance you have a 'D' Model jet tonight?"

The "D" Model F-16 was the trainer that had a back seat and allowed for a passenger. We had them at Luke for the training mission, but they were not authorized in the combat zone. He laughed and said, "Chief, you know we don't have 'D' models here in Iraq." Laughing together, I said, "I know, Major, but if you did, I'd be in your back seat tonight for this mission, no questions asked." He said, "Chief, if I had a back seat tonight, I would want you in there with me." Smiling, I said, "Sir, just know that I am always in the back seat with you no matter what." As he started to walk away, he said, "Chief, I know you are."

Tuskegee leaders ending the long day of site visits with the Airmen
of Al Asad Air Base.

Chief Dearduff and Major Gilbert taking a "hero" shot on the Al
Asad flight line.

Tuskegee Leaders enjoying a meal with the Kuwait leadership.

General Rand addresses the new members of Detachment 3 before they started the mission.

6
REPORT TO THE COMMAND POST

Sunday gave me a chance to catch up from the holidays and all our travels. It was definitely time to wipe down the inside of the quarters and remove the film of dirt and dust covering the walls. Even with closed windows and doors, the place always seemed to be dirty and I did not want to get sick from the smell of the air from the burn pit.

27 November 2006:

Monday morning always started the same way, with the meeting of the "Sergeants Major." Every senior enlisted leader on the base, regardless of service and sometimes regardless of pay grade, met over breakfast to discuss operational issues.

Everyone in attendance was expected to bring up issues or topics that would apply to the others on the large base. Some talked about safety while others talked about concerns for their basic needs. Conversation around the room was interactive and improved relations between units. We always brought the senior enlisted member of the Law Enforcement Unit to discuss police actions transpiring during the week. It allowed all the enlisted leaders to keep up with trends in discipline concerning law enforcement, and they had a direct contact to work through issues. The new Law Enforcement NCO was someone I knew and trusted from the past. Senior Master Sergeant Joe Bovair had worked with me on the headquarters staff at Air Mobility Command many years before; and I knew how talented he was. There were concerns about some of the briefers speaking out of turn, but I did not have that concern with Sergeant Bovair.

Great relationships with the civilians who worked for the Army and Air Force Exchange Service (AAFES) were formed. Some of them had been in Iraq since the beginning, and they were now on their third consecutive year of serving the military in this capacity. They had a tough life, worked hard, and showed more dedication than anyone could possibly expect. We were blessed to have Sylvia Stoudamire as the Exchange Manager at Balad, and she always brought valuable input to the meetings. Sylvia was on her third year of duty and had no plans to leave. When I asked her one day why she stayed so long, she said, "Chief, this is my family and I am here to take care of them." Wow, I never knew our civilian force in AAFES felt that way. I could see she was serious. I grew to know and trust her and the AAFES staff and would have many encounters with them throughout my tour.

It was my turn to speak and I decided to take a different approach than normal. I opted to show some of the real human feelings I had inside and share my thoughts about family back home and the brotherhood we shared in combat.

Some were surprised and showed it as I discussed the upcoming holiday activities and how much time and effort we should pour into them as enlisted leaders. The room was silent and nobody moved an inch. It became very uncomfortable, like I was a preacher delivering a tough sermon to the congregation, and nobody wanted to be the first to move or be noticed. I encouraged everyone to truly come together as one family, regardless of service. Our success in combat depended on everyone supporting the person on their left and right and nothing short of it was acceptable...we were a family.

Thanking them for service and leadership, I closed with sharing my hopes for the peace of families back home. The meeting ended, we departed and headed for work.

"All Red Tails, report to the Command Post." Something felt real bad, my heart sank, and my eyes began to water. This felt like a hard punch in the gut and a kick to the head at the same time. Not knowing what was coming, and not being close to the headquarters building, I had to endure several minutes of agony trying to get through the traffic, past tactical vehicles, and back to the parking lot.

Arriving at the building an eerie feeling brought me to a stop at the back of my vehicle. I leaned over and grabbed the corner, holding myself up. It felt like I was about to pass out, and there was no reason why. I was not sick, had just eaten breakfast and actually had had plenty of sleep the night before. Gathering myself, I noticed the General's truck was not in the parking lot, but I also knew I had not seen it back at Red Tail Village before I left. He must be flying this morning to make up for the sortie he lost over the weekend.

Entering the building nobody spoke a word, they just looked at me with blank stares. The entire building seemed silent as I made my way down the hallway into Colonel Renfrow's office. We made eye contact for a brief second, then he looked down at his desk. I could see a stack of fresh notes and he was shuffling them around almost as if he did not know what to say. I saw him swallow even though he had not drunk from the empty cup on his desk.

I wanted to know what he had to tell me, but it seemed as though time stood still. Finally, he looked at me and simply said, "Chief, we just lost a jet..." before he finished his sentence my mind went crazy. The General's truck, not seeing him at Red Tail Village, flying on a day outside of his routine...was it possible? Was he the reason I was standing here possibly about to face my worst fear. Then I focused back on Colonel Renfrow and heard him say, "Chief, it's Trojan."

My heart sank into my stomach and I fell backwards against the door. I was lightheaded, but gathered enough strength to ask, "Is there any chance…?" And before I could finish my sentence, Colonel Renfrow said, "No, Chief, there is no chance." He then said "Gather yourself; we need to go and brief the General who was just recalled from his takeoff."

Pain like this was new to me. I wanted to scream, I wanted to hurt somebody. How could Major Gilbert be gone? How could something have happened to such an incredible human being? Where was this enemy, I had to go and find them and destroy them. So many things went through my head, and once again I felt like passing out.

Suddenly Colonel Renfrow said we had to go as the General was heading back to the squadron. It seems he was about to take off when the news of the accident came across the radio. They passed a call sign to him without a name. He only knew it was a fighter pilot, a fellow Tuskegee Airman, and a brother in arms. He had no idea it was Trojan. We needed to be there when he found out.

We headed down the flight line, past several entry points without stopping and explaining so we could get to the General first. The moment we made eye contact with him, it was apparent he already knew.

General Rand was standing tall and moving with purpose. He looked like a man who just received terrible news and was determined to do something about it...the same emotions I had just minutes before in Colonel Renfrow's office. He told us he knew and we needed to get back to the headquarters and work this issue just like we had all of the others. We had jobs to do and as leaders, we needed to stay focused on the task at hand.

We jumped into our vehicle and he entered his. The drive back to the headquarters felt like it took forever, and I knew our minds were traveling a hundred miles per hour. We were dealing with this tragedy in our own way, and each felt pain without saying or sharing it.

The leadership team was now assembled at the conference room and after a brief stop in his office, the General came in for the official briefing. The room remained silent and the briefer began. Sharing the details of the event, it became clear to all of us that he was in a tough battle with insurgent forces on the ground, and his actions before the incident likely saved the lives of 15 Special Operations Forces who were pinned down by the enemy.

I thought to myself, "I wish I was in the back seat with him on this mission." I wanted to mount up and head out to find and kill the insurgent force myself. Emotions were running high inside me and others in the room knew it.

When the briefing was complete, the General looked at all of us and said, "We will mourn when it's time to mourn, we will cry when it's time to cry, and we will laugh when it's time to laugh. But right now it's time to concentrate on the mission and what we can do for the Gilbert family."

The room was silent; you could hear people breathing. General Rand looked at Colonel Renfrow and said, "Gary, you got this one, I have some calls to make." He walked out of the room with the confident look of a determined leader, but inside I knew he was a man who held in great pain.

I departed with the General and make it my duty to be near his side as he completed the awful duty in front of him. He had to notify General North and Brigadier General Jones, the wing commander back at Luke Air Force base and give them the horrible news. Then he had to wait for Major Gilbert's family to receive the official notification before he could make his own call. He got General North on the phone and discussed the details that could be shared over the insecure phone line.

When they were finished he hung up the phone and sat silently in his chair. He looked steady as a rock, but I knew inside he was torn up just like I was. We shared a few thoughts, talked about losing a fellow warrior and a brother, then sat silently in the office. I leaned back on the couch, the door closed, and he leaned back in his office chair. We were beyond tears at that moment. We sat silently, reading each other's mind.

Several hours went by and we had little to no conversation. Once in a while he would go to the conference room to check on the progress of the event, and then return. I did the same, usually clearing the office while somebody came in to give him an update. Several times I stepped into the conference room and stood in awe of the resilience of Colonel Renfrow. This was personal for him as well, but he remained focused on the task. I studied the live video shot from the scene of the crash. At one point I thought I could see the insurgents moving a large object from the area and place it into the back of a truck. I became infuriated and asked others if they saw what I did.

Shortly after my observation, it was confirmed that Major Gilbert's body was removed from the accident site by insurgents. Not only did this horrible incident cost the life of a fighter pilot, Airman and personal friend, it was now complicated by the removal of his remains. Seeing this happen on the video screen brought a strong emotional reaction I could not control. I left the room to be alone and hide my pain from others. An hour later I came out of my office and headed back in to check on the General.

The Operations Group Commander, Colonel Scott Dennis, stopped in to tell the General he was heading down to the unit and asked if we wanted to come along. Leaders have to be strong in front of their forces during tragedy, and this was something that needed to be done.

Reaching the flight line we were met by Major Gilbert's flying squadron commander, Lieutenant Colonel

"Crusty" Walker. Colonel Walker was leading the unit from Cannon AFB in New Mexico. The General asked him how he and the men were doing. Colonel Walker showed physical signs that he was taking this hard, but his voice remained steady. He responded, "Sir, I have talked with each and every member of the squadron, and although they are taking it hard, they are all focused and ready to maintain our part of the mission."

The General asked if they had cancelled any missions or needed some relief from missions before they took it back to the enemy. He replied, "Sir, we are ready to fly our missions and not skip a sortie. But first, there is something else I need to do and I would like you to join me." We all walked out of the squadron and headed across the taxiway to the hangar where the aircraft maintenance Airmen were formed up.

These were always tough days on maintenance teams because there was a full investigation had to take place to determine if something mechanical caused the jet to crash. There would be reviews of training records and personnel who worked on the jet would undergo scrutiny on their actions. Normally morale was extremely low in the unit following a crash. As we rounded the corner, we could see all 200 Airmen, both officers and enlisted, standing in a loose formation with their heads held low. There was no conversation, and little to no movement.

As we stopped in front of this large group, you could feel the pain and anguish among them. Colonel Walker took the lead and said, "All eyes on me." I watched as many in the back continued to look down. He said it again, "All eyes on me." Now they were paying attention and looking forward, but still drooping with sadness.

He said, "Today we have had a terrible tragedy. We lost an Airman and we lost an aircraft. But I want you to know I have not lost confidence in you. I trust you and I'm confident the results of any investigation will prove you did everything right in maintaining our jet today and all the jets you own. I am so confident in you, I just told the General we will not miss a single sortie. I told him we will gather ourselves and put the best jets out there on the mission and meet all of our demands." Then he said, "I have so much confidence in you that I have changed my schedule, and as soon as I have the proper amount of crew rest, I will fly the first sortie in one of your jets tomorrow morning." The formation stood silent.

I felt like this was one of the most memorable speeches I had yet witnessed. Then I heard him say, "Now, pick up your heads, pick up the Airman next to you, and get back to work. We need you and we trust you. That's all."

It was a moment I will not forget for the rest of my life. I watched in amazement as he, Colonel Dennis and General Rand walked away. The crowd stood taller, snapped to attention, shoulders back, chests out. They were pumped and ready to take the mission on head first. In my estimation, this was the most courageous speech I had ever heard, and it would prove itself to be a huge motivator for this unit who was suffering.

As we got back to our vehicles for the trip back to the headquarters, I pulled Colonel Walker to the side and gave him a battle hug. I told him quietly, "That was the best example of courageous leadership I have ever witnessed. Thanks, you were magnificent." We headed off to the headquarters to continue the agonizing duties we had to perform.

The tight bond between General Rand and I was growing closer by the minute. I thought about walking out and leaving him alone when he called Ginger to share his condolences, but felt it was right to stay and he agreed. Soon the call came from General Jones back at Luke AFB that his notification team completed their mission and we were now free to call Ginger.

The call to a spouse in a case like this is never easy, and although General Rand had completed it several times already on this tour, this one took on a different emotion because he knew the person on the other end of the phone. Over the next few minutes I watched as he dialed the phone, then spoke with a steady and heartwarming voice. His words could not have been more reassuring and heartfelt at a time like this. I sat in wonder at how he found the courage to remain focused while sharing the words I heard him say. I questioned my own ability to handle the situation with as much poise as he was doing right here in front of me. I knew I was witnessing something special from a leader among leaders. A man among men. A compassionate friend who hated making these calls, but handled them all with dignity.

My thoughts drifted back to Luke AFB and the family. I wanted to take the pain away from Ginger and the basketball team so they did not have to deal with it. There was nothing I could do from 8,000 miles away and it felt horrible. As the call ended he headed back to the conference room to get another update and let them know he had talked with the family. We sat in the conference room for a short time, getting info from others, and making sure we had a full understanding of the event.

I glanced over at the wall and studied the faces of the previous fallen Airmen from the wing. Sadness overwhelmed me after realizing I had to add a friend to the wall of heroes and write his name in my notebook. Again I wanted to scream and hit something, but I knew it was neither the time nor the place.

While the hours passed, back home the news media would be covering the fact that we lost a jet today. Although we locked down the communications and emails as standard practice, something always gets out. Our public affairs team did what they could to release the proper information and control the rumors, but something always finds a way around them.

I wondered what Mags and Kim Rand knew to this point. I needed to call her and let her know, as this was very personal for both of us. She deserved to know it was not the General and she also deserved to know that Major Gilbert was lost. I moved to my office and placed a short call to Mags' cell phone. She was at her volunteer work in a local hospital and although it was not the right situation for her to be in when she found out, she needed to know.

When she answered the phone I hesitated to tell her much. I asked if she had seen the news. She said the news reported the aircraft was from Baghdad and that she was not sure if it was one of ours, but she had a bad feeling. She asked if it was General Rand. I took a huge breath and told her it was Major Gilbert.

Her emotions took over and she nearly passed out in the hallway while leaning against a wall. One of her co-workers came out and found her nearly on the ground. She asked if everything was OK, and Mags told her no, that she just found out the name of the pilot who was lost in Iraq today, he was a good friend. She left right away.

Mags knew she needed to call Kim Rand to make sure she was OK. They needed to start working a plan of support. They had a strong network and would need to be informed before the news became public. Back in the General's office we looked at each other and knew what had just taken place. While I was talking to Mags on the phone he had called Kim. He knew she needed to know once Ginger was given the notification. This would be a tough day for our spouses, just like it was for us.

More hours passed and soon I realized it was nearly midnight. None of us had eaten during the day, and we had been locked inside the building for more than 12 hours handling this incident. Someone sent for food to be picked up at the DFAC and it was a great gesture. When it arrived we picked at it, but nobody really felt hungry.

The General knew he needed to get a little rest and get himself ready to lead through the next few days so we had better head to our quarters and get away from the building. By now everything that needed to be done on this end was complete. Colonel Renfrow assured the General he had everything under control and he would let us know if there were any changes or updates. He suggested the General head out for a little while and he would stay on until he returned. Colonel Ellis was also on duty and providing steady support for Colonel Renfrow, so we both felt comfortable leaving for a short time.

Walking together out of the building I was not sure what to say or if anything needed to be said at all. We hit our vehicles and drove to Red Tail Village. Once there, we met outside the gate and I asked the General how he was doing. He told me he was never good in these situations, but he would be OK, and just needed to clear his head. We decided on a time to rally back in the headquarters and then parted ways.

As I entered my quarters, my space, I finally broke down. My emotions could no longer be held in check and I was mad. In the minutes that followed I wanted to break things and howl at the moon. I challenged God to explain to me why he could let this happen to such a beloved Christian man who did nothing but good for those around him.

It was time to call and check in with my family. Mags picked up the phone and we both cried immediately. She had been dealing with this for hours, but hearing it from me again brought it even closer to home. Now it was real to her as well and many questions came to mind. What could she do? How would she be able to support Ginger and all the others who needed our support?

I told her she needed to do whatever she had to do to support them, travel to see them, or just help out. She told me how sorry she felt for all, but she was really worried about me. How was I taking this? She knew better than anyone that Major Gilbert and I shared a special bond. I tried to tell her about my last conversation with him, but emotions controlled the moment. She understood most of what I was saying, but clearly was more worried about how I felt and what she could now do for Ginger.

We talked about her attending the memorial at Luke. I encouraged her to go at all costs. She told me she would work it out and that I should not worry about her, she wanted me to focus on my own personal health and not let this loss drive me into a downward spiral. She also let me know Amber had come home from work and was with her after she returned from the hospital. Our future son-in-law Matt also came home to be with them and provide support. It was reassuring that my family would be OK together during this horrible time in our lives.

As soon as we hung up I lay on my bed and tried to write my thoughts about Major Gilbert so I could remember them later. It was hard, and my emotions interrupted many times. There was pain inside my body like never experienced before. I was angry at the insurgents and wanted to mount up and go after them. I was still mad at God. I could not grasp how he could take someone like Major Gilbert away so suddenly. I tried to find some understanding but there were no answers. It took an hour with all of the interruptions, but I finally captured my thoughts in a letter I would plan to share with others when the time was right.

The sound of the gate closing on the edge of Red Tail Village woke me up immediately. I jumped to my feet, still in uniform from the previous day. Lying on the bed was the letter, the pen still in my hand. The clock said it was time to meet the General and face the reality that we lost our friend and fellow Airman, Major Troy Gilbert.

Chief Dearduff and Chief Master Sergeant Bryce Maxson waiting for their turn at bat during the Chiefs versus Colonels whiffle ball game.

A Tuskegee Doctor catches a quick nap between traumas in the Emergency Department on the donated couch.

Major Troy "Trojan" Gilbert, killed in action, 27 November 2006.

General Rand and Major Gilbert taking a photo in front of the
Tuskegee block at the headquarters building.

7

I CAN ONLY IMAGINE

28 November 2006:

The first thing I did after arriving at the headquarters was to go into the command post and ask if there were any updates on Major Gilbert or location of his remains. They confirmed that our PJs were able to locate DNA remains at the scene when they initially responded, but they had nothing new or additional to report. Immediately I thought I needed to get out to the scene and start searching for his body. It was a dangerous mission, but it was one I wanted to take on. Locating the General inside his office, I told him I was rested and ready to head out to the area. He looked at me and smiled, knowing that I wanted this mission bad, and said he could not let me go. He had already formed an interim safety board and Colonel Ellis would lead the effort. He would not approve me going out to the scene since his Chief of Staff would already be there. I argued, but he had the final say. All I could do now was help those who were going on the initial trip to the accident site.

I could see several people moving about the hallway with great purpose. Among them was Airman Kellum, the photographer who captured Major Gilbert's photos on the day of his first flight. He was being prepped to fly to the scene and take photos to preserve the evidence. I became worried about him as I knew he had no combat training to prepare him if hostilities broke out while they were on the ground. I went over the operation of the M-16 rifle with him and made sure he was ready to protect himself under direct enemy fire. I felt like a protective father who was about to release his own kid into the world and I had failed to get him ready. Now I wanted to go more than ever, to care for the Airmen who were not combat experienced. I tried one last time and was reminded that I had been directed to stay back.

Four painstaking hours later the team returned and I peppered Colonel Ellis for information. He told me some of what they found, but reminded me he was now the Interim Board President and had to keep the information close hold. He assured me he would give me the details when the time was right. I understood the need to maintain the information and evidence, so I let it go. I was happy they returned unharmed, and needed to go and see Airman Kellum.

I spent much of the next few days in a fog, both literally and emotionally. Although we knew that we lost Major Gilbert and only recovered the small pieces of his remains, the time would pass slowly until we received confirmation of his DNA. He was still officially being listed as "Missing in Action, Whereabouts Unknown." Not being able to get closure on this issue made the pain in my stomach hurt more by the hour.

I failed to eat for most of the next three days following his tragic accident, it just hurt too bad to digest anything. I noticed things were bothering me more now. The cloud from the burn pit was thicker than normal. Black smoke covered a mile long area with a clear blue sky as the backdrop. The windows of my vehicle were covered in soot. My uniform smelled like I'd been in a small room that was on fire. The walls of my quarters needed a good washing. The smell bothered me like never before.

During these tough days, Colonel Ellis came by often and his words helped keep me focused. He also knew Major

Gilbert and had formed a personal relationship, so this was hard for him as well. His sense of humor, quick wit and ability to quote some of my favorite movie lines helped me stay focused during a very depressing time. Our friendship was growing stronger by the day as we helped each other mourn. Being a career fighter pilot and veteran of Desert Storm, he knew the pain of loss all too well.

Just two nights after losing Major Gilbert the base came under attack as it often did during the hours of darkness. Colonel Ellis was taking appropriate action to remain under cover inside his quarters and wondered why he always heard my door closing shortly after the attacks. On this occasion he decided to investigate. As he lay on the floor near his door, taking cover behind the rows of sandbags piled along the outside, he reached up and opened his door. He heard me walking away from my quarters and asked what I was doing. I told him that I was going out to check on the forces after the attack like I always did. As I walked around the corner and headed for my vehicle, I heard him say he was coming with me. Not wanting to place my friend in harm's way, I departed before he could get his gear on and join me.

The very next night, the rocket attack came again from several points of origin. Rockets impacted the camp and the flight line. As I began to move out, I found Colonel Ellis geared up and ready to roll. When I started to run toward my truck, I looked over and saw the Colonel, stride for stride with me, telling me he was going, and that I was not going to stop him. Although I still did not want my friend heading into the action, I felt better knowing a battle buddy was with me. Fortunately as we got to the scene, we found all the rockets had landed without engaging any targets, each falling harmlessly to the ground and creating small holes in the pavement and hard dirt of several parking lots. We evaded disaster again, and I for one was very happy— another night of attacks down and no loss of life or major damage.

3 December 2006:

I did not want this day to happen. I wanted to stay in my bed and sleep, hoping that when I woke up the whole thing would be a dream and we could get back to business. But reality took over and I knew I had to get up and get ready to attend a memorial ceremony for Trojan. During the days since his tragic loss, I spent time challenging my beliefs about my own mortality. I became keenly aware that tomorrow was not guaranteed. The only moments of peace these days was the official word on identification of the remains. It hurt differently now.

There was not much going on in the camp as I drove out. No aircraft noises, no construction sounds, and nobody scurrying about as normal. Those who were walking around did not have the normal pace in their step. Everyone seemed to be in slow motion, just milling around as if they were lost. There was an eerie feeling about the day and I hoped it would change.

Memorial services became the worst part of what we had to do in combat. They were happening far too often and none of us ever got used to them. In addition to the memorial ceremonies for our Fallen Airmen, we also attended many ceremonies on behalf of Soldiers assigned around Balad who were killed in action. The last one brought more personal pain than I wasn't prepared for. On that occasion, as we entered the chapel facility I made eye contact with a young Soldier whose emotions told me he lost a friend. When the long and emotional ceremony was over, I went over to comfort that Solider, only to realize that I knew him, and his face became instantly brighter for recognizing me.

He grabbed me with the strength of a grizzly bear and thanked me for attending. After a brief moment to catch my breath, I remembered how I knew this particular Solider. He was assigned to the Illinois Army National Guard and was activated after the attacks of September 11, 2001, and then came to my unit to support our operations. We reminisced quickly, I shared my condolences for his loss and we departed.

Another tough day of emotions added to the process of hardening me as a leader and person. Holding in my emotions would keep others from worrying about me. No matter how tough it was to lose a combat brother and close friend, I needed to deal with this in my own way and not become a drain on those around me.

On this cool December morning I was deeply involved in this memorial and had to gather my thoughts and muster the strength to face the day. I would need someone to lean on following this ceremony and the perfect person for that role was Chief Bryce Maxson. Whenever I needed to vent about this type of situation, it was Chief Maxson who came and stood by my side. I was counting on Bryce to be there with me.

Our friendship had grown significantly since we first met back at Luke AFB. I watched him grow from being a brand new chief master sergeant into a hardened combat leader. But I always knew he kept my best interest at heart and would be the one to keep me leveled on the tough days. I also knew he was communicating through email with Mags back home to keep her informed on how I was doing.

It would take every ounce of energy I could muster to hold it together while we honored Trojan. Thinking about Ginger and the kids back home, his mom and dad, in-laws, siblings and all of the unit members who would be attending similar events back in Arizona helped keep my mind occupied. I also knew I would feel the pain of my wife who would be attending memorial events with Kim Rand and many of our friends back in Arizona. They would all be there to help console the Gilbert family during their worst of times. Maybe the toughest part of the day was knowing we could not be there to help console them in person. There would be no travel home, because once the memorial service was over, we had to get back to the combat mission.

I felt no urge to eat, even though I could smell the distinct blend of odors coming from the DFAC that normally made me stop in and grab something before starting the long day. There was little conversation as people milled about in the camp, and very little exchange of thoughts when I got to the headquarters building and passed through the entry point, normally a high point of my morning. On this day, the young Airman charged with guarding the building and our safety knew it was neither the time nor the place to make small talk or ask how I was doing. We simply exchanged a quick pleasantry, he reviewed my badge and I went directly to my office.

Knowing I had several hours before the memorial, I closed my door and opted to remain quiet inside by myself and gather my thoughts. A few minutes later Sergeant Lizcano entered the office to check on me. I knew what Frankie wanted to say and he knew what I wanted to hear, so there was no need to have the exchange. About 30 minutes before the ceremony, he came back to make sure I was ready to go and had what I needed. He was one of the reasons I had to maintain appearances today, for he only knew the strong, confident chief, not the man who was being torn apart emotionally inside, and I did not want that to change.

Inside of the Town Hall tent over 500 people gathered to pay honor and tribute to a fellow Airman, a warrior, and a man who meant more to the wing than any of us could have ever known. Among those gather with us was the commander of the Joint Special Operations Command, a 3 star General. His presence was a clear indication of the respect that all of the special operators had for our fighter pilots, and specifically for Major Gilbert because of his actions on 27 November.

At all previous memorials and large gatherings, we all had concerns for the possibility of attack and mass casualties because of the large crowd being gathered in one small area. For some reason on this occasion it was not on my mind. It felt like we were in some worldly church with stained glass windows and hard wood pews. The wind howled and blew the sides of the tent so hard at times I thought the whole thing would come down on top of the crowd and cause another issue and many injuries. But it was not to be.

We seemed to be covered by something more powerful than the wind today. There was a presence I had not felt before. I could not explain it, could not describe it. I had no idea why I felt this way, but suddenly I became warm inside and felt a rush of strength take over my body. Right then I knew my emotions were in check and I would be able to maintain my composure. We were about to celebrate a life, not mourn a loss.

From the sharpness of the Honor Guard to the testimonials from fellow Airmen everything was perfect. The chaplain had the right words to say in Trojan's honor. His words were very appropriate for all that Trojan had given in service outside of uniform. Little did we all know how great his impact was on the chapel staff for all the time and energy he gave during his time off. Besides being a volunteer and active member of the church community at Balad, we also discovered how involved he had been at the hospital.

I remember the first time I saw him there and never once thought about asking him how often he volunteered. On this day we heard stories of his daily attendance at the Balad hospital and how much he contributed to their mission. Some days he was seen sweeping floors or standing by with a trash can to pick up the bloody materials laying around the emergency department during trauma cases. Other days he would join with other volunteers to stock the shelves in the makeshift storage containers behind the hospital. It was created by some innovative enlisted medics because of the large volume of support they received. It affectionately became known as the "Wal-Mart Closet" of the hospital. I knew from several of my own personal visits that it was well stocked and could rival a small store in any town USA.

What an amazing man we were paying tribute to. And now it was time for General Rand to give his testimonial. A tough moment for me to even think about, but once again, this man had the courage, the fortitude to go up and say what he wanted to say in Trojan's honor. He gave his personal recollection of times spent with Trojan. He reflected on the day we went to Al Asad. He talked about Trojan checking on him from time to time to ensure he was doing OK. He mentioned how Trojan never seemed to be without an infectious smile on his face. As he walked away from the podium I noticed he did not have any notes with him. I always knew he wrote out his remarks for a memorial from our previous experiences, but on this occasion, it appeared he spoke straight from the heart without any predetermined comments.

At the end of the General's words the small band, assembled from one of the regular church services, broke into song. Major James Lowe, the Commander of our Security Forces, was the lead singer. Something magical happened. I had never before heard the song he began to sing. The sound so smooth, the words so comforting. Although the wind continued to blow against the side of the tent, aircraft flew overhead, trucks steamed by to exit the base on convoy missions, and many other sounds could have detracted from their performance, the words came through to me like none before… "I can only imagine…" It was a heavenly song, and seemed so appropriate for this occasion and the man we were honoring. Major Lowe performed it with passionate perfection. Although he was done singing, somehow the song was stuck in my mind and it continued to play again and again.

When it was done, the General and I approached the front of the chapel, saluted as one, and then he went forward and knelt by the memorial and flag. After a brief moment he stepped back and it was my turn. I knelt, said a quick prayer and rose to my feet. As I came together with the General, we rendered a slow silent, final salute, then faced right and departed the area. In my mind the whole thing was moving in slow motion. I tried to convince myself this was only a nightmare and I would wake up and find my world still contained Major Troy Gilbert.

The 500 people in attendance remained inside to pay their respects as the General and I stepped out. We hugged and without saying a word, said everything that needed to be said. I retreated to my office and opened my notebook. It was extremely hard to write the name on that next line. Major Troy L. Gilbert, killed in action, 27 November 2006. I closed my notebook and laid it on the desk, tears covered my face.

For the next few hours I walked around in a fog. I wanted to call home and talk with Mags to make sure she had everything she needed for the trip to Arizona. Nothing else seemed to matter at the time.

The phone call was short because she had many people and important things to tend to. We shared our thoughts and I thanked her for being able to be there and help the others. I sat back in my chair and thought about taking a short nap to regain my energy before trying to move forward.

The radio sound came eerily across from the command post. It was the voice which told me something was bad. But I could not grasp another tragedy now: we were only days removed from the last one, and only hours from the memorial service. This had to be a mistake on my part, misinterpreting the radio call for "All Red Tails report to the Command Post." It could not be anything bad. Maybe the boss needed to get us all focused on things, and make sure we were all keeping it together.

Walking down the hall I could see the look on the face of Colonel Renfrow, and knew what was coming even before he said, "Chief, here we go again." I took a deep breath and collected my thoughts before learning the details of another tragedy.

We entered the conference room and began getting the details and watching a live feed from an unmanned aerial vehicle watching the scene of the incident. I heard the briefer say that a helicopter almost crashed into the water at Haditha Dam and some crew and passengers jumped into the water with full gear on. The initial reports said several were missing, including an Explosive Ordnance Disposal (EOD) officer, an Air Force captain. Additionally the briefer said recovery operations for the missing would take a considerable amount of time. For now, those warriors would be considered missing. I felt numb, but pain was stuck inside of me. I wanted to scream, but remained silent. The room went silent for a moment as we all took in this horrible news.

After about a minute of trying to ingest the thought of losing another Airman, my emotions began to build and a strong feeling of anger came over me. I leapt from my chair and departed the room so I could retreat to my office and not cause a problem for the other leaders who were trying to work this event. Colonel Ellis followed me out of the room, sensing something was wrong.

As always he brought me back to reality and told me what was best for everyone would be for me to get back to the conference room and see how I could help. I regained my composure and went back into the room to hear more details of the tragedy.

As the details became clearer, the name of the EOD captain was released and it stuck in my head like a knife. Air Force Captain Kermit Evans. I knew that name and something was fresh in my memory about it. I left again, this time going into the office and getting on the computer to check photos and emails from the past few months. There it was, an email from an Intelligence Chief who was assigned to the EOD task force in Baghdad we visited in late October. Attached was a photo of me with the task force team, including Captain Evans who had just perished in the incident.

I sat back in the chair, unaware of the warning sirens going off in the background signaling an air attack. I did not move. All I could think about was the words I shared with the captain weeks before. I remembered being very impressed with his leadership, and after visiting with them and passing out a few of my personal coins for recognition of excellence, I had asked the captain to come outside with me where I handed him a coin.

I said, "Captain, it's not very often that I coin a commissioned officer, and I never do it in front of their Airmen. But it's even rarer when I am as impressed with the leadership of a young company grade officer as I was today. You are an impressive leader and I want you to have this coin as a small token of my appreciation." He was grateful, smiled and thanked me for the coin and for visiting his team. It hurt even more knowing he was now gone from our ranks.

I felt honored to have met Captain Evans and experience his leadership of a multi-functional team in combat. He exemplified a true American hero.

Still reeling from the pain of losing Trojan, with a heavy heart I took a deep breath, reached into my pocket and wrote the name of another great warrior in my notebook. Captain Kermit Evans, killed in action, 3 December 2006.

Brigadier General Robin Rand and Chief Dearduff rendering honors to Major Troy Gilbert during a memorial ceremony in the Town Hall.

Chief Dearduff on bended knee reflecting at Major Gilbert's memorial long after the crowd departed.

Visiting with Captain Evans (4th from left) and his task force in
Baghdad in October 2006.
Captain Evans was killed in action 3 December 2006.

Staff Sergeant Frankie Lizcano checking out our vehicle before
moving out on a mission.

8
REFOCUSED EFFORT

4 December 2006:

Arriving at the wing headquarters for the morning meetings, I was hoping for a quiet, non-emotional day. After the meeting I planned to spend time walking around Balad and visiting with Airmen and Soldiers. Unfortunately the first update at the morning meeting showed that our Air Force PJs completed recovery operations at Haditha Dam. It was now confirmed; Captain Kermit Evans was deceased. Although we knew it in our minds the day before, now it seemed to hit us right in the heart. I did not hear another word from the entire meeting, I was lost in my thoughts about Captain Evans' family back home. His wife and 1 year old son, Kermit Jr.

The next 36 hours went by and I remained in a haze. I could not stop thinking about my recent encounter with Captain Evans, about how losing a warrior who was young, talented and full of life, could be taken from this earth so suddenly. I told everyone who would listen how impressive he was; an incredible leader.

I found myself snapping at people for no reason. I snapped on the wrong guy one time too many and he let me know. Colonel Ellis knew I was using him to vent my frustrations, but as a good friend would do, he also set me straight. He was bluntly let me have it.

After a brief counseling session led by Colonel Ellis, I needed to get out and check on the progress of the memorial. I pulled into the engineers' compound and walked inside to find several members of the shop working hard to finish the project. The shop foreman met me and said he heard about the casualty and expected I would be by to check on their progress. He assured me they were on schedule and would have everything done in advance of the ceremony.

A sense of relief came over me knowing these professional engineers took this project personally and would do everything in their power to ensure it was done on time and to perfection. My efforts could now be placed on the execution of the ceremony itself. No matter how much I wanted to stay in the moment and start planning for the memorial dedication ceremony, I could not stop drifting back to Arizona and Luke Air Force Base. Today, 6 December, the memorial service for Major Troy Gilbert would take place and both Mags and Kim would be in attendance. It would be the hardest day for many involved. While they would all have it tough, few could understand the pain Ginger and the kids would experience. They were my only focus today. The pain continued.

Captain Evans' memorial was upon us. We were about to honor another warrior for making the ultimate sacrifice on the fields of battle. We marched from the headquarters building to the Town Hall for the gathering of the brotherhood, one formed through trial and tribulation. Hundreds of Airmen, Soldiers, and civilians were gathered on an unusually hot and sunny day in early December.

Normally Iraq mornings had a harsh chill in the air, and we often wore jackets or wool undershirts to stay warm. On this day the sun was bright and strong. Heat came pouring through the sides of the tent like never before. The air conditioning units used to cool the inside of the tent could not keep up and the air became still, the heat overbearing. Everyone in the crowd sat sweating like we were outside in the intense heat of the summer, but I sat quietly unaffected by the heat. My body was chilled, my mind drifting off to that last meeting with Captain Evans, almost totally unaware of the discomfort of those around me.

The ceremony began with testimonials about the captain and his faithful service. Sweet songs of joy and praise followed. Some of his fellow Airmen talked about his young family back home and how they would be surrounded by so many during this most difficult time.

Throughout the ceremony the strength of the EOD brotherhood permeated around the tent. Being outside of their community made it hard for me to understand what I was sensing. The only thing I could relate to was the loss of one of your own.

As expected, the EOD community paid tribute to Captain Evans in an honorable and meaningful way. Everyone who spoke on his behalf helped validate my personal experience. This was a great Airman who would truly be missed. We ended the ceremony by moving to the front and paying our final respects. As I looked at his photo on the screen behind the memorial, I decided to recommit myself to focus my energy on the enforcement of standards. Captain Evans was a standards enforcer like me, and I would hope to make him proud with my effort.

Following the memorial service it seemed difficult to get back to business. There were so many places to go and so many things to do. Within hours of the ceremony we headed out to the flight line to welcome the Secretary of the Air Force, his wife, and a traveling staff. Normally allot of planning and preparation go into visits with dignitaries at this level, but frankly, the memorial service held our highest priority, so we just handled this visit impromptu.

The Secretary immediately expressed how happy he was to visit and spend the day with Airmen on the center of the battle field. He and his wife knew of the serious nature of the attacks, and both asked right away what they should do in case of an attack. We explained the expected actions, but hoped deep down inside it would not be needed. Our travels took us to the headquarters building for a photo opportunity with members of the wing leadership team. The Secretary obliged any and all who wanted to have their photo with him. The final photo was taken with General Rand, myself, and the Secretary and his wife. When we finished, everyone headed into the building for an update on the mission in Iraq from our perspective.

"Incoming, Incoming, Incoming" sounded on the public address system just after arriving inside General Rand's office. Everyone looked stunned. We just walked the Secretary and his wife inside the building and now we were under attack. Instinctively we all dove to the floor. The Secretary came around the corner and saw everyone on the floor, including his wife who was lying beside me just after I instructed her to get down. General Rand told the Secretary to get down on the floor until the attack was over and he responded immediately. Several mortar rounds could be heard hitting in close proximity to the headquarters building, but fortunately there were no injuries. As we rose to our feet, the Secretary looked at General Rand and said, "It's almost like you planned that attack so we could see what you go through!" We all laughed, dusted ourselves off and continued toward the briefing room. The remainder of the visit went well and our visitors got to experience a real day in the life of combat Airmen.

In the days following Captain Evans' memorial I reflected on his life and service each time I opened my notebook and read his name. The holidays were fast approaching, and I knew the General and I would be traveling to the far reaches of this war-torn country to visit our Airmen while his family and many others would be grieving at home.

My reputation was already set, and carried on from previous units and deployed locations. All of the Airmen knew I was a standards enforcer myself, and I would not walk past a problem. But none of them was prepared for what was about to happen. I briefed the General about my new leadership focus. I told him on this day I vowed to give every ounce of my energy, every bead of sweat, and every hour of the day to ensure I did everything within my power to ensure the safety of our Airmen.

Later in the evening I decided to have some chow by myself and drove to the DFAC, parked, and walked in from the side of the parking lot minding my own business. As I neared the entrance to the facility two young female Airmen were fast approaching, both apparently off duty and wearing their Air Force Physical Training (PT) uniforms.

PT uniforms were mandatory for wear when we were not on duty, and there was a clear standard for how they were to be worn. On this occasion, the two young females clearly had decided that following the rules was not in their plans. As they got closer, I noticed their shoes were not tied, their shirts were not tucked in, and both had jewelry hanging outside of their shirt. One of them had not made any effort to place her hair in a military fashion and clearly did not meet the regulations.

They came upon me just before the ID checkpoint, and I asked them to stop and talk with me before going in. After a brief conversation, I asked them where they worked. They both replied, "We're in the medical group at the immunization clinic." So I said, "OK, I assume you know the standards for wearing the PT uniform on this base?" They both replied that they knew. Then I said, "Since you know the standards and tonight have chosen not to follow them, I wonder what other standards you don't follow." There was a silence.

"When you don't follow the dress and appearance standards, the easy ones, it makes me wonder what you do on the really hard ones." They looked at each other with cold stares. One of them looked at me and said, "Yes, Chief, we know the standards for giving immunizations."

I said, "Well, now I have a problem. If you knew the standards for wearing the uniform but chose not to follow them, how do I know you will follow the standards at the immunization clinic when I come for my next vaccination?" The message was clear and there was no need to continue the conversation.

This encounter with the young Airmen proved my point about the need to focus on standards. I had to get all the senior NCOs and junior NCOs on this path and have them start correcting behavior contradictory to good order and discipline. Somehow this message needed to spread.

I walked in, grabbed some food and headed for the door, choosing to eat back at my quarters rather than enjoy a hot meal in the comfort of the DFAC. This was becoming a sad routine, but taking the chance of being in public and having to constantly correct standards violations was no way to enjoy a meal.

Our travels continued and there never seemed to be enough time to visit all the Airmen working around Balad. The General continued to fly combat sorties, and the days passed like hours. One constant among the chaos was the support from people back home. Combat warriors are tough people, but they always seemed to get a little emotional when they received things from back home. Holiday cheer never got old, and in addition to the individual care packages that came in, several programs provided boxes of goodies for any and all. We challenged ourselves to ensure everyone received a box from home, regardless of where it came from.

Mags gathered donations to support our deployed forces during our last two duty stations. This year she led a community effort to help send boxes of Christmas stockings for us to hand out to the Airmen around the country. Even our son's religious education class pitched in. She also continued to send blankets to share. The effort seemed endless and touched those inside and outside of the military community. My oldest daughter got involved and even became crafty, making a blanket and sending it over for our sharing. People in towns like Freeburg, Belleville and O'Fallon Illinois reached out to support our Airmen through these programs.

Kim Rand dug in as always and recruited many of her friends and family to pitch in for a cookie drive. By now we had received boxes of home baked cookies from people in and out of the Air Force family. Kim made sure all the boxes were sent to my office, and she trusted that we would get them out to the forces. We came to expect this level of support from our own spouses and their networks, but this effort really showed me a higher level of concern than I ever imagined from people we did not know.

My office was filled with donations. The hallway outside my office and down into the supply closet was filled with boxes. We had so much of everything from Christmas cards to playing cards it seemed impossible to get it all distributed. The chocolate and candy started to pile up inside the headquarters building and we needed to move it along before we had a major health problem on our hands. We loaded bags every time we boarded a helicopter and headed out, always coming back empty-handed.

15 December 2006:

The Airmen of our wing continued to impress us with their resilience and motivation. We traveled to Camp Speicher in northern Iraq. This base was named in honor of Scott Speicher, a US Naval aviator who was lost in Operation Desert Storm. Speicher was a huge camp with a great runway that provided a logistical hub for the US Army in this area. We planned to visit with the large contingent of Airmen assigned to the Expeditionary RED HORSE (Rapid Emergency Deployment Heavy Operational Repair Squadron Engineers) unit. They were a high speed engineering unit who took on the toughest projects.

After we had landed and taken some detailed briefings about what they had already accomplished, they asked if we wanted to go and see Airmen working on the job site. We both enjoyed meeting with Airmen on the job so off we went.

At the site we were briefed that this particular project would build the main road connecting several parts of the base. This single roadway would improve operations by creating safe travel routes for movement of logistical equipment. We each received information from different Airmen about what it takes to build a road. Then the General called me over and asked if I wanted to drive the asphalt paving machine.

This was one of the largest machines I had seen on a job and I was excited from the minute we arrived, hoping I could drive it and walk a mile with these hard-working Airmen. I practically ran to the machine and after gearing up, I mounted the seat and took my instructions from the Sergeant whose job I was taking momentarily.

His instructions were perfect, but still did not give me all the skills I would need. It seemed this skill took more than desire and instruction. Controlling this machine was not easy and quickly I had the line of asphalt skewed to the right. They told me to slow down so they did not have to come back and fix my work. The last thing I wanted to do was create more work for them. I slowed the machine and eventually got the hang of it.

I could see the General and the others were being whisked away for the next meeting so I waved to them; I would stay behind. Unfortunately I was directed to join them. I told the guys that I wanted to stay and work the rest of the day, but I could tell they were ready for me to depart also. Thanking them for allowing me to have this opportunity, I jumped down to the ground and had to run to the truck before they departed without me.

The remainder of the trip to Camp Speicher was uneventful and we made our way back to Balad. Another week of battlefield circulation was complete and we remained proud of everything going on around the country.

During a mid-December trip to Baghdad we made sure to visit the units with Airmen who frequently went outside the wire (OTW) on the more dangerous missions. One such unit was the EOD team stationed at the Baghdad International Airport. We spent time with them, learning more about their operations and the arduous route clearance missions they undertook each day.

Although the living conditions they had here at the airport were rough, with just basic tents, lots of trash still remaining from the initial invasion of the city, and the constant smell of sewage in the air, we also learned they had Airmen who spent months at a time out at forward operating bases had little to no support and very often, no other Air Force presence of any kind. Some of these Airmen were at the airport getting a break from the OTW operations for a few days. I spent time talking with each, getting to know them and where they were from. We laughed, told a few stories and I informed them of what was going on at the headquarters level and around the rest of the country.

I shared news from around the battlefield because each unit seemed isolated and knew only what they were impacting locally, without much knowledge of the bigger picture. They seemed receptive to hearing it, so I continued to share. Once I completed my update there was something I needed to say to this team. I told them, "I do not know how it must be to go outside the wire every day and perform the missions you take on. I have not done what you do. Therefore, I want to share my respect and let you know that I willingly support your efforts no matter the circumstance." These were tough times for the EOD community, and they needed support more than ever. As we departed, I shared some final thoughts with the team leaders and ensured them we would handle roadblocks standing in their way.

24 December 2006:

Christmas Eve came and went almost like any other day on the mission. My mind drifted back home once an hour, wondering what it was like for my family who were alone, celebrating the holidays without me once again. Fortunately the General, Colonels Renfrow and Ellis, and several others convinced me to go with them as we worked our way around the base, spreading more good cheer. Everywhere we went there were Airmen on duty. There are no holidays from combat, and this trip proved it.

My time to call home came around and I sat alone in the office, hoping the phone line would not be cut off while talking to Mags yet again. The last thing I wanted on this day was to add stress to their lives. Once on the phone, we laughed, then we cried. I wondered how many holidays we would spend apart in our lives. They shared the details of their day so I could remain connected. I shared a few stories with them, but failed to reveal the pain I was feeling and the strong urge I had to give up this fight because it was taking a huge toll on me. I could not share my feelings about the casualties or what it was like to work so hard at keeping everyone focused on the standards during the holidays with so much joy and celebration going on.

Later in the evening all the leaders assembled at one of the DFACs to support the troops. Some served meals behind the line while others greeted troops as they entered. Even though we were not actual family, we sensed the troops appreciated us being part of their family for the day.

You could see joy in their faces knowing they would be getting a holiday meal with trimmings, and you could see the pain in their eyes from being away from home; some for the first time while others had done this repeatedly. I hesitated to ask how many times they have been away, but often held on to the handshake longer and stared deeper into the eyes of the older NCOs, as I knew they were the ones paying the heaviest of prices, with the most left at home.

The strength of our brotherhood became clear. Not just in my own service, but across the services, and regardless of the color of the uniform, we each knew that this was about coming together as a team and accomplishing the mission. This was the largest family gathering I had ever attended, even though none of my own family attended.

Christmas morning dawned like any other day for the men and women of the 332d Air Expeditionary Wing. We continued to fly missions over the skies of Iraq. General Rand and Colonel Scott flew a 5 hour mission together, making sure they set an example for the younger aviators. EOD forces went out on patrols to ensure they cleared IED situations. Security forces provided base defense and firefighters prepared for emergencies that arose. Although everyone was in a great mood, you could tell they were missing their families and would much rather be with them.

We prepared for the arrival of General North and his team from Central Command Air Forces. He liked to visit Iraq on Christmas day and spend time with the Airmen who were always in harm's way. We knew he worked 20 hours a day, so this would be a long and fruitful duty for us. His team arrived late in the evening and we greeted them as always out on the flight line. Quickly we rushed them back to the headquarters for a few minutes of private discussion between the Generals, allowing me to spend time with his command chief, and let him know what we had been doing. Chief Todd Small was someone I had come to know from other gatherings and we often talked about how our Airmen were doing on this great mission.

Before long we were out visiting work centers with General North and his team. Airmen truly enjoyed his visits since he was not one to come in and inspect how things were going. He enjoyed hearing what the units were doing and if there was a demonstration or practical thing he could be involved in with the Airmen that was even better. Mostly, he just wanted to meet them and find out what their issues were. If there was something he could fix, his team took notes and got to work. On this trip we gave him some of the Christmas bags we had received, and he handed them out as we went. Some Airmen even referred to him as Santa Claus because he was being so generous. We all laughed.

Midnight came as we visited with Security Forces Airmen out guarding the base. This was one of General North's favorite parts and we all laughed and smiled while enjoying the enthusiasm of the Defenders. Their Commander, Major Lowe, and their Chief, Kevin White, were with us throughout this portion of the visit. They were doing a great job of leading this team and making sure everyone at Balad had the opportunity to work without looking over their shoulder wondering who was coming behind them. Major Lowe and Chief White had led through more than 150 base attacks to this point in their tour, and the stress on the unit was grueling. Morale remained high and it was a clear reflection of the active leadership they provided for this large unit. Every time I saw Major Lowe I thanked him for singing at our memorials. He knew how much we appreciated his effort, but remained extremely humble.

Watching General North's interaction with the Defenders, I began to wonder what he was like as a person. Was he always this way, friendly and enjoyable, or was there another side to the leader with such a hard reputation? Watching the team around him he seemed very genuine and he approached everything the same way. I knew there was much to learn from his leadership teachings.

Dropping the team off around 0200 at their quarters, another short night of sleep was ahead. As we neared the quarters I asked General North how he handled these long duty days and going from one base to another, often working well past the 20-hour mark in a day. He looked at me and said, "I'm not sure how we do it, but we can sleep when we are dead." I stood in awe listening to him and hoped to spend more time with him as the years went on. His leadership was inspirational to everyone around. His genuine concern for these Airmen gave me strength to continue moving forward.

We had to get the team on a plane by 0600 so they could visit Airmen in Afghanistan. I wondered how a leader could summon enough stamina for these long days and remain completely in touch like he does. It was all one could do to try and keep up with him. My admiration grew.

Most people found ways to enjoy the holidays even though they were in combat and far away from their families. I never got lost in those moments. All I could think about was the pain and suffering endured by the families of our Fallen Airman. I thought about the Clemons family, the Chavis family, the Gilbert family and the Evans family. How would they make it through a time like this? They had to cope with the reality that holidays would never be the same. I longed for answers to tough questions about life. The pain was deep. My life was affected in ways I never imagined.

30 December 2006:

A major world event took place not too far from our location at Balad Air Base. The former dictator, Saddam Hussein was executed by the Iraqi people following his conviction for crimes he committed. The event went mostly unnoticed by the wing and the Airmen who were serving in Iraq at the time. We wondered aloud what this moment meant in the history of the world. Would this create the positive turn for the Iraqi people and quell the insurgency, or would it spark more radical behavior and anti-American sentiment? Only time would tell.

Reflecting after hearing the news about Saddam, I remembered the day of his capture during a previous deployment, during the death of his two sons, and now during his death. It was a great victory for the Iraqi people and should bring them great relief.

I was glad to see 2006 come to an end. I hoped 2007 would be a better year for the Tuskegee Airmen, our fellow Soldiers, Sailors and Marines, and even for the Iraqi people. The New Year brought promise.

Captain Kermit O. Evans, Explosive Ordnance Disposal, killed in action
3 December 2006.

Chief Dearduff working with the RED HORSE Airmen to build a road
at Camp Speicher Iraq.

Lieutenant General Gary L. North, Commander, U.S. Air Forces Central Command, handing out Christmas stockings to the Airmen at Balad.

Lieutenant General North viewing the Fallen Airman Memorial during the design phase at the Civil Engineering Structures shop.

9
A TRAGIC ANNIVERSARY

New Year's Eve and New Year's Day were big deals celebrated by our families back home, but really did not get much attention here in combat. On 31 December, Chief Maxson convinced me to stop by the recreation center and see what our Airmen were up to. It seemed like an easy way to show some spirit and be around some happy people.

Arriving before midnight, I found the center manager Kiera Clark and her staff doing what they did best, entertaining the forces and making them feel like they were back home. She always had a way of bringing a smile to the faces of the service members even on days like this when they were missing home. Airmen were mixed with Soldiers, Marines, Sailors and civilians around tables playing Texas Hold'em. Movies were on in one corner, while others played pool and ping pong. Everyone in the center was engaged in their activities with friends and fellow warriors, so I headed off to my quarters. I ushered in 2007 alone.

New Year's Day was no different. It was a routine business day for Airmen around the wing. Sorties were flown, missions outside the wire took place, and everyone had mission focus. This was no holiday; it was just another day in Iraq, which just happened to be the first day of this New Year. With any luck, this year would bring different results to the mission in Iraq. New Year's Day was a chance to reflect what we accomplished in the previous six months.

During the last half of 2006 the fighting in Operation Iraqi Freedom had increased in all statistical categories. Balad Air Base had been attacked more than 175 times, a rate higher than it had ever been since opening up in 2004. There were more indirect fire attacks, more IED attacks, more small arms fire incidents, and more insurgent activity in the country than in any six-month period of the previous three years. Enemy activity was at all-time highs and the insurgency appeared to be gaining ground. The 332d Wing had flown more sorties, dropped more bombs, and eliminated more enemy than in any previous similar time frame. More cargo was transported, more service members traveled on tactical and strategic aircraft. The list of accomplishments was endless.

Unfortunately, the human toll was also bad. More US Service Members had been injured or killed than any other time in OIF. The human toll was rough and proved to be a great challenge for the medical professionals at the Balad hospital and across the battlefield. Our surgeons completed an average of more than 2000 procedures per month and still maintained a survival rate of better than 96%. Families back home owed a debt of gratitude to these capable medical professionals, but would never get the chance to say thanks.

The wing had grown to more than 8,200 Airmen, and many were serving in ILO missions outside the wire. More Airmen were in direct contact with the enemy daily than we had ever experienced, and it brought stress to the force. The turn of this New Year had to bring us some relief or at least let us see that we were making progress in the overall fight. We needed something to maintain the high state of morale and keep everyone focused.

General Rand often said things that made sense to the leaders on our staff. At the turn of the year he said, "January is going to be a defining month for the war in Iraq." He knew and saw what most of us were overlooking. Our wing and the other services fighting in Iraq were making progress and the country was improving each and every day. Although the costs were still high, our service and the completion of each mission were critical to the long term success of this war torn country.

7 January 2007:

January would represent a personal milestone for me. January 7th was the 25th anniversary of my entry into the United States Air Force. Back then I never imagined I would serve this long or lead Airmen in combat. But here I was, about to celebrate my anniversary directly in the fight against the insurgency, exactly where I needed to be. Never being one to publically celebrate birthdays and anniversaries, I was pleased it fell on a Sunday and the day could pass without any mention.

Our travels in the first week of January took us to see unit across the country. It was amazing to see how they were impacting combat operations. I decided as my new year's resolution I would make every effort to meet as many Airmen as possible, learn their stories and ensure I was giving them every ounce of support I could muster.

January also brought the rotation of forces and all the new ideas that came with new arrivals in Iraq. Having six solid months on the ground now, my tolerance level for new ideas was very short. I encouraged them to focus on learning the operation as it currently existed for the first 30 days, then if they found something to change or improve, they could bring it forward and we would give them our full attention.

I told them if they saw something that did not comply with the standards or violated safety, it had to be fixed right away. Normally it was the "I did this different at my last base, and …" It was a tough transition to get people to understand this was a combat operation and while things were fluid, they needed to be standardized for one team made up of people from 50 bases. This would continue to be one of the hardest challenges faced in trying to maintain the right combat mission focus across the force.

My heart wanted this day to be different. I wanted to control things but knew it was not possible. I decided to break from the routine and enjoy a long run at the fitness center. There was a unique sound coming from outside, and it appeared to be raining. We had not received much rain, but when we did, it would always stay around for a long time and create flood-like situations in the camp. I glanced out the window and saw the area around my quarters was filling up fast. There was nowhere for the water to go, so it filled the sidewalks around the area and created a lake. I figured I could go about my day and avoid the floods for now.

Stepping into the bathroom I found the water was not working in the sink or toilet. It happened, so we just moved on and knew it would be fixed in short order. Sometimes it just meant the water bladder was not filled on time and it needed to be corrected. I decided to head to the fitness center and get the workout in, hoping the shower would work when I returned.

Stepping outside of the quarters my feet were soaked immediately. Looking to the right I noticed that all of this water was not from the rain, but was compounded by a break in the water line heading into Red Tail Village. Stepping back in I called the Civil Engineering work center and asked if they could send someone out.

Two Airmen arrived and quickly identified the water line break. They told me it would take several hours to clean out the area and they were the only ones available to work this problem. I asked what could be done to help. They looked at each other and assured me they could handle it. I thanked them, and then said, "Pass me the shovel."

For the next two hours we dug in the mud to clear the area where the break was. Once it was clear they set up a pump system to move the water out of the hole, allowing them a place to work. It took about four hours, but in the end it was complete and all water service was restored. The three of us were covered in more mud than we cared to think about. I had no idea how I would get all this out of my uniform and boots, but right then I did not care. I also knew this physical labor could easily count for my workout and I did not need to head to the gym. Back inside my quarters there was laundry to do, a book to read, and a phone call to make back home. Otherwise, this would be a slow day.

The afternoon brought out the sun and blue skies. I decided to head out for a drive and maybe even take in some shopping at the exchange to see what was new. I checked in on the radio and there was silence. Normally there was an immediate acknowledgement of my status check, so something must be going on. What was the deal with this day? Seconds later the Command Post came on the radio. "All Red Tails report to the Command Post."

My heart seemed to stop, I began to lose the focus in my eyes, and I had to stop my truck. I knew the call, and did not want to face the news that we had lost another Tuskegee Airman. It had been more than a month since we had lost Captain Evans, and maybe, I hoped, this radio call was for something new and less impacting than the tragic loss of life.

As I walked in Colonel Renfrow met me in the hallway and said, "Chief, this is not good. We have two KIA and one fighting for her life."

I lost my breath for a second, stopped and leaned against the wall and felt like screaming. Not one, but two and possibly three Airmen lost in one incident. An IED would be the only thing that could take away so many at once and it was likely EOD or Security Forces.

Inside the battle staff I noticed a few extra faces in the room. I quickly realized these were leaders from the EOD career field and their presence told me what I feared. It was obvious they were hurting. I asked them if there was anything I could do to help comfort them for the moment, and they responded very directly with, "No, chief, we don't need any help."

They would not open up to me...an unbreakable wall existed that I could not breach. They were in a world all their own and would not let anyone in at this time of tragedy. As the details of the incident became clearer, my anger grew. As our third warrior fought for life in a combat hospital, I wondered what could have done to help prevent this.

As the briefer continued, someone interrupted from outside the room. The horrible news came about our third warrior losing her battle. They also reported that a fourth member who was with the team was also injured. He would be medically evacuated to the Balad hospital.

The briefer provided the names of the Airmen killed in action. "Technical Sergeant Timothy Weiner, Senior Airman Daniel Miller and Senior Airman Elizabeth Loncki, all from the 775th Civil Engineering Squadron at Hill AFB in Utah." I had already begun to write those names into my book when it hit me. These were the very Airmen who I had met in the tent at Baghdad during our last visit. I distinctly remember trying to pronounce Weiner and Loncki's names and we laughed as I got one right and one wrong. A strong bond between them existed, and it did not surprise me that if something happened to one, it would affect the others as well. Just like previous casualty reports, this one hit hard and I had to leave the room to clear my thoughts.

I was mad. Thoughts of tough issues were boiling inside of me. I thought there must have been something more I could have done to get inside the wall and help them as a career field. There must have been more I could have done to fix any issues they were facing. This was tearing me up inside. My head hurt and my stomach churned. There came a moment when I was lost in my thoughts with no answer to any of the questions I had for myself.

After several hours of processing information and ensuring we had everything in order for notifications, I decided to visit the EOD shop and see what I could do to help. As I entered the parking lot, I realized it would not be the right time or place to begin my efforts because of my anger. This was a close-knit brotherhood and they would all be suffering right now even if they did not have personal relationships with the ones who were killed.

I drove away and spent the next hour on my own, driving around the 22-kilometer perimeter, smelling the awful smoke from the burn pit, looking outside the perimeter and wondering how a country full of people could live in such poverty-stricken conditions. I drove past people who were milling about their day, totally unaware that three Americans were just killed and by the end of the day, several more Soldiers and Marines would also give their lives in service to the country. I became more incensed that nobody seemed to know but me. My anger filled the truck as my mind raced a hundred miles an hour looking for a solution to the problem.

Hours later I decided to go back to my quarters and try to get some rest. I could not, and just sat quietly in my room reviewing emails from the previous day. I sent a few notes to the leadership chain back home so they knew we had everything under control. I needed some rest for the events of the coming days and the multiple memorial ceremonies we would attend. I sat there quietly, hoping for answers to the questions still on my mind.

"Incoming, Incoming, Incoming…" and on the floor I went. This time I waited the mandatory 2 minutes to see if the attack made it through before I went out to survey the damage. I heard chatter on the radio like never before, and could hear the distant sound of sirens through the haze of the early morning. The entire time I was lying there on the floor I fought the urge to get up and respond immediately.

As soon as the minimum time passed, I headed out and drove toward the hospital, fearing the worst. Fortunately what I found on arrival was only minor injuries to two civilians and one Soldier. I did find several Airmen who were near the points of impact and who had stories to tell.

Included in those was a young female Airman who told me she heard the sirens and decided to run for the nearest bunker rather than hit the ground immediately as we were instructed to do on hearing the warning. On her way to the bunker she tripped on some loose rocks and fell to the ground, temporarily hurting her knee. Her incidental fall made her decide to stay in place rather than head to the bunker about 75 meters away. Lucky for her, as the bunker took a direct hit from a small diameter rocket; likely about where she would have been had she kept running. It was her lucky day and I made sure she knew next time she was to do as ordered and hit the ground.

For the next several hours I sought refuge in the emergency department of the hospital as I often did. On this night I was walking with a noticeable limp on my right side which caught the attention of the orthopedic surgeon, one of the best in the country. He said, "Chief, looks like you are limping tonight. What's wrong with your knee?"

I said I was just tired and had a long day on my feet, and everything was OK. But he was not buying it and demanded to look at my knee. With a quick exam of my knee he determined that I had major damage to the joint and would need surgery. He said, "Things are slow around here tonight, we could take you in now and have you back on your feet by lunchtime tomorrow." I laughed. He said he was serious and had a look in his eye.

Although it was tempting, I told him it would not be right for me to take the bed away from a battlefield wounded warrior nor would I be able to live with myself if he was tied up in the operating room working on me while someone came in with battle injuries and needed his attention. "Maybe later on Doc, but not tonight, I just cannot take you away from the mission at hand." He seemed to agree and told me any time I wanted to have it fixed to let him know. I felt like the brotherhood I formed with the Tuskegee Medics was stronger than ever before, and I would be taken care of no matter what happened on this battle field.

January 7th was now done and I never once had the chance to think about my 25th anniversary of joining the Air Force. There had not been one minute for celebration. Exactly as intended.

8 January 2007:

The rainy season was apparently upon us, something none of us were truly ready for. The sound of heavy rain woke me earlier than planned, and when I looked outside, I could see the water was already pooling around my quarters. I knew this would impact our ability to fly missions, which might negatively impact our overall ability to meet mission demands. I had to get around the base and see what damage had already been done.

Driving around Balad showed the full impact from rain in the desert environment. Everything seemed to be covered in mud. Water was collecting in the areas where our engineers had planned for it to go, and it was overflowing those retention ponds and impacting our ability to travel by foot and by vehicle. Everything came to a standstill. Flying missions were cancelled, convoys were slowed in moving outside the wire, and maintenance on the flight line became extremely difficult to manage. I spent the entire day going place to place and lending a hand with water damage or whatever they needed. Each time I entered the flight line I stopped and washed off my tires with the pressure washers placed by the entry points. The possibility of major damage to an aircraft engine from mud and rocks was high, so it was critical that every vehicle complete this process before entering. Airmen volunteered their day off to pitch in and help others. It was a great showing of teamwork that can only exist within a tight-knit unit, under difficult circumstances. I retreated to Red Tail Village for some rest.

Four hours of sleep was interrupted as the radio crackled with the sound of the controller's voice. "All Red Tails report to the Command Post." I hated that radio call. It was not good, but this time I did not have the same feeling.

As I went outside to see or hear if anything was unusual, I noticed a dense fog had appeared and visibility was severely restricted. Thoughts crossed my mind about an aircraft or helicopter accident because of the fog conditions, so my heart slowed to a very low rhythm. I hesitated to enter the briefing room and find out what was going on.

The briefer had a concerned look, but not one normally associated with the solemn nature of a death notification. Opening my notebook, I started with the first page, and went over the list of names annotated to this point. When I got to the end, I took a deep breath and hoped I would not be adding more today.

The briefer began once everyone was in the room and within seconds I could tell this was not going to be a briefing about another tragedy. He stated the weather was so bad that we had to close the runway and divert all aircraft to alternate runways and maybe even some non–US-controlled landing strips. This was a big deal and the reason for recalling the leadership team was evident.

Sending our aircraft to other locations brought many concerns and this explained my feelings about it being a long day. Many in this room would now plan to work well into the night, making sure our crews and aircraft returned safely and were secured at the alternate locations. We would also likely have to send maintenance crews out to recover those jets, but we could not do that until the fog cleared. There was much to do, and the day would grow longer with every hour. Following the initial brief there was not much more for me to do, so I departed and informed the General that I would be out and about, checking on our Airmen in case anything went wrong.

A loud boom came from the east. It sounded like an artillery barrage landing near the perimeter, but I knew we did not have active artillery units in the area, so it drew my attention. I headed toward the hospital, knowing that if anything was going to go wrong, it would end up having something to do with the hospital. I thought about generators exploding and many other possibilities that could have caused the noise, but could not lock into anything.

When I entered the hospital compound, the Defender told me he heard the noise come from outside the perimeter and immediately afterward he saw a large cloud of smoke. I decided to turn around and head in that direction and quickly saw the problem. A plane crashed just outside of the perimeter. The fog was beginning to lift and I could see the plane was still on fire. There were people moving around at the site, but I could not tell if these were locals or responding military members.

I hit the perimeter and took a position inside of a guard tower to get a better assessment of the situation. By now our units were being dispatched to respond outside the wire and assist where they could. Our fire fighters were the first to go and they took their aircraft fire-fighting equipment. They encountered problems maneuvering through the mud and found they could not reach the aircraft site with their large trucks. Only the Fire Chief's response vehicle could get close enough. Once he was on scene the reports started coming in about total destruction and loss of life. The news was not good, but the response had to go on.

Suddenly the call came in to bring our PJ teams to the scene in an attempt to rescue survivors. Our PJs were the best in the world, and if anything could be done to save life and limb, they were the ones to get the call. One after another the HH 60 Pave Hawk helicopters flew over the hospital and out to the scene. Knowing that I could do no good from where I was, I headed back to the hospital to lend a hand on what was to come.

When I arrived the team was moving about with precision. Teams were standing by at the helicopter pad to receive the patients when they arrived, and the emergency department was ready. Operating rooms were prepared, and the entire hospital staff was alerted to be ready for this mass casualty incident. I stopped and took it all in, wondering how many times they had all practiced this during base exercises back home, and if they would be fully ready for the reality that was about to hit them.

Calls came in alerting us to expect more than 30 patients come into the hospital, a number that would overwhelm most hospitals back home, but seemed very manageable to this team. I noticed the commander of the Medical Group, Colonel Bat Masterson and his team building a plan for setting up the triage area outside of the emergency department. This place was normally used by the staff to unwind by playing football or basketball after a long trauma situation. The parking lot was filling with gurneys, medical equipment and what appeared to be body bags. Staff members were lining up and establishing trauma teams to handle the business at hand as the first helicopter landed at the pad.

I made contact with the Chief Stephanie Cardozo at the hospital and told her I would stay out of the way, but I would be there to support the medics if they needed water or anything else. I had no medical capability so I planned to help where they needed me. I was totally impressed by their actions even though it was about to turn into the worst incident any of us ever witnessed with.

As the first two gurneys came running into the triage area, an unfamiliar smell came over me. The medics were not fazed, they continued to prepare for more. A nurse came over and told me the smell was coming from the charred bodies still burning inside those body bags. This was a clear indication that I was not cut out for medical work and stood in awe of what this team was doing.

It was a hard scene to witness. Doctors, nurses and medics opened each of the bags on those first two gurneys and went to work, looking for any sign of life in the patient. I could not do what they were doing, and as it progressed, I became more and more in awe of their ability and courage.

More bodies came in, and as the triage area filled, those who were checked and pronounced deceased were moved to a line at the edge of the area. The line was growing, and the smell of burnt flesh overtook the area. I noticed many of the medical team were sweating from the heat of the day and the stress of the action. I grabbed cold water bottles and started passing them around so they could try to stay hydrated. It would be a losing battle for some of them since they would not stop working long enough to take in the fluids.

After the first hour, Colonel Masterson implemented a rotation and started making the teams take short breaks to give them a chance to hydrate and clear their heads. I watched several go off to the side, shed a tear by themselves, and then move back in for more processing.

The bodies kept coming in, two at a time, and you could see the determination grow on the faces of the medics. They wanted to find someone alive and save at least one life in this large mess. Suddenly there was a new excitement in the air and you could see someone from inside the emergency department had just delivered some news to the commander. It seemed there would be a live body coming in and there was hope after all.

Each trauma team stood ready as the teams of volunteers who were delivering the bodies came running into the triage area. It looked like a movie scene as they reached the gurney. Items went flying around. Teamwork was incredible with each person knowing their role. The team quickly determined that a pulse was evident, albeit weak, so they ran off to the emergency department for more attempts at saving this life.

Details flowing in disclosed the plane was transporting contract employees, mostly of Turkish decent. They were on a commercial aircraft that attempted to land on the runway, even though it had been closed for the fog. Once they got under the fog they were too far off the runway and about to hit our Maintenance Group headquarters building, so they pulled up as hard as they could, but lost altitude and eventually crashed in the field just outside the perimeter. Had they been any lower or not able to maintain as long as they did, the plane would have crashed on the base and likely in one of the housing areas they just cleared. I stopped moving at that news, as I realized we could have been dealing with hundreds of deaths if the plane had crashed on base. I thought about the pilots who also perished and how they likely saved lives by their actions, even if the initial decision to land was in poor judgment.

The day for our medics would continue long into the evening until all the bodies were accounted for and moved on to the morgue. Everyone pitched in. Chief Cardozo and the first Sergeant, Master Sergeant Terry Schorer, were constantly rolling up their sleeves and performing alongside the medics with great confidence. At one point I was helping Sergeant Shorer load body bags into the mortuary van. Her resiliency would help me with the internal battle I was dealing with.

I left the hospital as the sun was setting and stopped long enough to take in the scene. Earlier in the day this parking lot was used for a game of pick-up football, transitioned into a triage area for a mass casualty event, and was now back to a parking lot, with only a few vehicles, and a very distinct smell burnt into my memory.

When I got to the office there were several notes about meetings I had missed during the day. One said work was complete on the memorial and it would be put in place the next morning. With the events of the past days; I completely lost track of the pending dedication ceremony for the Fallen Airman Memorial. I needed to focus and get ready for the ceremony.

As my night came to an end, I realized that my family would be awake back home and could probably use a word or two from me. I made the phone call and just wanted to listen to what they had been doing. I would try my best to avoid the conversation about what happened today.

Mags immediately asked about the plane crash. She never missed a beat on the news as it applied to Iraq. I took a few minutes and explained that a commercial jet carrying 35 civilians crashed outside the perimeter, but none were military or belonged to our unit. I refrained from telling her too many details, or my emotions would have taken over and I would have been a mess.

She went on to talk about their day, giving updates on the kids. Then the alarm warning started going off. She was talking, but heard the sirens in the background. She stopped and asked, "What was that sound?" I began to tell her it was the alarm warning us of an incoming attack, when a large boom sounded from a mortar round, and suddenly the phone went dead. The last words she heard from me were "It's the alarm for an attack…"

I knew I was OK, but she had no idea. Why had the phone gone dead suddenly, was there a direct hit on my quarters? Was I alive? I tried calling back with no luck. The phones were down and this would be a problem. Before I headed out I had to let her know I was OK. The round was close, but I was actually OK and was going to go out and do what I did to care for the Airmen.

I looked at the computer from my prone position on the floor and behind the sandbags and realized this would be my only chance. Crawling over to the desk I reached up and grabbed the mouse and keyboard. "Boom!" Another round had landed close by, so I needed to stay down. I did what I could to manipulate the computer and send her a quick email. I doubt that words were spelled correctly or that any grammar made sense, but getting a message to her that I was OK was the only objective. She got it and it brought some sense of relief. I'm just glad she did not know I headed out to check for damage or injuries.

Around 0500 I made it back to my room and passed out from exhaustion. I had three hours before the alarm and the trip to Baghdad for the first of several memorials to come in honor of three Fallen Airmen. I needed something to help shut down my mind so I opened my notebook. There were now three more names on the list. Technical Sergeant Timothy Weiner, Senior Airman Daniel Miller, and Senior Airman Elizabeth Loncki, killed in action 7 January 2007.

Technical Sergeant Timothy Weiner, Explosive Ordnance Disposal, killed in action 7 January 2007.

Senior Airman Daniel Miller, Explosive Ordnance Disposal, killed in action 7 January 2007.

Senior Airman Elizabeth Loncki, Explosive Ordnance Disposal, killed in action 7 January 2007.

The H6 housing area of Balad Air Base following a January rain storm.

332d Air Expeditionary Group's Tuskegee Medics in action during a mass casualty incident.

10
HONORING FALLEN AIRMEN

9 January 2007:

Rising early, I headed straight for the passenger terminal with all my gear for a quick trip to Baghdad by helicopter. What most people would think of as a fun and exciting day riding on a helicopter felt more like catching a city bus to get across town. There was always danger in flying at low level across the battlefield, but we were fully confident in the ability of the crews that it never seemed frightening. Flying in the daylight was not comforting. The insurgents could see us coming and could easily target us. With the added pressure of civilians walking around in the villages, it would be tough to effectively engage with the machine guns mounted on each side of the helicopter.

The rotors thumped as we started to lift off and it felt like someone was pounding on my head with a board each time they turned. I had not slept much, and over the last several days had not eaten much, causing a headache, now deeply impacted by the environmental noises around me. While flying low across the terrain and into the city of Baghdad, my thoughts drifted to my own health which seemed to be on a steady decline. There were more important things to worry about, even though I knew my own health was important to fulfilling my mission and taking care of others.

Focusing back on the moment, I knew it would be on each of us to defend ourselves if we were shot down, and I wanted to be ready. Traveling with my rifle and a full combat load always seemed appropriate in case we found trouble.

We pushed low enough over the rooftops to see trash lying in the streets and smell the awful stench that rose above the houses. We all wondered how these people could live amongst the trash but knew it was out of their control. The entire country was still reeling from the insurgency, and there were little formal Iraqi government facilities or services, including trash removal. A corner lot in each neighborhood became the place where all trash ended up.

Families appeared to be going about the business of their day and children were playing in the streets of some villages. Several times we came so close to the houses we nearly clipped the few power lines going into and out of the villages. Somehow the crew up front always saw them in time and maneuvered appropriately. We landed in Baghdad and were met by a large contingent of forces, much more than normal, which seemed strange.

Time was limited and we had to make tracks, so there was little time for small talk. On the way to the memorial service, General Rand asked the commander if everything was ready to go and all things were in order. He assured the General it was, and we could rest assured of no problems. When we got to the scene of the memorial, we noticed many of our US Army and Marine counterparts were on hand to honor our Airmen. The EOD career field was known across the services and earned great respect for all the things they did...they brought additional credibility to our service.

The ceremony started as all did, with posting of colors, a thoughtful opening prayer from the chaplain and some appropriate readings. Then the testimonials began, and a long line of Airmen formed up, ready to speak. It was more than we were used to, but keeping in mind this was to honor three Airmen it seemed to fit the situation.

Testimonials covered the amount of respect this team had earned among their peers. During this tour of combat, they completed over 100 combat missions into harm's way and covered the spectrum of problems to solve. However, some of the Airmen who provided testimony about the team went too far. Stories they told were not appropriate for the moment. I felt embarrassed and angered that they would use such poor judgment at an honorable time like this.

The ceremony was done and we completed paying honor to the fallen. We learned many things about the character of these EOD warriors and the pain inside continued to burn. Learning more about them personally made it hurt worse. Knowing they had families back home who were hurting made us feel closer to them as brethren.

On the helicopter ride back to Balad, I opened my notebook completed the annotation of names.

Technical Sergeant Timothy Weiner, Senior Airman Daniel Miller, and Senior Airman Elizabeth Loncki, killed in action, 7 January 2007.

I closed my eyes, not wanting my fellow passengers to see the tears welling up inside.

Arriving back at Balad I needed to take my mind off my own worries, so I headed to the one place where I could always get lost in the needs of others, the hospital. Entering the emergency department I could see how busy they were. Soldiers, including the Iraqi National Army Soldiers inside, were receiving care from trauma teams consisting of doctors from the active duty, Air National Guard and Air Force Reserve. They were assisted by nurses from the same. The most impressive part was watching the young enlisted medics handling business like true professionals, even in the face of dire injuries. They were treating four victims of a vehicle-borne improvised explosive device. Most were suffering from burns and shrapnel.

Watching these teams was like watching water run through a pile of rocks. I felt helpless to do anything except watch and thank them as they passed. At one point I noticed a young Army Medic trying to carry a large pile of supplies and his hands were full. It was something that I could do to help, so I took them from him and let him get back to work doing what he was paid to do. He smiled, handed me the supplies and moved on.

I came across members of several other squadrons who spent their day off or came after work to help the medics with patient movement, supply and re-supply, cleaning, organizing or whatever else came up so they could concentrate all of their effort on the patients.

After a short stay in the emergency department, I headed for the Intensive Care Unit where the Soldiers from an earlier incident were receiving care. Expecting to see the worst, once again my eyes focused in on the actions of the medics who courageously handled the task of caring for these wounded.

These Soldiers were involved in a terrible motor vehicle accident the previous day where they rolled into a large canal near the base and were trapped under water. We're not talking about good clean water like we are all used to seeing in canals and rivers. This is the most green, murky water you can imagine and just going into the water would be dangerous enough. But these Soldiers were wearing more than 60 pounds of gear and were tucked into this armor plated vehicle which immediately sank to the bottom of the canal.

One of the Soldiers got out immediately. A second Soldier was rescued by the first and quickly got to the shore where he was attended to by several other Soldiers from a trailing vehicle. Those Soldiers cannot remember the details of what happened next, but somehow they rescued the other two more critically wounded Soldiers. While we don't know the full details and may never know, it appeared all three were drowned and should have died on scene. Neither the second nor the third had a pulse and neither was breathing. Several of the attending Soldiers went to work doing CPR and trying to resuscitate their two fellow warriors.

The second one was able to regain a pulse at the scene and was prepared for transport to the hospital. The third was not so fortunate, as it appeared he was under water for a long period of time. But the spirit of the American Soldier cannot be easily defeated. Within a short period of time and with constant CPR being applied to the third Soldier, all of them were brought to the hospital for life saving treatment.

One trauma surgeon described it to me like this. He said, "Chief, this guy was basically drug in here by the collar of his shirt and his buddy asked us to save him." Against the toughest of odds, our medical trauma team was able to get a pulse and get him breathing again. In fact, both were now breathing on their own or with some assistance. I can only describe this in one way; they brought him back to life after drowning…nothing short of miraculous in my eyes.

There were three Soldiers being prepared for an emergency flight to Germany for more treatment. When I looked into the ICU, another team of professional military men and women, US Army and US Air Force working hand in hand to save these lives. There was an ICU crew, an aeromedical medical evacuation team and other critical care ward personnel working in concert to make sure every detail was covered before they were transported. Just outside the room was a team of volunteers waiting to move these brave Soldiers to the bus and ultimately to the C-17 aircraft that would evacuate them home.

Watching this was truly inspiring. My only conversations were with the staff as they passed or took a short break to clear their heads. I was speechless and could only think to shake their hands or put a hand on their shoulders and thank them for what they were doing.

At one point, I noticed two Soldiers standing in the room off to the side. I could tell they were associated with these men and so I had to talk with them. I reassured them we were and would continue to do anything and everything we could to get their buddies home and keep them alive. They were shook up, but mustered the strength to tell me how proud they were of the Soldiers and how happy they were to see our medical team handling the situation in the professional manner they were witnessing. There was one other Soldier at the other end of the ICU. It was their unit first sergeant and his pain was obvious.

Over the next few minutes, Chief Cardozo led me outside to help lift the patients into the bus to relieve the medical staff from this duty. We moved out to assume this honorable duty. Before we left, it seemed one of the three Soldiers was moving around and appeared to be doing well. One of the attending physicians gave a positive, yet funny response. He said, "Chief, I would say he is doing pretty good considering earlier he was upside down in a Humvee in murky water with his lungs full of gunk." What more could I say, I was speechless once again. He told me that one of the other Soldiers had to have multiple liters of fluid pumped from his lungs and the extent of his injuries would not be known until he was past the infectious stage in his lungs. These medical professionals take great pride in saving lives and fixing wounds. Pride in saving these men was swelling in this room like nothing I had ever felt before.

At the bus Chief Cardoza and I joined a small group of volunteers with the medical staff members and we lifted each man into the bus carefully, making sure not to move or bump the medical equipment attached to their gurney. It was a slow and careful operation and you could tell each and every person on the detail was focused. After loading the first three into the bus, we then loaded one additional victim into the bus who had severe burns. He had his wits about him though; as we delayed outside for a brief moment, he looked up, laughed and said, "I think I'm getting a sun tan!" It broke the tension of the moment and most everyone smiled.

Once loading was complete we headed to the flight line to help load them on the C-17. Once again we found another team of volunteer Soldiers and Airmen standing at the ready. Over the next 30 minutes, the team of volunteers withstood extreme conditions behind the aircraft. It was hot, but nobody minded, they just stood ready to handle the gurneys to make sure these warriors were safe.

As we were loading the first three Soldiers on the aircraft, the one who was conscious looked up at the Airmen carrying him and said, "Thanks, guys, for taking good care of us." What more needed to be said? Once on the aircraft there was a full team of medical professionals taking care of at least ten wounded Soldiers. They had equipment equal to any emergency room available and working. It looked like an emergency room inside the back of the jet. There were more Soldiers on the side seats, each heading home after more than one year in Iraq.

As this part of a long day ended, three US Army Soldiers were alive, breathing and with strong pulses who had faced death just hours before. They were alive because of the collective team effort of Air Force and Army medical teams dedicated to saving lives. While this was a life-altering experience for me, it was all in a day's work for them. Now they had to recover and wait for the next emergency.

There was not another crew waiting for them so they could take a break from their duties. There was no lunch break and no rest in between traumatic situations. They stood ready for the next grinding moment. These medical professionals had my respect before today, but now have my deep admiration beyond any level I could have ever imagined. It was a day I will long remember and something I badly needed. Maybe now I could muster the strength to go on another day and finish this mission.

The following day I went around Balad and found Airmen doing their jobs, walking their own miles. I jumped in when and where I could, and found out how much I did not know about their inner workings. At one location some Airmen were working on large generators to power the Air Traffic Control tower. I was amazed at the size and complexity of these machines. I was more amazed at the knowledge of the technicians we had working on them. Taking me inside of the generator control room, two very young Airmen showed me the entire operation from start to finish. They instructed me on how to start these generators in the case of power failure and the unit did not automatically start. They were covered in grease and oil from head to toe but did not seem to mind.

My next stop was out on the flight line to see the aircraft maintainers. I always liked to park my vehicle in one spot and walk the line to find Airmen working on airplanes without the supervisors worrying. I wanted to meet them and work with them for a few minutes and did not need any extra attention. There was only one issue. If I left my vehicle and did not take my battle gear with me, I would not be able to respond or protect myself if we came under attack, leaving me with only one option: I had to wear my gear while I was out walking. It would add to the physical fitness routine and might send a strong signal to the force about being prepared.

I came across a young crew of maintainers working on the wheel well of a C-130. The fuselage appeared to be sitting on jack stands and the wheels were off the ground. This caught my attention and I had to go see it up close. One of the Airmen turned around as I was approaching in full battle gear and looked alarmed. He said, "Chief, is something wrong, are we under attack?"

I reassured him that everything was under control and I just liked to wear my gear around when I was out walking in case we came under attack. He sighed and said he was relieved. I asked if I could join in on their operation and learn a thing or two. He smiled and said, "You can join us any time. We are changing out the wheel bearings and this is a very dirty job." The look of their coveralls and uniforms validated his comment.

Sitting on the ground next to the plane, they showed me what had taken place. Most of the work was done and they were wrapping things up for inspection. My confidence in them grew exponentially with each minute. These Airmen knew the importance of getting this right, and how much the crews and passengers were counting on them. These maintainers took great pride in knowing their jobs and that people trusted their work. I told them I would likely be flying on this plane during one of my battlefield circulation visits, and I was very happy they did their jobs so well.

As the operation concluded, I walked over to my vehicle and grabbed some of my coins. I went back over and asked each of them if they would accept one of these coins as a small token of my appreciation for what they did and how well they did it. There were many smiles in the small formation and they asked if we could take a picture. I departed the flight line to get some food and head back to my quarters so I could catch up on email and get ready for the days ahead.

Although we had already memorialized our three fallen EOD Airmen at Baghdad, we continued the tradition we started with Airman Chavis and held a second memorial at Balad, allowing everyone in the wing a chance to mourn the loss and pay their respects.

Early in the morning, as the sun rose above the massive airfield and many people went about their daily mission while General Rand, Colonel Renfrow, Colonel Ellis and I made our way over to the Town Hall. The crowd filled the tent to the limit. The scene was set and we were prepared for this hour of honor. Three battlefield cross memorials were on stage with the photos of our Fallen Warriors.

The weather cooperated and the airfield was unusually quiet. The ceremony went off without a flaw. Over 500 people had the opportunity to pay honor and respect to Sergeant Weiner, Airman Miller and Airman Loncki. I breathed a sigh of relief and wondered how their families were doing back at home. The memorial ceremony was flawless, with music and testimonials about their service and sacrifice. It became even clearer to me just how tight knit the EOD community was and how close this team of warriors had become on their 100 combat missions on the mean streets of Baghdad.

We completed our final salutes, placed coins at the flags by each battlefield cross, and slowly walked out of the tent. Standing outside we greeted everyone as they departed. The pain of sacrifice and loss was deeply engrained on each face. A considerable amount of time passed before the last person departed. EOD remained inside to spend more quiet time together as a team.

Walking back to the headquarters building, I opened my notebook and glanced at their names once more. Wiener, Miller, Loncki. Those names were now etched into my memory forever. I noticed something else. The first page was now full with the names of seven Airmen killed in action. The page turned slowly, and for a brief moment I silently hoped we could end the list there.

Back at the headquarters building I decided to check in with the General and see how he was doing after another tragic loss, so many incidents and attacks, and a never ending battle rhythm. We sat and talked for a while, then he asked me why I was so concerned. I told him I was concerned because of the incredible burden placed on commanders in combat units. He smiled and told me everything would be fine and we had to focus on the mission and all of our Airmen who continued to find ways to amaze us. Nobody knew more than him just how much we had going on.

I knew we needed a little respite from so much pain and misery so I made him an offer. "General, how about we postpone the Fallen Airman Memorial Dedication ceremony until we have more time to get everything together" I said. He looked at me and said, "Chief, the ceremony will take place as planned, we will not cancel anything. This must happen and you must make it happen." I headed for the door. Turning toward him I said, "OK General, I got it."

I departed and headed for the Civil Engineering unit and found Airman Ketchum hard at work putting the finishing touches on the monument. It looked incredible. Airman Ketchum designed and built this fitting object from scrap materials using some creative techniques he found by searching for ideas about bending and coloring metal on the internet. I smiled for the next 30 minutes as he described how he accomplished all that he did. I wanted to hug this young man and thank him for bringing the vision to reality.

There were other NCOs in the shop now putting the name plates and functional badges on the monument to represent all of the Airmen from the wing who had been killed in action since the start of Operation Iraqi Freedom. It looked perfect, and all I could do was stand in awe and tell them how much I appreciated their effort.

They assured me they would place the monument in front of the headquarters building and everything would be ready for the ceremony on 12 January. I walked out fully energized. We would dedicate a memorial to 32 Airmen who gave the last full measure on the field of battle.

I was excited about the ceremony and knew we had more work to complete the plan. I stopped in at DFAC #2, walked into the tent, washed up, and headed straight for the food line. I was finally hungry and needed a good meal. Arriving at the line, I was met by the DFAC supervisor, a retired U.S. Army First Sergeant who liked to see how I was doing whenever he saw me in there. We talked as the guys loaded food into a container for me. The first sergeant asked me to sit down and enjoy a meal, but I informed him how much I needed to get done for the ceremony. He understood and wished me well, stuffing a couple of extra cookies into my container as I headed for the door.

When I arrived at the office there was a note on my desk. It seemed someone had already finished the draft of the script for the ceremony, signed up all the volunteers for the formation, arranged the honor guard, the music and everything else we needed. I knew Frankie J had something to do with this, and I was grateful for his actions. I could now concentrate my efforts on executing the ceremony.

Around midnight I finally headed out to get some rest. Walking past the force protection Airman guarding the door, he wished me a good night with a huge smile on his face. I stopped and asked him why he was grinning. He just smiled and said, "You will see Chief." Out the door I went and there it was, the monument was in place for the memorial.

Airman Ketchum and several others were still there, having just completed the installation. They asked if I was happy. I told them I was really happy, but wondered why it was covered. The shop foreman looked at me and said they thought nobody should see it until it was officially unveiled during the ceremony. He was right, and this was perfect. I had great confidence that it was 100% perfect and there was no reason for me to see it until the moment. I thanked them one more time and reminded them to be in attendance at the ceremony as we planned to include them in the unveiling.

12 January 2007:

My eyes opened to a strange noise coming from outside. The memorial dedication ceremony was going to take place today and the weather needed to be perfect. Opening the door my worst fears were realized. That noise I heard was rain on my roof. Not a little rain, but a very strong downpour. I became angry and wondered how we would make this ceremony happen on a rainy day. The thought of cancelling immediately came to mind. I had to get dressed and get to the headquarters to discuss this with the General or Colonel Renfrow.

When I found General Rand, I began to ask him about cancelling the event. Before I could complete the sentence he looked at me and said we would press on, regardless of the weather. He was right and it was only rain,

Hours later the ceremony was about to begin and a crowd of Airmen gathered in the area of the monument. In addition to the crowd, there was a formation of 32 Airmen, each one representing one of the Fallen Airmen. The Airmen were from the same career fields, of the same gender; and whenever possible, were of the same rank as the Fallen. They were formed in order of the deaths from beginning of OIF through our most recent fallen.

General Rand and the other senior officers arrived at the area and we prepared to start the event. It was early afternoon but the sky had already turned dark as if it were late at night. The rain came down even harder now. It was a steady downpour again just like it had been when I first woke up. The scene was somehow appropriate for a memorial to those who were killed in action.

The Honor Guard was in place and the national anthem was sung by a chorus of Airmen from the Medical Group. The chaplain came up and delivered an appropriate invocation. Then, the narrator began with some opening remarks to give the audience a real sense of why we were here. Following the chaplain, it was my chance to tell everyone the story of the memorial vision and the history behind it. I spoke about the memorial at Tallil and how it was supposed to be moved to Balad. I talked about Airman Ketchum, Chief Kembel and the other Civil Engineers who poured so much time and effort into making this a reality.

When my comments were complete I stepped away from the podium and the narrator informed the audience that we would now conduct a roll call of the Fallen Airmen. Standing in the rain each person in the formation appeared ready and undaunted by the conditions. The names were called. As each name was sounded, the representative in the formation came to attention and took one step forward. Bowing their head, they assumed the position of parade rest. After a momentary hesitation the next name was sounded. This continued until the last of the 32 names were called.

Following the last name being called and the movements complete, General Rand and Airman Ketchum moved to the monument and prepared for the unveiling. Taking a cue from the narrator, we removed the cover from the monument and everyone looked in amazement at this fantastic creation. General Rand and Airman Ketchum stood together silently admiring the monument.

After a minute of reflection we moved back to our seats and the Honor Guard firing party snapped to attention. Three volleys of seven rifles sounded. Taps was played over the speakers and everyone snapped to attention and saluted toward the memorial. There were no dry eyes anywhere at the event. The chaplain came to the podium and offered a benediction. His words brought us peace. It was a reflective time in our lives. We stood in the rain, honoring our brothers and sisters and we felt the strength of the brotherhood.

The ceremony officially ended. One by one, everyone in attendance made their way to the monument to pay their respects. My heart warmed as I watched Airmen walk up to this memorial, render a salute, move forward and place their hand on one of the plates. In that moment of silence for them, they were paying tribute to someone they knew and had been associated with. Everyone was impacted by loss in combat, now there was a place they could go to show their respect. To reflect and to remember.

My day was done and I needed some rest before we traveled again. Sitting on the edge of my bed, I thought about the sacrifices made by the Airmen we paid tribute to during the ceremony and I wondered about their families and how they would approach a new year without their loved one. The magnitude of those thoughts weighed on me and I could not control my emotions any more. I was mad. I cried.

Working with a C-130 maintenance crew as they changed a wheel bearing
to keep this vital cargo aircraft flying tough missions.

(L-R) Chief Dearduff, Brigadier General Robin Rand and Colonel Doc
Ellis preparing for a battlefield circulation trip in January to visit Airmen.

The official unveiling of the Fallen Airman Memorial at Balad Air Base took place on 12 January 2007.

A formation of 32 Airmen, each representing one of the 32 Fallen Airmen from Operation Iraqi Freedom from March 2003 – January 2007.

11
WALKING THE MILE

Waking to the sound of silence it felt very hot inside my quarters even though I could feel the cool air being pumped out of the window air conditioning unit. I was sweating like I had just finished at the gym and could not control my breathing. Something was wrong with me, and I knew I needed help. I put my hand on the phone next to my bed thinking about calling but must have fallen back to sleep from exhaustion before I could make the call.

I woke up feeling better and trying to wrap my mind about what happened earlier. Maybe it was a bad dream. Maybe it never happened and I just needed some rest. Maybe battle fatigue was settling in and my body and mind needed a break from the action. I closed my eyes and drifted off to sleep again.

Hours later I was startled out of the bed by the sound of CRAM defensive guns firing rounds to protect us from incoming fire. It sounded like it was right outside my window, and all I could do was roll onto the floor and hope for the best. I had no idea it was a monthly test of the system that takes place on the same day and time each month. I had no idea what time it was until I looked at the clock and saw 12:00. It was noon and I had overslept by at least 5 hours. Exhaustion had really set in.

As my head cleared, I heard the command post come across the giant voice and say, "Test fire complete." I moved about in my room gathering my uniform and gear so I could get something to eat and find out what I missed on this day. As I drove to the DFAC, things seemed rather strange, like there was not much going on within the camp. As I approached the entry point and two sturdy Security Force Defenders, I wondered what was going on. Had there been some attack and everyone was hunkered down? I stopped as I always did to greet the Defenders and as they approached I detected nothing wrong. In fact they seemed happy to see me and provided me with the most motivated post report I had received in some time.

When they were complete with their reporting actions, I asked them what was going on. The leader said, "Chief, nothing new here, just a quiet Sunday afternoon with lots of planes flying out to kill the enemy." I realized I lost complete track of the time and date and had not missed anything…our battle rhythm on Sundays was much slower. There were no meetings or briefings to attend. As I cleared their post and moved toward the DFAC, it hit me; this was the very first day I slept in since arriving last July. It was really my first day off and yet I almost did not have clear enough thinking to take advantage of it.

I reached the DFAC and found several chiefs eating and laughing. I happily joined them and got caught up on what they were doing. They talked about their travels and the great Airmen they had encountered. I just sat and ate quietly, looking intently into their faces as they glowed about the things they had been doing. This was the refreshing break I needed; I enjoyed every minute of it. I sat with Chief Maxson and he asked how my family was doing back home. I said, "That is a great question, and one I cannot answer very well, so I had better get going and make a call."

Mags answered the phone with excitement in her voice. There was something she wanted to tell me, making the call easier for me, all I had to do was listen. She updated me on all the things happening at home, including the news about our son being the last one cut on the 7th grade basketball team. I was confused but I let her go on.

At the time he was not a basketball player at all, but he decided to become one. He trained himself hard to make the team against all odds. The previous year he suffered a major ankle break and his orthopedic surgeon said he would never play competitive sports again. But that would not stop Sean, and being the only kid who has not played more intense basketball in the AAU program would not stop him either. He made all the cuts until the final day. Rather than get mad and not play again, she said he has had a basketball in his hand every waking hour since. And considering current weather conditions in the Midwest this winter, it was quite surprising he was outside shoveling the street of snow so he could dribble and shoot.

She was obviously proud of him, and I shared with her how proud I was. Not only about his effort, but of the effort she made in helping him and ensuring he maintained a positive attitude. She reminded me that he overcome a real tough obstacle by making the baseball team earlier in the fall. He worked his way into the starting rotation and hit the ball as well as any other kid on the team. Almost making the basketball team against many odds showed the resiliency he had developed. Needless to say I was a proud father.

I asked her how she was doing and if she was OK. Like the tough military wife that she is, she told me she was OK. But I knew differently, and could detect something about her voice that changed when I asked. I pressed the issue, but she refused to share anything, knowing I had enough going on and did not have the capability of fixing any problem she had. She simply told me I needed to get home on my mid-tour leave and spend some time with her because she really needed it. I reminder her that I would arrive home for two weeks of R&R in April, getting us closer to the end of the tour and my safe return home.

Before we hung up she asked me how I was doing following the recent tragedies. Words were stuck in my throat and I wanted to tell her the entire story and how mad I was, but knew it was not the right time or place to discuss these situations. I told her I would explain some things when we were together, but for now I was just doing OK and had a tough mission to focus on.

As we hung up I noticed there was a thick coating of dirt on the walls inside of my quarters and an awful smell coming from outside. I opened the door to find myself covered in a dark cloud of extremely odorous smoke. It could only be from the burn pit and the wind was blowing just right to send it toward Red Tail Village. For the next two hours I washed the inside walls and tried to do a little preventative maintenance on my quarters, hopefully preventing any illness.

Late in the evening I ran into Colonel Ellis. We talked about all the things that were going on and what we needed to accomplish. He also reminded me he only had a couple of months left in his tour and he wanted to spend more time on missions out to see our Airmen.

I had grown really close to Colonel Ellis and respected him unconditionally. He was a true battle buddy for me; and with his experience in combat and other missions in the Air Force, he became a great friend and confidant. I assumed he and I would have other opportunities to circulate the battlefield before he completed his mission.

15 January 2007:

Monday morning came quickly with an early departure on a C-130 heading for Al Asad Air Base and the ceremony to stand up the 438th Air Expeditionary Group. Before we departed I met with the new Mission Support Group Chief, Dave Halverson. Dave came in from the Air Force Reserves and brought with him a civil engineering background which was perfect for everything going on around Balad. My first impression of Chief Halverson was that he would be a great partner in improving our operations each and every day. We shared a passion for a late afternoon cup of coffee, so I knew there would be many hours of conversation ahead with him.

Back in November we had made the trip to Al Asad to check out the grounds and figure out the best use of their facilities so we could bring in the mighty A-10 Warthog. It brought a capability that our F-16s did not normally bring, and would prove itself valuable in the terrain out west. The US Marines operated in the area; and they were quite familiar with the A-10, so this would be a win-win situation. This would be our day to officially set this unit forward on their mission of providing ground cover for Marine forces in the region and it would be a great honor for our wing.

Colonel Pat Malackowski was brought in to lead this group. We had a real hard time finding a chief to fill the role of group superintendent from back home. Several dropped out for medical reasons and others who wanted to come were not qualified for the particular mission. An idea came to me and I needed to brief the General and see what he thought. We had Chief Maxson working in the Mission Support Group and he was about to finish his tour. Although he came to us on short notice and was only supposed to serve here for 6 months, I was sure we would have no trouble convincing him to stay and help start this unit. When his replacement arrived, we could relieve him and send him out to Al Asad with Colonel Malackowski. The General trusted my judgment and liked the plan so the moves were made.

Our C-130 loaded with cargo made the trip to Al Asad much shorter than we had previously taken in the Army Sherpa. We carried pallets filled with critical supplies needed by the maintenance team and others within the unit. Landing on the massive air strip, we were greeted by the contingent of US Marines who controlled the base. They had nothing but positive comments about the new team and the arrival of the A-10s. Marines always seemed excited to have additional air support in the area, and this team let us know how much they appreciated our presence.

The team at Al Asad was set and they were on the ground making things happen. The weather was not being very cooperative. The wind was blowing and the status of this outdoor ceremony was in jeopardy. We decided to place Airmen behind the stage to hold the flags so the wind did not knock them over during the ceremony. General Rand conducted the Assumption of Command ceremony for Colonel Malackowski and the ceremony went on without a hitch. The unit was well on its way to bringing Airpower for America, Right Here, Right Now with the mighty A-10.

We spent several hours walking around the unit and meeting with some of the warriors. Their enthusiasm was easy to detect, and felt like this was a success from the start. There were several encounters with Airmen who knew me from previous assignments.

Chief Maxson told me that one such Airman insisted on seeing me and catching up. We arrived at their new headquarters building and walked around the concrete barriers protecting them from indirect fire. Standing before me was Senior Airman Paulson Nez. Airman Nez and I first met at Luke Air Force Base when he was working in the munitions storage area. He asked me a question that led me to tell him a story about taking pride in all that you do. He engrained that story and made significant improvements in his professional life. It was easy to see he was continuing to uphold a high level of professionalism even here in the combat zone. We caught up for some time and I thanked him for finding me and sharing this moment.

Before boarding our C-130 and heading back to Balad, we wished the leadership team well and told them we would be back in a few months to see how much progress they had made and to ensure they had everything they needed to complete the mission.

2 February 2007:

The next day was dedicated to the Operations Group and missions they were responsible for. The new Operations Group Chief, Tim Ruenning was on board and he encouraged me to go out and be a part of these missions every chance I could. He suggested I start with the C-130 Hercules crews and fly several sorties with them so I could fully understand what their mission demands were.

I arrived late in the evening at the C-130 operations building and joined in the preparation for the mission they assigned me to. After receiving necessary gear and mission information, I was paired with one of the aircraft load masters.

Air Force load masters were responsible for everything that happened on the back end of the aircraft while the crew took care of the flying. This crew worked like a well-oiled machine. Briefings were detailed and timely. Actions to prepare the aircraft were handled promptly and you could feel the cooperation with the aircraft maintainers on the ground. Before I knew it we were off and flying, heading for our first stop of eight we would make tonight.

My load master showed me how we loaded and locked down the pallets and went on about the other portions of the cargo bay. Within the first hour I knew more about the C-130 than I had ever known, even though I had been in them hundreds of times. This was shaping up to be a fantastic mission opportunity.

Our first stop was a remote airfield that required us to park off in the distance without benefit of airfield lighting. We quickly offloaded the first load to the four Airmen who worked this aerial port and remained in place. After several minutes of sitting there idle, I asked the load master if we were waiting on pallets. He said we were about to handle special cargo and it would not be on pallets.

One of the crew members in the cockpit informed us via the radio about inbounds. I was not sure what we were about to do, but it sure caught my interest. Suddenly several individuals appeared at the back of the plane and joined us inside. We began working with them to lay plastic out on the floor and secure it with gray duct tape. I finally figured it out, we were about to transport detainees to one of the confinement facilities.

Once our preparations were complete inside, those two unidentified individuals departed and came back within minutes. This time they had armed guards marching more than 20 prisoners into the cargo bay. I was told to stand back and not engage with the insurgents; this would be handled by the guards. The process of sitting them down and strapping them into place for their own safety took about 30 minutes. They could not see us and we did not engage with them. This detailed process had to be followed to the letter and my crew was highly experienced at this mission.

Our takeoff came quickly and we made great time getting to the next location for the drop off. The process was repeated in reverse and the insurgents were offloaded. Once they were done we conducted a cleanup of the cargo bay. This was no easy chore, but working together we had it ready in 20 minutes. Before I knew it we had several cargo pallets waiting at the back door on a fork lift ready to be loaded. Once loaded we were off again. After they were gone, I began to wonder if any of those insurgents knew of or had anything to do with Major Gilbert's remains being taken back in November. I could not clear those thoughts from my mind.

I marveled at the speed and efficiency of the C-130 crews and how they went from moving critical cargo and supplies to transporting detainees. Their flawless execution impressed me beyond belief. My appreciation for these Airmen was positively impacted tonight. I was so proud of the Airmen who took on this C-130 mission and moved cargo around the battle field.

Moving around Balad the next morning, one of the first sergeants informed me they would be gathering at the OSI TOD for a BBQ to say farewell to several who had completed their tours. I wanted to thank each one of them personally for their service and sacrifice so this was a must do for me. Arriving at their building, I made my way onto the roof where I met with the superintendent of the OSI, Special Agent Stu Nichols. Agent Nichols and I were previously acquainted from an earlier deployment, so there was no need to do any forming—we just got down to business.

I asked Agent Nichols point blank why we were not stopping insurgent attacks from hitting the base. After all, it was their job to counter the insurgency and defeat enemy threats to the airfield before they became successful. He was blunt himself and told me he had complete trust in his agents and the work they were doing, but there was a big problem. He said there were no direct support elements assigned to them, and each time they needed to go into the local villages for intelligence gathering or meetings with sources, they were at the mercy of other ground units in the operating area who would "...take them along." while they did their own missions. He said it was even worse for the agents at Kirkuk Air Base. For some reason in their area, the senior commander of ground operations determined that he did not have enough forces available to support OSI at all. Those agents were forced to provide their own security on every mission. They were not properly trained for this tasking, but handled it to the best of their ability.

Agent Nichols described several missions to me where they had source meetings arranged to gather intelligence, but the available maneuver unit commander determined there was not time to stop and allow the OSI mission to get in his way. The maneuver commander terminated the mission and forced everyone back inside the wire. Lack of support for the OSI mission was becoming routine. When it was available, the support came from units that were not highly trained ground infantry units; rather they were units made up of troops who were tasked to perform missions after their normal duties had ended. They were mechanics, transporters, and food service workers. They were all well-meaning Soldiers, but they were not infantrymen and did not have the skill set to provide the level of support needed for this critical mission.

Then it hit me. I told Agent Nichols what he needed was his own squad of Defenders to protect his agents on every mission. An entire team solely dedicated to the counterterrorism and counterinsurgency missions. His stunned response said it all; "Do you really think they would give us our own squad of Defenders for this mission?" I told him we might hit some resistance; but we had to make the effort and get this support established, thereby hitting the local insurgents where it hurt and stopping the attacks on our bases. He said his detachment was not the only one needing this assistance, but every detachment throughout the country was in the same boat. This problem was far reaching and needed immediate attention. Every location with an OSI Detachment in Iraq needed support, not just the Balad team.

I needed to discuss the matter with General Rand the next day. Our business done, we went about the BBQ and enjoyed the rest of the evening with the First Sergeants sitting on the TOD, listening to the stories about their time in Iraq.

Being the highly experienced, trusting leader that he is, the General said he would support the initiative. However, he needed first hand validation from me on the level of support being provided and the possibility of our Defenders being trained to complete this mission. Before he could even start the next sentence, I told him I would be cleared for a mission immediately and go outside the wire and validate the need for improved support.

I had focus again, and felt like there was an immediate need for my leadership and personal motivation. Momentarily I forgot about the problems of the previous weeks and the casualties we had suffered. I departed the General's office and went to share the good news with Agent Nichols and the OSI team so we could begin planning for the mission.

7 February 2007:

Several days passed and it was Wednesday night. After a full day of meetings and seeing Airmen in action, this night brought the General and me to the Operations Group for the opportunity to walk a mile with them. Colonel Dennis had arranged for both of us to participate in a mission with the Expeditionary Rescue unit outside the wire. It was an opportunity I longed for and would have made great sacrifice to fit into my battle rhythm.

We arrived at the rescue unit's compound and immediately went to the equipment room to get all the required gear for the mission. They wanted us to be fully ingrained and we would have it no other way. Next we made our way into the briefing room and prepared for the mission brief. The crews came in and once introductions were complete, I studied the room.

There were distinct groups within this room, but you could feel the absolute synergy of the team. Each of the rescue helicopters had a crew of four, consisting of two pilots, a flight engineer and an aerial gunner. These were hardened warriors who had flown hundreds of rescue missions in combat and we felt comfortable in their capable hands.

The crew also included a team of Para-Rescue specialists. The officers were known as Combat Rescue Officers and the enlisted Airmen were simply known as PJs. This was one of the most storied and well decorated career fields in the Air Force and rightfully so. PJs and rescue crews had proven themselves time and again in direct combat actions and several had paid the ultimate price over the years. PJs trained harder than any other career field to ensure they could rescue fellow service members who were hurt on the battlefield. It is truly an honorable profession that performed tasks only few could do.

We each linked with a crew and began the mission preparations. Once the briefing material was covered, the Rescue Squadron Commander asked if we had any questions or comments. The General told them how proud he was of their efforts and much he appreciated trained and prepared warriors like those in the room to rescue him on the battlefield. He was right; these teams were highly trained and truly lived by their motto, "That others may live." It took nearly three years for an Airman to gain full certification as a PJ and I am sure the helicopter crews had an equally difficult certification process. I simply thanked them for allowing us to take part in this mission and walk a short mile with them.

Flying out of the controlled area of the base, a warm feeling came over me. If something happened during this mission we would have to participate in an actual rescue while staying out of the way of the rescue actions. My assigned PJ gave me a full detailed briefing of the actions he wanted from me in case of contact with the enemy or during a rescue lift operation.

We moved out and headed for an area where they would practice retrieving someone from the ground. There were requirements they needed to perform in order to maintain proficiency. If they went weeks or months without needing to perform a rescue, lack of practice could impact their success. Keeping these skills fresh was important.

The average PJ was a physical stud. I noticed both of the PJs on my team were smaller than me, but I had little doubt about their physical capability. I knew they could bring me out of the fire if something happened. Their individual equipment weighed at least 80 pounds but they bore it easily.

We arrived at the location and began preparations to lower one member to the ground from the General's helicopter. My team would complete the extraction so we hung back. As they dropped the first PJ off to secure the area a spotlight hit the helicopter from a short distance off. This was a technique used by insurgents to target our helicopters so this was deemed an immediate threat. Insurgents often spotlighted aircraft before they began firing at them. We needed to depart the area immediately.

The mission was called off and the helicopters moved away from the threat source. There was one PJ on the ground, but he was not worried, he could handle himself. The spotlight came on several more times, but there was no hostile fire from that location. After several minutes of tense flying around, waiting for the start of hostilities, the lead team swooped in to pick up their PJ. It appeared the suspect had departed the area and was no longer posing a threat. A decision was made to return to the base and conduct the extraction inside the flight line area and the protection of the base.

Flying back into the airfield we needed to take on extra fuel in order to conduct the second attempt at the extraction. Both teams completed refueling actions and we were soon off flying toward a remote area inside the flight line. As we reached the area and the PJs began preparing the rope for insertion, we heard the other team report an issue. It seemed they had a jammed gun on their helicopter and it would now be impossible to complete the task. I was disappointed but knew this was the right decision. The PJs on my team had just informed me they would be lowering me down and using me as the person they would rescue. But now we needed to return to base, the mission was scrubbed.

Back at the unit they apologized for not being able to complete the mission. We were grateful to take part and everyone seemed pleased. After some photos and coin presentations, the General and I departed. My appreciation for the Airmen of the 332d Operations Group grew higher.

Meeting with Senior Airman Paulson Nez, formerly of Luke Air Force Base.

Chief Dearduff and Chief Maxson (far right) meeting with Airmen who were building a maintenance shack at Al Asad Air Base.

Chief Dearduff prepares for a combat search and rescue mission with the para-rescue (PJ) crews from Balad Air Base.

An Air Force Loadmaster trying to complete more push-ups than Chief Dearduff while they were flying at 15,000 feet.

12
ESCORTING JEREMY

The month of February was passing quickly. Operations were being conducted at record pace. Insurgent activity was out of control, impacting the lives of every Iraqi citizen. Despite all of our efforts to control areas around Baghdad, the situation seemed to worsen by the day. Leaders at all levels understood something had to change quickly or we could lose control of the entire battle space.

Every day brought new challenges. Travel was continuous and the lack of sleep was taking a toll on our bodies. Every day since the dedication of the memorial it was my ritual to start and end my day by stopping at the memorial and reflecting on those Airmen and what they gave to defend freedom. It became my escape from the hardships of war and being far from family.

11 February 2007:

Regardless of how busy our schedules were we always made time for visits to the Balad hospital. The emergency department was busy and the Tuskegee Medics were handling everything the enemy was throwing at them. We worked our way around the hospital and ended up in the ICU. I talked with staff members and received updates on the wounded Soldiers occupying the beds. Regardless of the level of care, the news was never good.

We came across an Airman who was wounded on the battlefield, but we never received information on before our arrival. Once we were inside the ward area, the staff brought us to meet an Air Force Videographer who was working with a Special Forces unit in Baghdad. She described the operation she was recording with her team as they engaged the insurgents. We both stood looking her in the eye, listening to her story and paying keen attention to every detail. The entire time she was talking, I was looking for something. It appeared she was uninjured, or at least I could not see any visible injury.

When she was done, we both looked at her and near simultaneously said, "What happened to you in the firefight?" She looked at us, somewhat embarrassed and said, "A sniper shot me in the hand." She lifted her hand and showed us the bandage keeping her wound wrapped up. The General told her she had nothing to be embarrassed about, and the fact that she lost part of her finger was a significant factor. Then he asked her, "Where was your hand when it was hit by the round?" We both knew the answer and when she said it was on the camera, and the camera was next to her face, I think it became clear to her just how lucky she was. Yes, her finger was shot off, but it was only inches from her head and that would have been an entirely different set of circumstances. We breathed a sigh of relief and thanked her for the dedication and sacrifice she gave to the effort in Iraq.

The General was whisked away by the nursing staff. They wanted him to meet with an Iraqi family currently inside a special ward for enemy casualties. I caught up with him and found him talking with the mother and grandmother of a 20 day old Iraqi boy named Hussein. Through an interpreter, General Rand shared his compassion for the child and their situation. His actions gave them reassurance that little Hussein would be given the best care, even better care than he could ever receive from a local Iraqi hospital. He also assured them they could stay with Hussein and that while they were inside our hospital, they would be fed and cared for. I watched as an elderly Iraqi woman smiled and reached out to hug my commanding general.

As we were walking out he said, "I think we made a few friends tonight." It was like him to see beyond the moment and think about the big picture. He knew that little gestures of this kind would help us in our dealings with the Iraqi people. We headed to our vehicles and back to Red Tail Village. There was obvious fatigue in both our actions, and a little sleep was well in order.

15 February 2007:

Another day of formal visits around Balad took us to the supply warehouse where our Airmen prepared aircraft parts and other essential materials to sustain the war effort. After meeting with many great Airmen and hearing their stories, the General linked on to one particular Airman who caught his attention. I listened in as they talked and could tell this story would really intrigue the General.

Senior Airman Ed Camacho explained that he was from Venezuela and came to America during his early college years to make a better life for himself. He mentioned that his father saved up more than a year's wages to give him a plane ticket and some money to sustain him during his transition period.

Once the money from his dad was gone, he would be required to earn money and provide his own support. He found work cleaning a church in the town of Boston, Massachusetts. When the General asked him why he went to Boston and not some other place where there were many Spanish speaking Americans, Airman Camacho told him that it would be too easy to lean on his native language. By going to Boston, where there were fewer Spanish speaking people, he would be forced to learn English which would help him survive in his new country.

After four months of cleaning that church, Camacho

said he was contacted by an Air Force recruiter. Intrigued, he did not think he would qualify for the Air Force but he talked about it at length with the motivated NCO. Several months later, and many cartoons on TV to hone his language skills, Airman Camacho took and passed the entrance exam to join the Air Force. Not only had he been successful to this point, he had a proven record of outstanding performance and superior grades in every school he attended. The General was so impressed he pulled a commander's coin from his pocket and shook the hand of this proud American warrior. He asked Camacho if he had any new goals in the Air Force. Camacho hesitated, then told the General, "Sir, I would like to go to the Air Force Academy and become a pilot." I'm not sure what was said next, but somehow I knew the General would work as hard as he could to provide an opportunity for Airman Camacho if there was a way to make it happen.

By the end of this night I was tired, but filled with motivation from the excitement of meeting with Airman Camacho and the others. I was pumped with a new level of fight inside me, and I wanted to make more good things happen in the months remaining on our tour. The Iraqi insurgency was growing stronger by the day and we needed all the positive energy we could muster.

Once I arrived back at Red Tail Village I saw a message from CSM Mellinger's office in Baghdad. He wanted to talk to me about spending some more time with our great Airmen. I returned the call and talked directly with him to see what he had in mind. He left it up to me, but I knew he always liked to visit the hospital while he was at Balad. Whatever else we did from there was completely my call. He also told me he had a civilian news reporter coming along with him as part of the national level effort to spread the word about what we were doing to make Iraq a better place. That made me think even harder, and knowing that the sergeant major had been in country for more than two years, there was not much he had not seen or done.

I asked him if he had ever seen our medical evacuation teams in action. He said; "Only at the hospital while loading the patients, but not their entire operation. Bingo! I wanted to spread the word to the world about how incredible our medics were and the huge impact they were having on the mission to change Iraq. I asked if he could give me three days to walk a mile with the medical evacuation teams, and would he mind going to Germany? I think I detected a big smile on his face through the phone, maybe even some excitement, when he said, "Let's do it. Just tell me when."

Immediately following the call I went to see Colonel Masterson at the Medical Group to start the clearance process. There were very strict controls on who could fly with the medical evacuation missions, as the maximum amount of space was needed for the wounded and their critical care teams. I found him walking about the hospital late at night and told him what I intended to do. He clearly understood the value of having the senior enlisted member in the country complete this mission and know the full value of our medical teams. He assured me he would get us clearance and make it happen.

18 February 2007:

Colonel Masterson cleared both of us for the medical evacuation mission. I called CSM Mellinger and told him that we were good to go for a medical evacuation mission on 23 February. I informed him that in order to experience the entire chain of events for our wounded, he would have to arrive at the hospital several hours before the departure time. This would allow him to be integrated into every step of the mission if he was willing. He assured me that he was on board and was looking forward to the opportunity. Plans were set, and I was excited about showing off our great Airmen.

23 February 2007:

CSM Mellinger and his protective service team known as the "Lion Patrol" arrived on schedule, and we met at a pre-designated rally point. I asked if he needed me to do anything for his security element, the same guys who take him on every ground mission he completes. He laughed and said, "They are well taken care of, and will be happy you are taking me away for a few days, because now they get time to themselves, and maybe a day off." I could see their relief, and even received a few thanks from some of his security team members before they departed. We had plenty of time before the mission departure time, so we headed for the fire station where he could meet the joint team of warriors who performed this critical mission. In addition to meeting the teams of firefighters and medics, they offered to let him drive their newest fire truck. They told him that it was a 250,000 dollar vehicle, and that he would have to back in into the garage when they returned. I believe I saw him smile for the next hour as he handled the task of driving that large fire engine, shooting the water cannon as they went. Soon the visit was complete and we headed to the hospital.

We arrived with plans to go through the wards before we linked with the medical evacuation team for the mission. However, as we passed through the Intensive Care Unit, we could not help but stop and see what was going on. Chief Rudy Lopez was now the Medical Group superintendent. He described the patients who would be traveling with us on the mission to Germany as they were being prepared for the movement.

We could see at least three patients who appeared to be badly wounded, and there were teams at each of the beds. The ICU nurses, several doctors, and medics worked in and around the ward, making preparations and taking what appeared to be life-saving actions on two of the Soldiers. I thought it would be best if we stepped back out of the way and watched from a distance. I motioned to the sergeant major, who looked at me, and then moved forward to the first bed, asking some questions to the attending nurse.

I saw the look on his face change from the excitement of the mission, to the pain of death. The doctor told him the Soldier's name was Jeremy, and he would not make it. The entire effort to sustain him on life support was designed to get him to Germany with his parents before he expired. It was the humanitarian thing to do, and one every family would appreciate, even if they did not know it. The sergeant major turned to me and said, "I will stay with Jeremy." It was a simple statement, but was meant with all seriousness. He was now escorting Jeremy.

I found the attending nurse from the medical evacuation team and told her that CSM Mellinger was going to accompany Jeremy to Germany and she looked stunned. She asked, "Does he know Jeremy is not going to survive?" I told her he was aware and that he would end up meeting with the family at the other end, trying to provide them with some level of comfort.

Things progressed rapidly over the next hour, and there was constant movement around the room as they prepared all the patients for transport. While we stood speechless in the ICU, other patients were being loaded on the bus and taken to the plane for the ride home. ICU patients were the last ones out and the plane was buttoned up once they were on board, reducing the amount of time they were exposed outside of a hospital. These missions were very carefully planned and executed.

I noticed the ward nurse bring the phone over to Jeremy's attending doctor and listened as he explained things to his father. I heard him say, "Sir, I am sorry to tell you that we have done everything we could to help Jeremy, but his injuries were so severe we could not bring him back, and cannot give him a positive prognosis." I then heard him say, "Please get to Germany as fast as you can so you can see Jeremy before he expires." The phone was pulled away and the doctor went right back to work. Then I noticed CSM

Mellinger take the phone from the nurse and speak directly with Jeremy's father.

I asked him later what he said, and he said; "I told his dad that we would be with Jeremy every step of the way and he was getting the absolute best medical care available." I could not help but think about the level of courage it takes to speak with the father of a dying Soldier at a moment like this. It was courage I only hoped I would have in the same circumstances, but until I was tested, I would not know.

We departed the ICU when the other patients had all been loaded. Jeremy would be last. A large formation of medics attended to him, carrying his support equipment through the tight hallways of the hospital tents. As we got to the bus, I noticed the sergeant major up front, hoisting Jeremy onto the bus along with the medics, and then jumping on to ride to the flight line. Chief Lopez helped me onto the back of the bus and said he would take care of my vehicle and get our gear to the plane.

Once we arrived at the flight line, we saw the ramp of the C-17 was lined with at least 30 military members, all of whom were volunteers on their time off. They were standing ready to load the last three passengers onto the ramp. Although this line of volunteers always did the carrying onto the back of the plane, this time the carrying was done by the sergeant major and several members of Jeremy's unit who made it out to see him off. I asked the volunteers to step aside and let this happen; it was the right thing to do. They each stood back and made sure the load procedures were done safely. It took a simple word from me and this team of volunteers went from workers to coaches, making sure every step was taken with care.

Once on board Jeremy was loaded onto the medical racks lining each side of the large and versatile deck of the C-17. The medical evacuation team turned the plane into a hospital room and made Jeremy as comfortable as possible. I secured our gear and made room for us to sit on the side rails near Jeremy's position. We were about to take off when the aircraft's loadmaster had to ask the sergeant major to take his seat as it was not safe to be standing during this part of the flight. Reluctantly he sat, but he was so close to Jeremy he could still touch his hand.

Once airborne we were part of a fully capable hospital cruising at 30,000 feet above sea level. The ride was smooth and the air evacuation crews operated as if they were in a regular hospital. Throughout the four-hour flight there were many complications going on around the deck, with some of the patients needing medication, asking for food or water, and a variety of needs. But Jeremy lay quietly. His 3 person team and CSM Mellinger by his side every minute of the way. When I asked him if he needed something to eat or needed to get off his feet, he replied; "I'm good to go."

As the plane leveled off and settled into cruising speed, the nurse told CSM Mellinger it was time to let Jeremy rest, and we could all take a short break. For a few minutes I watched as this highly resilient battle-tested leader sat down and rested. Somehow he slept for 30 minutes among the chaos. I knew he was mentally and physically exhausted. Now he was also being tested emotionally, and this trip was not going to be easy.

During the flight I talked with the other patients, crew members, and the fantastic medical evacuation teams working around the makeshift hospital floor inside the plane. I was impressed at the youth of some of our medics and the extent of their experience in this current combat situation. Some of them had been on as many as 100 medical evacuation missions and proudly stated they've never lost a patient on any mission.

I was pleasantly surprised to find out how many of them were from the Air Force Reserves and Air National Guard and had experience working in trauma hospitals back in the States. They were happy to be on this team and said nothing they did back home could compare to what they accomplished on these missions. Bringing the wounded home gave them a sense of satisfaction and made a direct contribution to the overall mission. I could feel the pride and enthusiasm, and just stood there smiling.

Four hours after take-off, the C-17 landed and the doors opened as soon as we stopped and engines were shut down. The patients would be offloaded in the opposite order from the load plan and Jeremy would go first. I grabbed the bags and CSM Mellinger went to transfer Jeremy from the plane to the bus.

The ride to the Regional Medical facility was short, but seemed to take forever. Anything could go wrong, causing them to proceed carefully. A bump along the road could undo the great work done back at the theater hospital. The bus moved slow, ensuring the comfort of all the wounded.

At the hospital there was another team of volunteers standing by to offload the patients. They would not stop the sergeant major from doing his part and having a hand on Jeremy's gurney. When we arrived at the ICU, Jeremy was placed in the first room and another team of medical professionals immediately went to work preparing the equipment and making him as comfortable as possible. They were very accommodating to us, allowing us to remain in the room when they usually would not.

We stayed for an hour before everything was done and the staff was moving on to the other patients. We thanked them for all their actions and decided it was time to get checked into our room and get something to eat. The night was over and we were expecting to meet his family in about five hours, rest was needed.

There was finally some time for me to sit down and get to know the reporter who was traveling with us. His name was Michael Yon and he said he was a former Soldier himself. He was now a freelance reporter traveling around

Iraq with different units so their stories could be told some day. We both knew that a story was being written directly in front of our eyes on this trip. He and I shared our thoughts on many issues as we headed to our quarters for the night. He seemed like a great American, and I was glad to have him with us on this trip.

We arrived back at the ICU and checked in with the charge nurse. She informed us Jeremy's parents and sister had arrived and were in with the chaplain now. They had not been in to see Jeremy, and we could visit with them first if we wanted. The sergeant major led the way, and once the chaplain was done, we went right in.

The room was cold and had no character. The walls were plain, the chairs were simple. The family was all situated and yet they did not seem to understand why we were coming into the room. I watched as this battle-hardened Soldier walked right over to Jeremy's mom and held her tight in a hug for what seemed like several minutes. He whispered into her ear words that only they know, but by her reaction I could tell he said the right thing. We greeted the rest of the family and sat down to talk. They appeared tired, but attentive to what he said. I was sure they had not slept since receiving the news of Jeremy's injury.

The sergeant major began by explaining to them who we were and where we had come from. He told Jeremy's dad that he was the one who spoke to him on the phone after the doctor and we were with Jeremy the entire trip, witnessing the care and concern he received at every step. He described the scene inside the C-17 and how the critical care team never left his side throughout the journey. There seemed to be a great calm in the room at this time, and even though they knew it was hopeless, they somehow appeared comfortable now, knowing Jeremy was not in pain.

Several minutes passed, questions were asked and answered, and finally the knock came at the door. It was the charge nurse and she was ready to take the family in to see

Jeremy. They collectively decided that his mom would go first and she would go alone. Earlier we had discovered she was a nurse herself and had a good idea what to expect when she went into the room.

We stood as she departed and collectively held our breath, knowing there cannot be much in this world more painful than for a mother to see her child lying in a bed being sustained on life support with no hope of survival.

The room was quiet, the door closed. Everything in the ICU seemed to come to a halt. Seconds later, with the ICU completely still, we heard a very loud scream that chilled us to the bone, "JEREMY!"

It was painful for all of us, but none could imagine her agony at this very moment.

She came back into the room where we stood. She looked at us; we froze in place. CSM Mellinger walked over and extended his arms. She grabbed him and held on tightly. It was a comforting moment. I stood speechless. I would remember this day for the rest of my life.

A team of volunteer Tuskegee Airmen load patients off the bus as they prepare for the medical evacuation flight to Germany.

Jeremy is loaded on the C-17 as the last patient in preparation for the medical evacuation flight to Germany.

Medical Evacuation teams hard at work on Jeremy and the other wounded warriors while in flight. This C-17 was transformed into a fully functioning Intensive Care Unit.

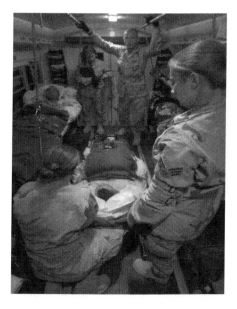

Wounded Warriors being transported on the bus from the flight line to the hospital for the next level of care.

13
NO REST, NO RECUPERATION

We left the hospital and began the trip from Germany back to Iraq which would hopefully bring some peace and a little sleep. Boarding the small C-35 Lear jet, we all hoped to make it home without stopping for fuel so we could just sleep through the seven-hour journey, but it was not to be. The crew informed us that because of the altitude they needed to reach, we would have to stop for fuel in Bulgaria.

"Now if memory serves me correctly," I asked, "Bulgaria is one of the former Soviet bloc countries and we probably won't be too welcome there?" They said not to worry, we would land at a military air strip and they do this all the time. "Yeah, right," I thought. I survived a trip to Iran back in 2003, another to the Soviet Union in 1998, but the third time was probably not going to bring me any more luck than I already had, so I told them I planned to stay on board during the fuel stop.

Arriving in Bulgaria was a little shocking, seeing the snow-covered runway and harsh cold wind blowing snow sideways toward our plane. The place was completely isolated, with no movement by vehicle or pedestrian. It was everything we've seen in movies about this region and our bones were chilled. We were not allowed to remain on board during the refueling operation, so walking into the desolate terminal and using the bathroom seemed like a great idea.

Once inside, we were met with some mighty tough stares, mostly by old men wrapped in furry parkas and large furry boots. There were no exchanges of conversation, and no questions about the location of the latrines. We just walked until we found them, took care of our business and returned to the plane. As cold as it was outside, it felt warmer than standing in the terminal with those cold hard stares peering upon us.

A few hours later we landed back in Iraq and CSM Mellinger thanked me for the experience. He summed it up well. "I have never been as impressed in my 35 years of military experience as I was on this mission. Please pass along to those Tuskegee medics my thanks on behalf of so many families who will never meet them, understand what they do, or get the chance to thank them in person themselves." Those words would ring loud and clear in my mind, and I would share them often in the future as situations permitted. As usual he was spot on.

As we parted ways and he told me to make sure I made plans to attend a ceremony in May in which he would hand over his duties to another Soldier. He also said he had something for me, which peeked my curiosity.

After a quick shower and time to unpack my bag, I was off to handle whatever I had missed during the previous days. I knew what I had to do so the office was drawing me over. I knew there would be plenty of administrative work to do and Frankie lined everything up to limit the amount of time it took. He knew I had other things to do.

For once, sitting in the office felt OK, and brought some sorely needed peace. I decided to spend more time in there and get caught up with all the things I had been neglecting so I could head back out at full speed. After several hours of tedious office duty, I retreated to my quarters. Arriving well after dark, I met with Colonel Ellis inside Red Tail Village. We sat and talked for a short time so I could bring him up to speed on the trip to Germany.

We were about to knock off for the night when suddenly, Boom! "Incoming, Incoming, Incoming!" We both instinctively hit the ground, faces down in the dirt. We wondered aloud if these attacks would ever end.

Two minutes later we were in our gear driving toward the flight line because this one sounded like it hit near our transport aircraft parking ramp, and could be big trouble. On arrival we saw a complete ghost town, with no movement around the three large aircraft waiting to depart or be offloaded. As we entered the area, the Defender said at least one round had impacted very near the second jet and there had been several Airmen and civilians in that immediate area. Our worst fears were possibly about to come to fruition. We knew we had to get there immediately.

When we arrived, more Defenders were checking out the scene and assisting those who were in the area. They went person to person and checked inside and even under the aircraft for injuries but could not find any. We all took a collective sigh and they radioed the information in to the command post for follow-on emergency forces. There were no injuries from a round that landed so close...we were very fortunate.

The rockets caused holes in the parking ramp near the jets. Upon close inspection, there were also some small holes in the tail section of one C-17 aircraft. But those small problems would not stop the aircraft from taking off, and the crew wanted to leave right away. They hurried with the offload and asked for clearance to taxi with lightning efficiency. People get real motivated when the enemy attacks. We were very lucky on this one; and although I wanted to count my blessings, I also did not want to curse us either. So we decided to not think about it and spend the next several hours out on the flight line with these Airmen.

Before long there were Airmen from the civil engineering squadron arriving to repair the taxiway and parking ramp. We were amazed at how fast they worked to ensure the planes could take off and more could land and load critical battlefield supplies.

While the parking ramp was fixed, Airmen from the Logistics Readiness Squadron, known as aerial porters, were finishing the loading of the C-17 sitting near us. Once it was finished, the crew boarded and the plane departed. The attack resulted in a 15 minute delay for the plane; considering what could have happened, we were lucky. I told the aerial porters I would come back out soon and spend some time loading planes with them to get a better appreciation for what they did.

Colonel Ellis and I headed back to our quarters knowing tonight the Tuskegee Airmen escaped a huge tragedy. We breathed a collective sigh of relief.

27 February 2007:

Knowing General Rand would depart for his well-deserved R&R the next day, I hoped the night would end quietly. Unfortunately the enemy got a vote, and as we came to expect, they knew we had important flying operations going on after dark. They often attacked at night hoping they would interrupt our mission. I left the recreation center after a short check in to see how the Airmen and Soldiers were doing and had gone back to my room, hoping to watch a little television myself when the first mortar round hit. It was close and I knew that sound too well. Once you are within 100 meters of a mortar or rocket landing, you never forget the sound.

This one did not knock me off my feet, but I could feel the concussion through the concrete walls surrounding our housing compound. Hoping it was a single attack, I headed to the area I believed had been hit. As I ran down the roadway looking for damage or injuries, the second round landed near me and the attack warning came across the giant voice system, "Incoming, Incoming, Incoming." I had to choose whether to dive behind some concrete on the ground or keep searching for the injured. As always, my training kicked in and I ran at full sprint now, unaware I was running toward the target area.

As I neared the recreation and fitness centers, I noticed people milling about like nothing was going on. I began to scream at them to "Take cover, NOW!" To my left I noticed several Soldiers who were standing up near the smoke pit, acting as if nothing was happening. I approached at a fast pace and told them to get down before they were hit by the next round. Without saying a word, they looked at me like I was crazy and continued to stand outside the bunker enjoying their smokes.

Quickly I broke left and headed straight for them, instinctively diving to cover them in case the next round came even closer. I grabbed both of them and we all hit the ground with a thud, just seconds before the next round hit. BOOM! Another close one...probably 50 meters away and with nothing in between the point of impact and us. As we dusted ourselves off, the two Soldiers crawled into the bunker without a word, and thanked me for coming to their aid.

I was off again in seconds and shook my head at their inability to understand how important it was to take cover during these attacks. I knew there would be injuries in the camp and I needed to help find them. Security Force Defenders were all around searching and finding damage. They radioed in points of impact, evacuated buildings and assisted the wounded. By the time I reached the row of living trailers that was hit, two Defenders were already on scene providing life-saving treatment to an Airman who was struck by shrapnel while sleeping in his bed. The quarters were destroyed, but luckily there was no fire or damage to the adjoining trailers.

Firefighters and medics from the hospital arrived at the scene expecting to find casualties following the attack. Moments later we heard the sirens again and the warning of incoming. As we directed everyone to take cover again, the defensive systems around the base went off and the last incoming round was stopped short of its intended target.

I needed to find my General and the Colonels. They might have been out moving around the base and directly in harm's way. I needed to make sure I could keep my promise that nothing would happen to General Rand and I felt the same commitment to the colonels. I headed straight to the General's quarters where I found all of them safe. They were OK. They laughed and said; "We knew you were out there and that nothing bad would happen."

I wished they were right, but knew I could not stop attacks coming in from indirect fire or other sources. I told them what had happened within the housing area and what we found at the point of impact. I did not tell them the path of the rounds likely flew directly over their location, and just missed 200 meters long. They were reassured that all responding forces were on scene and secure. I knew they were safe, providing some relief, so I moved on.

Within minutes the entire situation changed. The attack was over and the base was quiet. Aircraft were taking off and landing, vehicle and foot traffic resumed. The resiliency of our Airmen was impressive...nothing could stop them.

Reflecting on this attack and how accurate those rounds were made me think hard about the help we needed to get for our OSI Agents. Their ability to stop these attacks was directly related to their ability to conduct counter-insurgency work outside the wire without looking over their shoulders. Attacks on the base were up, and accuracy was increasing. We needed to get OSI outside the wire more often so they could stop these attacks on the base. I needed to visit the OSI detachment soon and find out what I could do to help. General Rand departed for his R&R time back at home.

Colonel Renfrow and I would spend the next two weeks side by side meeting with our Airmen. The nature of our duties normally kept us going in separate directions. But now we would attend meetings and luncheons together along with visits to work centers and FOBs. I came to realize just how dedicated a leader he was. Talking with Airmen at luncheons, he started to divulge more about his past. During one such event at DFAC #2, he revealed to the crowd that he was an enlisted Air Traffic Controller before going to OTS and becoming an officer. I had just spent 6 months in combat with this colonel, and I had no idea about his past. I was happy to hear about his enlisted roots and some of his leadership philosophy forged while serving as an NCO. It drew me closer to him than I already was.

I made plans to spend time with the aerial porters before we started our travels again. Since most of the cargo missions took place at night, I would get ready for a long 20-hour workday. I arrived at the flight line and met with the NCO in charge of the port operations. I told him I was there to load planes with his crew. He smiled and walked me out to the area where the next cargo plane was due to arrive. After a short explanation of the safety precautions, we readied ourselves for arrival and off-load.

I decided to wear my battle gear, including my gloves and protective eyewear. Within minutes there were two C-17s parked on the ramp and two C-130s heading that way. We jumped out of the truck and I told him I would work the first one. I climbed up the side of the 60-K Tunner Loader, a commonly used piece of equipment that was named in honor of Lt General William Tunner, the architect of the Berlin Airlift back in 1949. This one machine was capable of handling six fully loaded pallets and significantly eased the loading process.

Once inside I latched on to the youngest Airman I could find and got a briefing from him on what we needed to do. Within the next 30 minutes we pushed 17 pallets off the plane, each weighing more than 5,000 pounds. We locked them onto the Tunner loaders and off to the yard they went. Just a few minutes later we had new loaders at the ramp being backed into place. Each of the loaders was expertly placed in line to create only one movement at the back of the plane. The other loaders would match the first loader and the pallets would be rolled all the way into the aircraft.

The process was a thing of beauty. I was also getting tired as this work was difficult. It was not normally performed wearing full combat gear, and they all told me I could take it off. But I wanted to prove a point. If this old Chief could offload these pallets with combat gear on, so could they. Maybe the next time there was an attack, they would not hesitate to wear their gear and protect themselves even better. The experience was enlightening for many, and I thanked them for allowing me to join their operation.

The days continued to be long. I found myself trying to accomplish a routine of meetings throughout the day while spending time with different units around Balad at night. Friday night finally came and there would be only one meeting the next day. I figured this would be a great time to find another group of Airmen working in some back shop. Making my way around the flight line, I found Airmen preparing F-16s for take-off and Airmen who were completing long term maintenance. Each one provided a unique perspective on how they contributed to mission success. I felt better each time I met another Airman who was truly attached to our success through his or her own actions.

17 March 2007:

General Rand arrived safely back at Balad ready for the remaining months and whatever tough times waiting for us. The situation in Iraq continued to get worse by the day, placing more of our Airmen in harm's way, facing the enemy on a regular basis. The official word coming from Washington that a troop surge was going to happen in order to give the MNF-I Commander sufficient forces to counter the insurgency in a new way. We started hearing the term "COIN" being used and had no idea initially what it meant. Apparently this was to become the new method of implementing the Counter Insurgency effort. There were not many details, but we knew it would impact the mission of the US Army, and entire units were being told they would stay past their original tour of 12 months in country. Rumors were abound that all Army units would stay a full 15 months in country before being relieved and sent home.

We took a couple of hours to get caught up on what happened while he was gone. He told me about the time he spent with Kim and how relaxing it was to have a few days away from the battlefield. He also admitted that while he was away physically, he never left mentally. He told me how hard it was to leave and not remain attached to everything going on back here in Iraq. I could tell he carried the weight of command with him every day, but I hoped he did find time for some rest. He appeared ready to go, and was focused on getting his next combat sortie complete, but first we had to say goodbye to Colonel Ellis, not be an easy thing.

The Red Tail Commanders and Chiefs gathered, the food was prepared, and the air was thick with smoke. American aircraft could be heard taking off in the background and helicopters were pounding the air overhead, likely taking wounded warriors to the hospital for care. It was the perfect atmosphere to pay tribute to our warrior and friend who had once again deployed to combat, leaving his family behind. Going away ceremonies in combat are not always high spirited, and rarely have gift exchanges. We told stories about the warrior who was leaving, while thanking them for all they gave to the fight. Colonel Ellis would be the first person from our Tuskegee leadership team to depart, so this was uncharted territory.

I kept my emotions in check, but knew that I was losing a battle buddy, a confidant, and someone I could count on to give me the honest truth at the times when others would not. I watched from the back as he humbly accepted the kind words from the other colonels. They told stories about their times with him during the past seven months. We laughed, but deep down inside, there were other emotions in play.

General Rand had the last words about Colonel Ellis. He told everyone about the long relationship they shared, and about the connection between their families. He talked about service and sacrifice and shared the story about calling Doc on short notice and telling him that he was in need of a Colonel to become the chief of staff, and his name was Ellis. We all laughed, but most had similar stories about their willingness to deploy to combat. General Rand reminded us that combat brings out the best and the worst of the human spirit. But when it came to Colonel Doc Ellis, he said most of what he brought to the fight was the best of that spirit. He concluded his remarks by telling us it was our duty and our burden to fight our nation's wars, and Colonel "Doc" Ellis knew that burden well.

I embraced him in a battle hug and we parted ways. He left a few short hours later, and I needed some rest. I was starting to understand the emotional drain of personal relationships, the brotherhood, formed in combat.

24 March 2007:

Soon I would be going home on my mid-tour leave to spend two weeks with my family, and I needed to prepare myself and the office for that time away. I knew Chief Tim Ruenning was a very capable leader who would be able to fill in during my absence. His character was superior; and having watched him in action with the Airmen of the Operations group, there were no worries about his ability to handle the additional responsibility.

I went over to spend some time with the base Honor Guard at their practice and talked with Tim about the program. Chief Ruenning took on the responsibility to mentor the Honor Guard and provide them with guidance and support. I was very appreciative of his work in this area and noticed our Honor Guard program was significantly improved. He gave all the credit to Technical Sergeant Richard Rositas, my new assistant who had taken over from Frankie J. just weeks before. Sergeant Rositas used his previous experience with the Air Force Honor Guard and brought the base Honor Guard members up to speed rapidly.

The Honor Guard would remain a highly motivated team with Chief Ruenning watching over them. His humble leadership style gave me great confidence in his ability to fill in my shoes while I went on R&R – time I badly needed. I felt worse physically and mentally than I had at any other point in my entire career. Tim reassured me he had everything under control and he would take good care of the General and all of my duties, so I could go and unwind.

Days flew by, and I was really looking forward to my pending departure. I knew there was much to do before leaving; but my anticipation was growing, and the strain of traveling back across the ocean was adding to my overall stress. After this long day ended, I decided to stop in at the recreation center to see how things were going, and maybe catch a few minutes of the Balad Idol competition, which was patterned after the very popular TV reality show. I figured a few minutes of entertainment at the end of the long day might help me unwind before heading home.

As I entered the recreation center, I was surprised by the huge crowd gathered and the incredible amount of noise. It seemed more popular than I ever imagined, and that this definitely might be worth seeing. Making my way to the back of the room I found the General, several colonels and some of our chiefs enjoying the night with their favorite soda or Slurpee in hand. They told me to pull up a chair and enjoy as this was the semi-finals and the competition was going well. Although half of the acts had already performed, there were some good ones to come and things would really pick up.

The emcee came on and announced an intermission, but before we did there was one act who had been disqualified because he did not appear in the previous week's competition. He was back now and they wanted to let him participate as a special act, not a part of the competition. They had my attention, and all of us turned to see what this was all about.

A US Army Major walked on the stage and took the microphone, set up his guitar and prepared to sing. He made some statement about being disappointed about being disqualified from the competition, but I was not paying him any mind, just waiting for him to start singing. To my surprise, he was quite good and had the full attention of the crowd.

Once he was done, the emcee came back on stage to put everyone on the intermission, but the major pulled the microphone back. He began to excite the crowd, saying he got a standing ovation and should be allowed to get back into the competition. The emcee again tried to grab the microphone, but the major insisted and began to incite the crowd with chants of "Let him in," "Let him in."

He now had my attention since he was no longer taking direction from the emcee and appeared to be taking over the event. I listened intently as he ranted on. "I should not be eliminated from the competition because I have a real job and have to go on missions outside the wire," he said. Now I was irritated, because this was some kind of reference to the Army versus Air Force battle we often dealt with. Then he said, "You Air Force don't go outside the wire, and you all have easy jobs. That's why you get to stay in the competition, but I have a real job!"

At this point he crossed the bridge of respect and was clearly offending my Air Force and the men and women who have incredibly tough missions, both inside and outside the wire. He offended me because many Airmen in our wing spent more time in harm's way than he likely did on any given week. I started toward the stage and fully expected to be held back by the General or one of the colonels. Somebody had to stop this insanity so I headed his way.

The General looked at me and said, "Go get him, Chief." When I reached the stage he was still chanting to the crowd to let him back in and he refused to give the microphone back to the emcee. I walked to the edge of the stage, motioned him over, grabbed the microphone and stated very clearly for the crowd, "We are now on a 15-minute intermission." I handed the microphone to the emcee and told the major to join me outside.

As we exited the door Colonel "Omar" Bradley, our newly arrived Chief of Staff, was on his way in. I stopped him and said, "Colonel, I need you as a witness to this discussion with this major." He looked at me and said, "Chief, just don't kill him!" Over the next few minutes I explained to the major how important it was to maintain good order and discipline in our events, even the off-duty ones. I explained that his comments were completely out of line and he needed to cease and desist. Somewhere in the conversation I told him I did not appreciate his comments about the Air Force and the criticality of our jobs. I told him there were many Airmen protecting him at that moment in places he had no idea they were performing missions. I also told him about those Airmen who had made the ultimate sacrifice and given their last full measure so he could have an Idol competition.

The conversation went fast and furious and I would not remember everything I said. Certainly I made my point and he stood by speechless. My point was made loud and clear and he did not care to belabor the discussion. I looked at Colonel Bradley and told him I was done with the major and it was over to him. I listened as he told the major to press on, and not to go back into the recreation center, as his night was over. This was not the kind of stressful event I needed before heading home, but it was done and it felt great to have Colonel Bradley stand firmly by my side. I needed some rest.

There were no real days off, and very few days without competing demands on our schedules. I was scheduled to leave on a medical evacuation flight around 0400 and needed to be at the passenger terminal by midnight. Before I could get there and begin the travel home to see the family, the General and I had to visit our Security Force Defenders at Guardmount before they took to their posts.

I was late arriving for the Guardmount formation because a careless Airmen who was somewhat distracted, pulled out in front of me, almost striking my vehicle. When I tried to get his attention, he simply waved at me and continued on his way. It would have been easy to let this go, but I was worried he was so distracted that he may hurt himself or someone else along the way to wherever he was going. I stopped him and engaged in a conversation hoping to bring him back into focus.

Once inside the Guardmount room, we both thanked the Defenders for their courageous efforts each and every day in the direct line of fire with the enemy. Some of them would be completing their combat tour soon and would head back home. We wanted them to know the impact of their service on the defense of the base and the safety of the Airmen and Soldiers who lived there. As we departed from the unit I said goodbye to the General and headed for the passenger terminal. It never crossed my mind that something could happen to him while I was gone, he was my General and seemed invincible. The goodbye was simple and I kept all of my emotions in check.

As I began this long trip home, from Iraq to Kuwait, and then through the civilian airport at Kuwait to St. Louis, I felt pain and anguish, not knowing what it would be like to come home from this hellish place. Coming home from combat would be no different than it had been previously. Adjusting to life at home and fitting in with the family was always a challenge. I had no idea how tightly I was wound and how much stress I was showing. The family knew it, and they were prepared to support me during this short visit.

It would not be easy to compartmentalize how I felt. My mind would not shut down, it kept me from sleeping along the route home. During the final leg of the trip from Washington D.C. to St. Louis, I passed out from exhaustion. I'm sure I looked like hell when I walked off the plane, but seeing my family sparked me up like never before.

Damage to the inside of an Airman's living quarters following a 27 February 2007 rocket attack. The rocket motor ended up on the bed next to where the Airman was sleeping.

Airmen from the civil engineering squadron perform rapid runway repair following a mortar attack on the flight line.

Colonel "Omar" Bradley observing aircraft taking off from the Balad flight line.

Chief Dearduff addressing the Security Force Defenders at guardmount.

14
A MIRACLE TO BEHOLD

The welcome home was as special as ever. I found my family adjusted to their life and they were operating well without me. There was no need for me to be in charge of anything, I just needed to be there and enjoy. I tried to hide my pain and stress, but they could see through the disguise.

The transition from working extremely long 20-hour duty days with tons of responsibility to being on R&R with no responsibility was harder than imagined. My only duty was to sit back, relax and enjoy some quiet time...my mind could not make the adjustment. It was great to be home around my family. In order to decompress and enjoy the time, I would hide my pain and deal with it once the tour was over and I had time to process it all.

Mags provided for me as she always did, ensuring I was pain-free and had all the emotional support needed. She knew there were things I wanted to tell her about the first 9 months of the tour but it was best to leave it alone for now. We pressed on quietly, and most important, we pressed on together.

Sitting on the back deck of our home one evening we were enjoying a cup of tea and catching up on the people in our lives. She told me about the chiefs back at Balad who thought enough to send a care package to the house in case I became homesick for the deployed environment. The care package contained items we used around Balad, like plastic utensils and napkins from the DFAC. It brought a smile to my face and gave us both a good laugh. I was sitting there thinking how great it was that my fellow chiefs took the time to worry about me while I was on my R&R when I sensed something out of the corner of my eye.

I did not turn right away because I was looking through the care package with Mags, but I felt something was creeping up on us. Suddenly I heard this thumping sound coming from the corner of the house and as I turned to see what it was, a projectile smacked me in the side of the head. I jumped across the deck and started in that direction, thinking I had been shot. My adrenaline was pumping so fast I could not tell if I was bleeding or in pain, I just knew something hit me. Seconds later my eyes cleared and I could see Sean laying on the ground holding a Nerf grenade launcher and he looked scared. I had no idea how intensely I was bearing down on him.

Mags caught my attention by yelling my name. I came back to the moment and realized that my son was playing a game we had played many times before and this was not the battlefield. But on this occasion, fresh from the battlefield, it seemed like a real attack...I was lost in the moment. My heart was beating faster than normal and I was sweating. Mags had to physically grab me and bring me back to the porch, calming me down the entire time. Sean was scared, and had no idea what just happened. Once I was back in my chair and breathing normal, Mags brought Sean over and explained to him again that he had to refrain from sneaking up on me while I was home because moments like that would scare me. I knew he meant no harm by it because we were used to scaring each other on many occasions. We all sat and took a deep breath to settle the scene. I was lucky Mags was there with me and was able to control my actions, both physical and emotional. I came to realize how tightly wound I actually was.

As each day passed during my R&R, I showed more of the stress that I knew was contained inside. My attitude was horrible and my actions were worse. I had no tolerance for anyone or anything they did. I wanted things done immediately and with no room for error. After this continued for a few days, Mags was finally fed up. She sat me down and told me in no uncertain terms that I could not act like this at home. She reminded me I was no longer on the battlefield, and they were not my troops. She would not tolerate me acting the way I was and if I continued, I might as well return to Iraq and not come home until I was done. She was right. It was the slap in the face I needed. I had to change and compartmentalize like I had planned to do.

These two weeks were the fastest of my life. Days flew by and before I knew it, my departure day had arrived. Although I was going to stop in Philadelphia for a three-day formal training course before departing back to Iraq and Mags was going to accompany me, I had to say goodbye to the kids. My daughter was used to seeing me leave, so it was easier for her. But my son had never really experienced me coming home and then departing again so soon.

We rose early on the last morning to make sure he had everything he needed for his day of school. He knew something was different about the day, but never fully understood until now that I was leaving again and would not be back for several months. His eyes watered and his demeanor rapidly changed.

Although it was time for me to leave, he began blocking the way to the door and refused to get his stuff ready for school. We both walked him toward the door, carrying his stuff and trying to reassure him it would be OK and I would be home soon. He was not convinced and grabbed me by the neck, holding on with a strength I had not known from him before. After a few minutes, Mags tried to convince him it was time for him to go to school and that his friends were coming up the street. He would not let go, but held on with more power than ever. She began to pull him away, but he resisted. His anger toward Mags was strong because she would not let him go to the airport and say goodbye. She knew it would be even harder to have this moment in public at the airport.

My heart sank. Did he know something I did not? Did he have a feeling that I would not be coming back and this would be the last time he held his father? It all worked me over pretty hard, and he held on with great perseverance. As she pulled to attempt a separation, his fingers sank into my neck, scratching me on both sides as he was moved toward the door. Once he landed on his feet, Mags said his friends were there and standing just outside the door. That was the moment we needed, because he was a proud young man and would not be seen crying by his friends. He tried hard to compose himself and waved goodbye as he departed through the door. Although the week would be especially hard on him, we knew Amber and Matt would be there to support him while Mags joined me in Pennsylvania. Mags closed the door and her emotions took over. She carried the full emotional load of what this family was going through.

My heart was breaking and I had to have a few minutes to myself. Why was I doing this to my family, to my son and to myself? I was putting them through so much, and they were asking and getting so little in return. This would be the hardest thing I had ever done in my life, leaving to go back to combat again. How many times could my luck hold out? What was my fate and when was my bill due?

Before we departed for Philadelphia, Mags checked in with Sean's school to ensure he was OK. They reassured us that he was OK, and his friends were by his side. The R&R was over and now we needed to get to Philly where I would drop Mags off at her parent's house before heading to Gettysburg for the leadership course. It was only three days, and then I would have a full day with her before heading back to Iraq. The longer I could put off another goodbye, the better I could deal with my agony.

When I returned to her parents' house, Mags informed me we had a visitor coming for the day. It was her friend of the last 25 years, Mo, her kids and Mo's sister Francie. On this day Francie wanted to sit and talk with me about Iraq. We had never met, but we each knew things about the other. Her son Bobby was deployed to Iraq with the 82d Airborne Division and he was not able to share much information with her about his mission, living conditions, or much of anything else. She just wanted to talk with someone who was actually living what Bobby was dealing with.

We spent a great part of the day talking and watching the kids play in the yard. As they were getting ready to leave, Francie asked me if there was a chance that I would see Bobby in my travels. I told her there was a possibility, but I would need to know where his unit was assigned. She told me he was at Forward Operating Base Loyalty in Baghdad and she gave me his unit designation.

I reassured her I would make my best effort to find him and let him know that I had spent time with his mom and that she was doing great. Then I pulled a coin from my pocket. I handed it to Francie and explained to her what it was. I asked her to hold it for Bobby in case I did not see him in Iraq. She could hold it for him until he came home on his mid-tour leave and present it for me. She seemed touched by the gesture. She shed a tear as we exchanged hugs and they departed. Spending the day with her and feeling her love for Bobby made my efforts in Iraq all seem worthwhile. I was inspired to return and get back to the mission.

Departure time came before I was ready. I wanted to cherish every last minute I could before leaving. Something came over me and I had an awful feeling. I needed to get to a computer and check email because I sensed that something was wrong and I needed to find out what it was. I had not checked email for several days, and it was worrying me that something bad had happened, and I wanted to know, I needed to know.

Finally we made it to her brother's house and I got access through a computer to check my email. There it was, a casualty report. I knew something had happened and only now wondered what was going on. I read what little I could find in the report, and immediately sent notes to the chiefs back at the headquarters to find out what the details were. All I knew at this point was that an IED had hit one of our Police Training Teams and several Airmen were injured, including one who was critical with not much expectation for survival.

The report said it was a Staff Sergeant named Scott Lilley. The report also said he received multiple wounds and his status was unknown. From previous incidents of this nature, I knew the results would not likely be good, so I assumed we would have another KIA. At this point I wished I had my notebook handy so I could jot down the information I always recorded when these notifications came in, but it was in my luggage and I could not annotate the notebook.

Soon the emails started to come back from Chief Lopez at the medical group and there were more details. He told me Sergeant Lilley would be sent to Germany via medical evacuation soon and would be stabilized in the Landstuhl Regional Medical Center Hospital. A thought came to mind and a plan was hatched. I needed to stop in Germany and see Sergeant Lilley. Since I had not been around for his arrival at Balad this would be very important. All I needed to do now was get General Rand to approve the diversion. I started to make arrangements in Germany to get picked up by one of my old friends, Dave Spector, who was serving there as a command chief. I could catch a military flight later to get me back to Iraq, but right now it was more important to get to Landstuhl and see Scott.

All of this preparation took my mind off of saying goodbye in just hours. It did not take away the stress and anticipation of that moment. Mags was fully supportive and got to see how deeply involved I was when Airmen were injured on the battle field. She saw a side of me she could not have experienced while I was deployed, so maybe this was happening in front of her for a reason.

The moment came and we had to part ways so I could head off to the gate for departure. Mags held on to me with a sense of warmth that provided great comfort for me. It told me she trusted I would be OK, but if something happened and I was hurt or worse, she would be OK herself. She did not have to say a word, but she gave me the greatest sense of security that it would be fine. I doubt I gave her anything close in return, as I was numb thinking about what I would find when I got to Germany and saw Scott.

The flight from Philly to Frankfurt was a blur, and I believe I slept the entire time. When I arrived, my checked bag did not. At the moment I couldn't be bothered with minor details like luggage. I wanted to get to the hospital and find out what was going on. Chief Spector arrived to pick me up and I was grateful. I did not have to catch a taxi and find my way to the hospital, but had my own friend to get me around the country. We arrived and he dropped me at my room, allowing me time to get cleaned up and changed into uniform before he took me to the hospital. I checked in with Mags to ensure she made it home OK. I was not prepared for the answer she provided. Unfortunately her flight out of Philly was cancelled and she had to have her dad pick her up from the airport because the next flight out would be the following day. She had no luggage and more importantly, she had to call Sean and tell him she was not coming home as she had promised. More emotional drain on the family that would take a toll on everyone.

When I arrived I was met by a sergeant from Scott's unit in Baghdad who had come with him as an escort that I knew from previous years. My presence seemed to provide some comfort for him and he gave me a warrior embrace, letting out a sigh of relief, for somehow he knew things would be better now that his chief was there. Before going into the room, we talked about what Scott had been through. He told me it did not look good, but they were hopeful.

I walked into Scott's room not knowing what to expect. Would his body be badly damaged like some I had seen from IED blasts? Would he be so wrapped up so much I could not see his features? To my surprise he looked pretty good for someone in his situation. Besides the tubes and hanging bags all around his bed, there was a solid white bandage wrapped securely around the top of his head. I asked what it was for, and that's when the hard news arrived for me to ingest.

Scott received a shrapnel wound to the head during an IED blast. One piece of the shrapnel entered on one side and made its way across the centerline of the brain and was lodged in the other side. This was a terrible injury, and the medical professionals gave a low probability for survival. Scott was laying there motionless on life support machines and had been placed in a medically induced coma. I knelt beside his bed and quietly said a few prayers that I often said when the moment was right. I touched his arm and it felt cold. There was no brain activity and no signs of Scott coming out any time soon.

Several hours went by and we sat in the room making small talk about the Police Training Teams and the trip he and Scott had made to Germany. After a while a nurse came in to check on Scott and we exchanged greetings. She asked how I was involved with Scott and I told her about my position as his command chief. She brought a brightness to the room, and her smile was something I would take notice of; it brought a reassurance of things we had not considered.

Something about her was not normal, but then again, I felt like all of our medical professionals brought something special to these situations. She informed us the neurosurgeon would be coming by to check on Scott soon because she had reported earlier that he was coming around and was responsive to her. I was shocked because I had not seen any signs of life in Scott, and really had given up hope for his recovery. Now I was somewhat cautiously and slightly optimistic. She prepared us that the surgeon would not be a friendly type when he came in, so we should not try to engage with him, just stay back out of the way.

He arrived and we heard them talk outside the room. He yanked the door open and walked up to Scott with the clipboard, and a facial expression told me he was not thrilled. He got up close to Scott and began calling his name with a loud and deep voice. "Scott, can you hear me? Scott, this is the doctor, can you hear me and feel my hand touching you?" After several attempts, he made a quick annotation on the chart and looked away in disgust. As he departed the room he handed the chart to the nurse and said, "See, I told you there was nothing going on here. This man has a severe brain injury and is in a coma." He walked off muttering something under his breath. We sat quietly in the room thinking this was a real bad sign.

Seconds later the nurse came back and asked if we saw anything when the doctor was talking with him. We said there was no reaction and it seemed hopeless. Then she smiled and said, "Come with me and watch this."

A warmth came over me like never before and I knew something special was about to happen. She walked to the side of the bed and placed her hand on Scott's right arm. We gathered on the other side and closed in tight. I watched as she began to rub his arm gently with slow and purposeful strokes. Her words were soft and comforting.

"Scott, I know you are in there and listening to me, and I am sorry about that last visit by the doctor. But it's time for you to give me a sign that you are with me." I wondered what she thought would happen since we just witnessed a lack of response from the previous attempt.

She went on, "Scott, I know you are strong and are capable of fighting through, so give me a sign that you are hearing me." Again, I wondered what she thought would happen, and we all stood breathless hoping it would.

She made a third attempt, "Scott, how about you give me a sign that you are with me, like a thumbs up." And then it happened. Scott's thumb on his right hand came up, straight up into the air, and a smile came on his face! I was so thrilled I thought I would jump through the roof.

I looked at her standing there smiling and I wanted to give her a great big chief hug. We stood in awe as she told Scott it would be OK if he opened his eyes, as there were some people here to see him. We waited about 10 seconds in hopes he would open his eyes, and bam! It happened, he opened both eyes wide and the smile continued on his face. Standing closest to his head, I took the lead and said, "Scott, this is the chief and I am so proud of you for fighting through. You are in the best hands and they are going to take great care of you as you head home."

You cannot prepare yourself for a moment like that. Scott's eyes told me he heard me and this seemed like nothing short of a miracle to everyone in the room. Here he was, lying in the bed, eyes open and moving his extremities with a severe brain injury. We were thrilled and could hardly contain ourselves.

Suddenly, a nurse entered the room and said Scott's father was on the phone and needed to talk with someone. After a brief introduction, I told Frank Lilley I could not speak for the medical status of Scott as that would not be the proper thing to do; I needed to leave that for the professionals. But I did want to share with him what I had seen with my own eyes just minutes before. It may have been an anomaly and that he should not increase his hopes, as Scott remained in a dire situation and could turn bad at any time. But I wanted to share what we had seen.

Recounting the event for Frank brought a huge lump to my throat and I could hardly get the words out. When I finished the story there was a short silence. Then Frank asked, "Chief, was the nurse good looking?" I thought for a brief moment and then told Frank she was. Frank laughed out loud and said "That's my boy; he always smiles and listens to pretty women."

We laughed together and shared a precious life moment over the phone from 8000 miles away. I felt an instant connection with Frank and his wife Jolene. Frank informed me of their travel plans to Germany. Unfortunately my time would run out before they would arrive. We parted ways on the phone in hopes of meeting some day in the future.

Scott would soon be loaded on the medical evacuation flight to the US and I headed back to Iraq without having to put another name in my notebook. I took a deep breath and thanked God for this outcome. My faith in God was being restored after a long struggle to find answers from the events of the previous months.

As I boarded the C-17 aircraft from Germany, I took one deep breath and fell fast asleep. I did not move a muscle until we were on final approach back home at Balad Air Base. I was back to the fight.

Medical teams inside the Balad Hospital Emergency Department work
feverishly to prepare a wounded warrior for surgery.

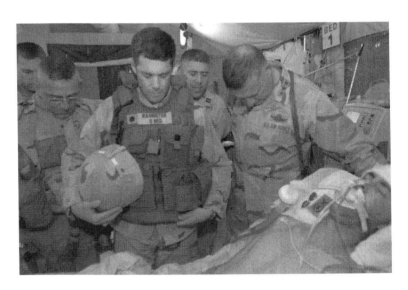

Lieutenant General Gary North and leaders from the 332d Air
Expeditionary Wing say a prayer at the ICU before Staff Sergeant Scott
Lilley was transported to Germany.

A wounded patient being loaded onto a bus from the Balad Hospital ICU
for transport to the waiting C-17 and trip to Germany.

This appropriately named patch of concrete leading into the Balad
Hospital is where every wounded warrior, including Scott Lilly, passed
through.

15
FINDING NERO

18 April 2007:

Less than 10 hours after my arrival at Balad, we traveled to Baghdad for a visit with Detachment 3, Police Training Team, Scott Lilley's unit. It was great to look them in the eye and relay the story of the miraculous moment back in Germany. Sharing what I witnessed in Sergeant Lilley's ICU room, the smiles on their faces grew. Several of them asked questions, while others sat quietly as tears rolled down their cheeks. You could see the light in their eyes get a little brighter as they prepared for the mission at hand. Somehow it seemed as if this piece of information about Sergeant Lilley gave them some additional strength to carry on against the toughest of odds.

Our travel team sat through their mission brief. For some it would be the first one they had witnessed. It was a well-orchestrated machine, each member knowing their responsibilities. Each answered in time when their team leader, Technical Sergeant McBride, called on them. We were all impressed and the pride was swelling inside the tent. Once outside, the General told me again how impressed he was with the briefing format and the professionalism of these Defenders.

He said all pre-mission briefings should be standardized so that we could ensure all Airmen were ready for the task at hand. He compared Defender mission briefings to the one F-16 pilots get before combat missions. He remarked about the similarities and how so many items were interchangeable between the two. The correlation was obvious to me now, and I agreed with him. I always believed Defenders and fighter pilots were much the same, we just had different roles to perform.

Hours later we mounted back up on the C-130 and headed back to Balad. Maybe I would finally get some rest.

26 April 2007:

April 26th came up fast and I had spent little time preparing myself for this speaking engagement that I was asked to take on. During the previous two Dining In events for our rotation of forces, the guest speakers were General North and Colonel Dennis. Now it was my honor to be the speaker, and I wanted to get it right.

All preparations were complete and the team had put together a great event. We received all the RSVPs from the sister service representatives and it appeared the crowd would exceed the capacity of the 500 seats in the DFAC. I arrived early to help with the final preparations and to take a few minutes to go over the formal part of my speech. On this occasion, I had something special planned and wanted to make sure I had it down.

The entire DFAC was decorated with Tuskegee memorabilia that included the large model of a P-51 Mustang, the signature aircraft of the historic unit. The model was normally kept hanging in the Town Hall, but on this occasion the team disassembled it, transported it to the DFAC and reassembled it once inside. It was easy to see how much effort the committee had put into their preparations.

During events like this, the food contractor went way out of their way to make things special for all US service members, but nothing like what we saw on this night. They prepared a cake for us that was fit for serving 500. It did not appear there was any way we would eat all that cake before the night was over.

The crowd poured in all at once, in keeping with tradition of the Dining In, you must arrive within 10 minutes of the appointed hour or you are in violation of the rules of the mess. Rules violators were to be punished, as the tradition goes, by visiting the grog bowl which contained an awful concoction of things all mixed together for your drinking pleasure. There was one change to tradition tonight, as we do not allow the consumption of alcohol in combat, so there would only be a non-alcoholic grog for this Dining In.

Once the crowd was seated the head table marched in with the Honor Guard leading the way. The leadership team stood there proudly looking over the crowd, each reminiscing what had transpired to this point in our tour. We all knew there was much to celebrate because of all that our wing had accomplished.

Following dinner there was a video that captured what we did each day, interspersed with clips from the motion picture depicting our Tuskegee forefathers. It was well orchestrated and made everyone feel the pride in being a part of the modern day Tuskegee Airmen.

Following a short intermission the audience was once again seated and ready to go. The emcee told everyone to prepare themselves for the Honor Guard's performance. I knew we were about to be amazed and I could hardly contain my excitement. They marched in dressed in the combat zone Honor Guard uniforms and carrying M-1 Carbine rifles, complete with bayonets fixed. It was an impressive sight.

They came in step, placed themselves and snapped to attention facing the audience in a small formation. Music started, and they began to make a series of slow movements with their rifles known as close order drill. As they went through each sequence, the pace and the music got faster. Then faster and the rifles were now flying back and forth and around the formation. All of a sudden one of them stepped out front and began spinning the rifle on his right hand. It was going so fast that you could not keep up with it, and it appeared to vanish.

As he finished that display of precision, Airman "Indiana" Jones stepped out. Indiana performed a flawless rifle twist and toss reminiscent of the best I have seen from any Honor Guard Drill Team and he learned to do this all on his own. By the time he was finished, the entire audience was on their feet clapping louder than I have heard in some time. As he completed his moves and rejoined the formation, they closed the performance with a four-man rifle toss. It was a breathtaking performance and we were speechless.

I looked over at Chief Reuning and we both smiled. He promised it would be right and he came through big time. I also knew this performance was due largely in part to the training provided by R2. My pride in the entire Honor Guard team soared to new heights. For a brief moment in time, I lost track of the fact that we were in combat and could be attacked at any second.

When it was my turn to speak I promised the audience that in honor of the 332d Air Expeditionary Wing, I would keep my speech to three minutes and thirty-two seconds or less. Indicated we were off on the right foot. But then I told them before I could start the speech I needed to make a few administrative remarks and when I completed the speech I would need to make closing remarks. They knew at that point it would take longer than some three minutes. A few in the audience groaned, but those who knew me figured I could keep their attention for at least 20 minutes before they would become bored. After thanking all of the sister service leaders in attendance, talking about how impressed I was with the Honor Guard, the committee and the entertainment, it was time to get to the speech.

"Before you tonight stands a humbled leader, thankful for your pursuit of mission accomplishment, grateful of your dedication, and amazed by your loyalty. You left your friends, family and the safety of your base perimeter, armed yourself to engage in a fight against terror and oppression, willing to sacrifice so that other nations could transition to democracy. You came here willing to set aside your personal identity and agenda, taking on the legacy of our forefathers, the famed Tuskegee Airmen."

"They bore the burden of terror from afar and oppression from within their own country, just as you take on those same burdens from different sources. You have looked the enemy in the eye and brought airpower to bear when the call came in. Like those famed Red Tails who escorted bombers in 1945, today you fly different airframes and escort Soldiers and Marines moving on the ground rather than bombers in the air."

"But you do it with the same passion and fire, the same commitment and sacrifice as that given by Colonel Benjamin Davis and his men. Today, under the leadership of the latest great Commanding General of the Tuskegee Airmen, you face the enemy like never before, filling roles well beyond the core competencies of the Air Force as we close the door on our Service's 60th Anniversary."

"Today you suffer losses like never before in this battle. You have given your own defense of the ideals of freedom. You have remained focused on the objectives set forth by our national leaders even as you mourned the loss of fellow Airmen. The acceptance of new missions, addition of new locations, and the unfortunate lack of support from some back in our own country, did not deter you from providing Combat Airpower For America, Right Here and Right Now."

"Your chapter in the history books is almost written, just a few pages to go, and you continue to write positive paragraphs that will someday be read by our grandchildren and school kids around the world. You continue to fill the pages with evidence of your initiative, with data showing the records we set for missions, cargo, passengers, air traffic, patients and much more. You've written chapter upon chapter that will hold a place in history, you did it together and you did it behind the scenes. And you did it behind a series of courageous leaders who cared for you with relentless passion."

"Be proud of what you have gained from this combat experience, finish strong, return with honor and then give something back from this experience to someone who will follow in your footsteps. Continue writing chapters in the annals of history in the name of the Tuskegee Airmen."

The speech was done in less than three minutes and thirty-two seconds as promised. It seemed to hit the mark and was well received by the audience. I closed shortly thereafter, having said my thanks and told all those great Airmen how important they were to me. The ceremony was almost complete, the night almost done.

When the President of the Mess declared the event over there was still more to do. The committee had determined they would give a commemorative coin to each and every person in the mess and they gave me the honor of passing them out and shaking hands with each of the nearly 500 who remained. I was honored to do so. It took nearly two hours to complete this great honor. My hand was cramped, but it was well worth the pain.

Finally, well after midnight, I headed back to my quarters for some needed sleep. Checking email before hitting the bed allowed me to read up on what they were doing back home. I detected a change in their words, and could sense their worry about me. Their words about the end of the tour were cautious, their tone was guarded. Would I make it home or would something happen beyond my control before I could get back to them? My mind wondered as I drifted off sitting in the chair at my desk.

2 May 2007:

The General and I planned to make a long-awaited trip out to see the Supply Detachments and Logistical Airmen who were far from the flagpole. We would be accompanied on this trip by Colonel Omar Bradley, our new Director of Staff. While we were sad to see Colonel Doc Ellis depart, it was refreshing to have an equally qualified senior officer fill his shoes. We had spent time getting to know each other in the weeks since his arrival, but this would be the first trip out to the battle field for Colonel Bradley.

All of the FOBs we would visit on this trip were located at small Marine or Army locations. In some cases they were only a few Airmen assigned to the base, a very small portion of the population. It would take us two full days and at some of the locations we would only have a few hours on the ground, but I knew from past experience these Airmen would appreciate our visit.

At the first stop we were met by a team of 35 Airmen who performed the entire logistical mission for the base which contained 3,000 Marines. Airmen were in charge of the aerial port mission to get Soldiers and Marines moved to and from the battlefield. They also controlled the command post, aircraft maintenance and vehicle maintenance shops as well as running a new team called Redistribution Property, Accountability Team or RPAT for short. The RPAT team was responsible for finding, fixing, repairing and replacing military equipment for units across the entire country. If they could not accomplish the above, they would also remove the equipment from the country and get it to Kuwait for a determination on how to dispose of it. It was a huge job, and they seemed well qualified to accomplish the mission.

The first thing that struck me was how much they appreciated what little they had. We viewed their quarters and found they had made the best of a tough situation. Since the Marines were in charge of this installation, they received support at the Marine standard for a forward operating base, which was different than at an Air Force installation. They accepted what they had and improved it to the best of their ability, and it seemed to bond them into a tighter group.

I felt the same way the first time I came into Iraq and we had not been able to establish much in the way of quality of life for our people. I saw how motivated Airmen could be using cans filled with water for weight lifting apparatus. We did not need treadmills and indoor basketball courts to get a good workout, and these Airmen were proving it every day.

When I met with the sergeant major for the garrison command unit, he could not say enough about the things being done by our Airmen and how impressed he was with their spirit of cooperation. I could feel the sincerity of my fellow senior NCO and I sensed he really appreciated the effort of this group of Airmen. We laughed and shared stories, and I made sure he had my contact information if there were ever any problems. He assured me he did not anticipate any, but he would gladly call from time to time and check in for issues. It started the trip off with a great sense of how we were doing at these detachments, and I hoped we would see more of the same.

Several stops later we encountered the most motivated group of Airmen I had seen in some time. Immediately they greeted us with an audible and visual passion. They were just glad to see anyone with the same uniform on and feel the love from an Air Force brother. This unit of 9 Airmen was being led by a chief master sergeant and 5 others who were from the Air Force Reserves in Guam. They had engineers, logisticians, and other specialties represented, but each and every Airman knew he or she could pick up the slack on any job and make sure the mission happened. They were at the tip of the spear, but they operated with no fear.

They were flat out impressive. After the General gave each one of them his commander's coin, I presented one of my Red Tail Chief coins to each person. It was the first time both of us had coined an entire unit at the same location. From the limited hours we spent with them, I walked away with a renewed energy I wanted to harness and take back to Balad. I really wanted to go around the base and find all those who routinely complained about things like not enough flavors of ice cream in the DFAC and bring them to this FOB for a one week reality check. Before we departed, General Rand presented the Iraq Campaign Medal to each Airman. It was one of the most moving ceremonies we had taken part in since the beginning of the tour. Nine Airmen on an isolated airfield, with few creature comforts, and tons of pride.

As we closed this visit and headed back to the C-130 for the return trip to Balad, I stopped and looked around the massive empty flight line and runway area. I wondered why we had not moved more of our operations out to places like this for the security it provided and the distance to the enemy. Then I thought back to 2004 when the wing headquarters was moved from a location like this in Southern Iraq to the present one in Balad. I knew then and realized again now that it had to be about location, which made it easier for our aircraft to get time on target.

Balad was the most centrally located installation, and our fighters could reach out in all directions with ease and be at the farthest reaches of the enemy lines in less than 30 minutes of being called to action. That could mean life or death for a warrior on the battlefield, so it made good sense. Being near the insurgents was one of the prices we would have to pay in order to meet mission demands.

The team loaded up and locked into the cargo seats, passed the boxes of food down the line and began to get some rest before we landed back at headquarters. Minutes after takeoff I opened the box of food given to me and found a sandwich had been prepared with cold cuts and cheese, kind of the standard thing. But since it had been sitting on the plane waiting for us, and it was over 100 degrees outside, it was like having a hot ham and cheese sandwich ready to go. I attempted to eat it and found there was something about the taste of the meat, and the color was not enticing. I figured I could wait until we landed and go get something else to eat. I loosened the strings on my boots, placed my feet on the railing across from me and faded off into a deep sleep for the 45-minute ride back to the base.

Arriving back at Balad the General, Colonel Bradley and I headed straight to the hospital to check on a military working dog handler who was hurt earlier in the week while supporting the Army at FOB Normandy.

General Rand and Colonel Bradley met me at the CASF and we all went in to find the wounded warrior, Staff Sergeant Zeb Miller. The nursing staff directed us to his bed and we all gathered to meet him and find out how he was doing. Sergeant Miller told us he was OK, but there were some things he needed and did not feel good about asking for. I broke away and found a staff member so I could ask for him, and make sure he was getting all the right care for his injuries. He was about to be shipped out of country for a little recovery time from his injuries, with plans for him to return to the battle field. He should not have concerns or requests unfulfilled.

After a short conversation with Sergeant Miller about what happened, the General asked how his military working dog was doing after the attack that led to his injuries. Sergeant Miller became quiet, took a deep breath and informed us he was unsure. He was not with his partner Nero when the attack happened and he was whisked away to a waiting helicopter without him.

We all recognized how close the relationship was between a military working dog and his handler. This was a tough moment for Zeb and we could see it. After reassuring Sergeant Miller everything would be OK, we headed out of the CASF. Walking to the vehicle, Colonel Bradley asked the General if he saw the look on Zeb's face when we talked about his dog. The General said he knew it was a tough conversation to have, but he did not fully understand the depth of the pain shown by Zeb. Colonel Bradley insisted that we should look into this situation deeper, and if possible, we should do something about it. The General walked to my truck and told me to locate Nero and the very least, provide an update to Sergeant Miller before he departed. I told the General we could make something happen, and we should go directly to the kennels and find out. I said, "Let's go make something happen."

Arriving at the front door of the kennel I found it locked down tight. I pounded on the door to make to get their attention. The administrative offices were located down a hallway, and if the kennel master was tending to the dogs in the back, it would be hard to hear a knock at the door. Finally, a U.S. Army NCO opened the door and before he could speak I looked at him and said, "We're here to find Military Working Dog Nero who was at FOB Normandy with Sergeant Zeb Miller. The NCO looked at me and said, "Sergeant Major, Nero is here, but we were told we could not take him to the hospital because they don't allow dogs inside the patient areas. I walked past the kennel master and said "Come with me and show me which one Nero is."

The kennel master quickly pointed to a 100 pound German Shepherd with a huge coat of fur and really bright eyes and said, "That's Nero right there, the one who looks sad." "Mount him up" I said, "We're going to the hospital." Nero was placed in an appropriate leash and we headed back to the CASF for a personal reunion between dog and man.

Military working dog handlers became very attached to their partners, even sleeping in the same quarters out at the FOBs because there was no kennel facility. The handler was the only one who trained the dog, fed them and spent 12 or more hours per day on patrol with them. Together they made great teams capable of providing a service no other asset in our inventory could provide. Apart, they were depressed and alone, unsure of what to do. It was clear to all of us that Nero was lost without his handler.

We arrived at the hospital parking lot and heard the giant voice; "Incoming, Incoming, Incoming!" We were feet away from the doors of the hospital and there were huge concrete barriers in front. We decided to seek shelter inside rather than go into a bunker. Seconds after we reached the concrete barriers the first round hit and it sounded close, then a second. We crawled inside for safety. Inside, the medical technicians told us all the patients were in the back under cover and they were secure.

I asked them where Sergeant Miller was, and they indicated he was in the back room with the other patients taking cover. We crawled toward the back of the ward with Nero in tow. The staff looked at me like I was crazy, but nobody questioned what we were doing.

Before we reached the door to the back room, Sergeant Miller was seen crawling through the doors, almost like he knew something special was about to happen. His injuries looked bad, but he managed to keep moving toward us. I made eye contact with him and said; "We brought you something."

Not another word was spoken, but for the next few minutes we all witnessed something powerful. There sat a young injured NCO on the floor of the hospital with bandages covering his wounds, and by his side was his partner, the 100-pound K-9 Nero. It appeared both of them were crying as they hugged. The General told us all to back off and let them have some room.

After what seemed like an eternity, Zeb called out to me and said, "Chief, thanks for bringing him back to me. I didn't know if he made it after the explosion and nobody could tell me where he was when I was loaded onto the helicopter." There was a lump in my throat so thick I could not speak, but simply nodded my head in his direction and blinked my eyes so he could tell I was happy for them. He got to his feet and grabbed me in a battle hug. He said, "Chief, I will never forget what you did for me today."

Members of the Balad Air Base Honor Guard practice their routine for the final show at the Formal Dining In.

General Rand and Chief Dearduff standing behind the P-51 Mustang model used as the centerpiece for the formal Dining In.

Chief Dearduff speaking to the crowd of more than 500 in attendance at the Formal Dining In.

Staff Sergeant Zeb Miller and his Military Working Dog Nero in the CASF after they were reunited.

16
BROTHERS IN ARMS PAY TRIBUTE

The General and I talked as we traveled and he suggested we start using the term, "Finish Strong" with all of our Airmen. This would become our focus point to get everyone to the end of their tours, and help fight off complacency. It was the perfect phrase to use and would come in handy when we were trying to motivate the masses to stay focused on the mission. Nothing should distract their attention until they are safely on the ground back at home, and this would be our goal.

We talked about the losses already suffered, and collectively we yearned to make sure there would be no more. Attacks from the insurgents had increased and now reached an all-time high for Operation Iraqi Freedom. Very few days had gone by in the past few months without an attack on the base, and the days to come promised to be just as challenging based on the intelligence reports. OSI predicted sustained attacks on the base. Although we still had not solved their issue of getting support teams, they remained focused on outside-the-wire missions to thwart attacks. They updated us on insurgent activity daily.

We planned to travel throughout the entire month. There would be change of command ceremonies and other unit visits, along with some travel to spend time with our joint partners. Careful planning was essential to make sure we met all of the demands and ensure the Airmen at Balad did not take their focus off the important tasks. In order to get it all done we would have to work 20 hour days, 7 days per week until the end of the tour.

In addition to all of the travel we planned for our Air Force units, I also had a promise to keep to Francie. I had to get to Baghdad and find Bobby's unit to check on him personally and report back to his mom. General Rand understood the need for me to attend the Multi-National Forces Iraq ceremony where CSM Mellinger would turn over his responsibilities to CSM Marvin Hill. He also knew about my connection to Bobby, so he told me to travel and take care of my business.

Landing at Baghdad International Airport, I was greeted by one of the young NCOs from Detachment 3, Staff Sergeant Charlyn Grayson. As we drove away from the flight line, she reminded me we served together on a previous combat deployment, and I was her Chief then. It took me a second, but then I remembered she deployed into my unit back in 2002 as a 19 year old Airmen two weeks out of technical school. Now, 4 years later, here she was serving as a staff sergeant, leading Airmen on combat patrols...a long ways from her previous deployment. I was impressed by her and told her so.

Sergeant Grayson said that Chief Gammage was away on his R&R so they planned to bunk me down in their Chief's cot for the night rather than get me one of those fancy DV rooms. I definitely appreciated bunking down with them so we could continue to bond. I told her before we went to our tent area, I needed to stop by FOB Loyalty and take care of a personal matter.

I arrived at Bobby's unit's location on FOB Loyalty and met with the unit First Sergeant, explained to him why I wanted to see Private Bobby Dembowski. He asked me if something was wrong. I eased his worry and told him about my connection with his family, and I was just trying to see him and relay a message. He seemed relieved, then told me that his unit was out on maneuvers and may not be back in for a day or two. I had missed my opportunity to see him, and would have to get back there again. It was very frustrating knowing I was this close and yet could not make eye contact with him and share my recent visit with his mom. I really hoped to bring a smile to his face and share a laugh or two with this young warrior. I figured I would meet him on my next trip to Baghdad.

Arriving at Detachment 3's compound, we met up with a team returning from an all day mission. You could see the guys were tired and really wanted to break down their gear, get some chow and check in with their families back home. Everything changed when they were told that I was the chief who got to see Sergeant Lilley in Germany and suddenly they wanted my attention.

We talked for a while and I filled them in on what I had seen. They asked the same questions as the team did several weeks before. Hopefully sharing this story would help bring peace of mind to these brave warriors. It had been an extremely hard tour for this unit with six members injured during the first five months of action.

I always enjoy my time with the Defenders. I was envious of these teams, and told them so. Had this mission been around when I was a young Defender, I would have volunteered just as each of them had. Although I did not get that opportunity, I told them how much I enjoyed being with them and taking care of their needs.

It was now time to get in the cot and grab a couple of hours of sleep. It would have been easy, except for being in this large tent with more than 40 people, all of whom either snored or stayed up through the night watching movies and surfing the web, so I lay awake and listened. It made me think of home, the great time experienced on my R&R, and the many nights I longed for in the near future. After being so involved in combat over the years, it would be a great thing to just sit on the porch with my family and listen to them talk about their days or what was on their mind.

For a few hours, these guys were my family, and I just sat and listened to them. Each one a younger brother or a nephew who had grown up and had many stories to tell. The atmosphere was memorable. There were no bunkers to take cover in should an attack come, for these warriors spent their days on the streets and considered this inside-the-wire area like the comforts of home. I even asked what the procedures were for an attack and I was told, take cover the best you can, rally back at the tent, mount up and be ready to roll. That was all I needed to hear. These were warriors and my heart was warm with pride. Before closing my eyes for a few hours I reflected back to the completion of my first Iraq deployment, three years earlier almost to the day. Then my mind turned back to the present and I focused on the past 10 months. My brain hurt from the emotional drain.

Morning came quickly, and after a quick bite of chow with the Defenders, I was transported to the Al Faw Palace to attend the ceremony. Arriving at the palace took me back to 2003 again. Back then this palace was in bad shape, having sustained some heavy bombing from coalition forces in the early hours of Operation Iraqi Freedom. Now the palace held the headquarters for Multi-National Forces and Multi-National Corps, Iraq. The palace was massive, with clear indications of the wealth of its former owner. At least now it was serving a purpose as the main planning location for improving things for the Iraqi people.

The lake which surrounded it was starting to regain some of its original beauty and the fish that adorned the lake were well fed and extremely active at the top of the water. Most who visited the palace for the first time were amazed at how many and how large the fish were. Prior to 2003, this was a weekend resort for the former dictator's family, all of whom were lovers of wildlife, fish included.

Once we got inside the palace's 20-foot-high doorway and entered into the main ballroom, we could see a crowd had assembled in excess of 1000 Americans, and quite a few Iraqi military members. There were general officers from all services, several friendly foreign nations, and senior enlisted as far as the eyes could see. I knew the two sergeants major would be busy with preparations for the ceremony, so I made my way to the seat, and began talking with some of those around me.

The ceremony was dignified. I had never attended an Army ceremony of this nature, so I was intrigued. It rivaled the change of command ceremonies the Air Force held for unit commanders, but went above and beyond. It was nice to see how much emphasis the Army placed on their top enlisted position.

When the ceremonies were complete and the long line was forming to meet the new CSM Marvin Hill, I made eye contact with my battle buddy CSM Mellinger and we closed ranks through the crowd. When we finally got together, we exchanged a warrior hug and he said, "Hey, I have something for you." He reached into his pocket and pulled out a well-worn copy of a book; so worn the cover was held together by layers of tape. He opened the book and showed me the inscription on the inside. "To the best warrior I have encountered in the Air Force, thanks for your leadership." Signed, CSM Jeff Mellinger, Multi-National Forces Iraq, Aug 04 – May 07.

The book was called *Into the Mouth of the Cat*. It was the story of the Air Force hero Captain Lance P. Sijan, a Medal of Honor recipient from Vietnam. It's a story of true heroism and one that Mellinger cherished. He had received this book in the 1980s and read it often as his own personal inspiration to continue serving. He said it should go to a warrior who is deserving of this personal copy. I was stunned, speechless and highly honored all at the same time. I told him I would cherish this book and read it often as well. We exchanged goodbyes in the warrior way.

Departing Baghdad in the daytime by helicopter would be very different from the many nighttime flights of the past. This one provided full opportunity to see how things had changed in the towns and villages since the last daytime flight over the landscape. As we flew low over the horizon, I could see many more children playing in the streets. It appeared that some normalcy had returned as people were moving around conducting business. We flew so low to the ground we could see stores with products on the sidewalks, and people standing around buying their goods. Cars moved about, and the highway running through the city was bustling with fast-moving traffic. There were so many signs of progress in the lives of the Iraqi people, and yet nobody back home was hearing about them.

Landing at Balad brought a sense of relief because I thought I would have a couple of hours to catch up on things. Sergeant Rositas, who had earned the nickname R2, picked me up and on the drive back to the headquarters he reminded me about my mission outside the wire with the OSI team in a few days. He said they wanted to do some training in advance. That took care of the extra hours I thought I had for catching up. This OSI mission was critical, so I set my attention in the direction and began mental preparations to ensure I would not be a distraction to the team.

8 May 2007:

The OSI mission would be conducted at night and I was stoked. Being outside the wire on a ground combat mission was where I felt most comfortable. Arriving at the OSI compound I was met by Major Matt Modarelli, the Detachment Commander. He thanked me for taking on the issues for his teams and for going out with them to validate their needs. Agent Nichols took me to meet with the agents for the mission, and we quickly became acquainted. They knew about my background and reassured me they would focus on their duties and not have to worry about me. They needed to focus on the target and not the chief.

We arrived at the pre-combat check area with the Army unit assigned to this mission. The team leader was informed that I was a new agent and would be going to observe their techniques, and I was fully trained on combat operations. I was dressed in the Army Combat Uniform as was the rest of the team, with no rank insignia, and no other explanation of my rank or position. I simply blended in with the team and began to observe. I needed to validate for the General that our security forces could handle this mission and not jeopardize our agents' safety.

Following the tactical briefing and pre-combat checks, we loaded into our vehicles. I asked the agents if this was how it always went, and they indicated that it was fairly status quo. I became concerned because it was a far cry from the pre-mission briefing and safety checks our Defenders completed prior to missions outside the wire.

Once I was comfortable with our planned emergency actions, I asked them if they had anything for me. They shared their concerns for their security element and the need to focus on their own safety while trying to complete the mission of gathering information from sources. I could feel their frustration. This was a major concern and it would become a huge part of the justification for pushing this issue up the chain.

When we arrived at the source contact point near a local village, the agents and I departed our vehicle and walked into the darkness on a dirt farm road. The road was lined with very tall weeds, making it very hard to see to our left and right. Although we had night vision goggles with us, we had to stay as low key as possible so as to not scare the source away. It was dark and eerie for several minutes until the cell phone of one of the agents buzzed, letting us know the source was approaching. This seemed like a perfect place for an ambush.

We walked forward and greeted him and began to talk quietly. When the conversation was over, the agents rewarded the source for the information he provided about the most recent shooting incident on the base. They removed two five-gallon cans of gas from our Humvee and walked toward his personal truck. After emptying the cans into his truck, they gave him a case of water and some small food items as further compensation for his valuable information. The source was so elated by this payment that he hugged each of the agents and thanked them vehemently before jumping into his truck and moving on.

I looked around while this was going on and took some mental notes about the unit who was providing security for our mission. Several things stood out as different from the tactics practiced by our Defenders. I formulated my thoughts about how to capture the right words to send up the chain of command. In my mind it was simple. Our Defenders could do this mission and would be dedicated to the protection of our agents as their only mission. This had to be done; it had to change before something went horribly wrong and people were hurt or worse. Once back inside the wire and done with the mission debrief, I immediately went to my office to record my findings, preparing to share them with the General first thing in the morning.

The next morning we discussed the mission and my findings for about five minutes, and then the General got on the phone and called General North. In a matter of minutes he convinced General North to reach back to the Pentagon and advocate for our Defenders to take on this mission.

The General called Major Modarelli and told him we made some progress and the request for Defenders was being pushed up the chain with great support. During the discussion, Major Modarelli mentioned that some of the agents at the other detachments were now being told that support from Army units would no longer be available. The agents would need to provide their own support.

Their plan going forward was for the agents who were not working a particular case to work as the support element and provide security for the agents leading the case. This would mean the agents were completing missions outside the wire almost seven days per week with no breaks. Once again, I reassured General Rand that this mission belonged to our security force Defenders and we just needed clearance to get them assigned immediately.

13 May 2007:

We landed at Tikrit and made our way over to the compound for Detachment 7, Police Training Team. They had the same mission as Detachment 3, but performed it in the town of Tikrit. It was not Baghdad, but it was also not a safe place. This mission was just as dangerous, and they displayed high levels of unit focus. Everyone in the unit from the commander to the youngest Airmen, demonstrated high levels of motivation.

During the next several hours, we received their mission briefing, viewed their quarters and work areas, and finally ended up in the preparation yard where they mounted up for missions. When we arrived there were several teams assembled. I looked at the young faces in the formation and was amazed at how combat hardened they looked.

Following a mass briefing and words from the General and myself, one team headed for their vehicles to get geared up and prepare for departure. We mingled with the other teams and got to know some of the Airmen. I found myself talking with the youngest of the Airmen, all of who seemed to be eager to get back out on the mission. Many of them were so pumped with adrenaline it was almost painful to remain inside the wire and take a down day. There was one particular Airmen who stood quietly in the area, listening to our discussions, but not offering much himself. I made it a point to walk over and shake his hand as we finished talking. Senior Airman Jason Nathan told me he was from Lakenheath England and he was happy to be on this mission. He also told me he was proud of his team and what they were doing, even though it was extremely dangerous. I was immediately impressed, and knew he carried a quiet confidence about him.

We finished the visit and loaded back on a C-130 for the return to Balad. I could not help but think about those young Defenders and how tough it must be on them to perform those missions. I must have dozed off knowing they were being safe and executing the mission well.

14 May 2007:

The morning brought more travel and visit to units at the FOBs. Landing at Camp Speicher and meeting with the Air Force leadership on the ground, we quickly went about visiting units around the massive airfield. From the first stop it was evident this was not going to be a good day. Airmen were clearly not excited to see us, and that started a negative trend. On more than one occasion I had to pull NCOs aside and ask them what was going on. I got the impression we were bothering them with our presence and they wanted to get back to their routine. While that could be admirable, there was certainly a better way to go about it. To me this was a reflection on poor leadership at their unit level. Others noticed that something was out of the ordinary.

By the third stop we met with a group of Defenders who were tasked to perform law enforcement operations around Speicher. They did not even try to hide their displeasure and began by speaking to the General in a disrespectful tone. He quickly departed and I stayed. We began a one way conversation where I explained to them how they were coming across to us. I also explained that we were not the enemy, and as their chain of command, it was our responsibility to visit them and see what we could do to help. Having a negative attitude toward caring leaders was never going to be productive. When I finished what I had to say, I walked out and not a word was said. On the flight back to Balad, General Rand told me he would follow up with the commanding officers of those units and express his disappointment in their leadership.

R2 picked me up and had planned some time with the aircraft maintainers later in the evening after my meeting with the first sergeants. The day was moving fast and I was on my way to the flight line when the call came across the radio: "All Red Tails report to the command post."

My heart sank…this was not good news. Not since January had we suffered any casualties, and on some days, I felt like we were operating on borrowed time. Was this the day it would all change, or could this be something far less important like news of a pending visit from some dignitaries? Could it be one of those Airmen we just visited at Detachment 7 who departed from our presence and took to the streets of Tikrit? My mind was racing fast.

As I walked into the building, I could feel the stress in the air, could sense something bad had happened. The force protectors normally kept things under wraps, but today Airman "Indiana" Jones knew about my passion for the Fallen and he wanted to be the first to tell me but knew it was not his place. As I made my way past him, he said, "Chief, I am sorry, I know this won't be an easy day." Inside my office R2 waited to tell me we had lost another Airman.

Another kick in the gut…a feeling I hoped to never experience again. I held it together and thanked him for his comments. Then I asked to be left along in my office for a quick breather before reporting to the room and getting the official news. By now I could figure was either EOD, OSI or one of our Defenders, because they seemed to be the most vulnerable Airmen doing the toughest ground missions. Regardless of which career field they came from, I did not want to get news about another fallen Airman.

The briefer began with the situation report and gave us the horrible news; another Defender was killed by an IED in Baghdad. In addition to the one Airman killed in action, there were also 3 Airmen wounded in action, all members of the same team who were traveling in the same vehicle. This all too familiar report burned a hole in my heart.

The details revealed that this tragedy came from Detachment 3 in Baghdad. Staff Sergeant John Self was identified as the casualty. He was well known for being a team leader who took great care of his Airmen while always allowing for a sense of humor to come along.

We learned that he had just returned from his mid-tour leave and while home had proposed to his girlfriend, with plans to get married when he came home from the mission. Those details always put more human context into the situation. "John was a strong leader who was well liked by his fellow NCOs and Airmen alike. He will be sorely missed," said his commander. This guy was a leader with a great future, and the unit members will take this one real hard.

Quietly I pulled my notebook from my left pocket and turned to the page with the list of fallen Airmen. I began to jot down the details letter for letter until I could not write any more. Something stopped me, and made me look at the time difference since the last casualties. A huge whirlwind of emotions was stirring inside my brain and I could not shut it down. I thought others would detect what was going on inside and look at me funny, but I soon realized that nobody saw what I was compartmentalizing inside. I was not sharing it with anyone, this was neither the time nor the place to vent; they needed me to be the chief.

I came back to consciousness inside of the room and listened as the details of the memorial were spelled out. I knew we would have to work real fast to figure out our travel to Baghdad for the first of two memorials for Sergeant Self.

I left to seek the solitary comfort of my vehicle, and took a long drive around the base perimeter. I needed to clear my head and think about how to lead through this and keep the wing's Airmen focused during these terrible times. Thoughts kept running through my head about what I could do or say to the families of the Fallen. Nothing would bring them back, but we could never let them be forgotten.

Soon the news came in that two of the injured Airmen had arrived from the combat hospital in Baghdad. The first one I encountered was Senior Airman Melanie Manley, a Defender from Offutt Air Force base. Fortunately a master sergeant from Offutt was deployed to Balad and was on duty. He was rushed to the hospital to be the first one to see her once she arrived. When I entered the ICU, he introduced me to Airman Manley. She shared her thoughts about what took place, then said she needed some rest. We left her alone and asked the nursing staff for her prognosis. One of the nurses said she would be transported out that night on the medical evacuation flight and would be in Germany in just a few hours.

In another area of the ICU, Senior Airman Joshua Brooks was being prepared for surgery. He suffered a serious leg injury and although some surgery had already been performed at the combat hospital, there was work left to be done in order to save his leg. The staff told me that Colonels Smith and Richardson were doing the surgery, and I knew they were the best in the business. Between them, many warriors went home from the battlefield with increased chances for a better life. I planned to come by in the days to follow and check on Airman Brooks until he departed for Germany.

18 May 2007:

Another huge crowd was packed into the Town Hall and the Balad Defenders were out in force. Heavy armored vehicles stood vigilance outside the tent with the youngest of Defenders manning the M-240 automatic machine guns on the turrets. If the enemy wanted to disrupt this ceremony, they would have to go through a tough and determined force. We had just returned from Baghdad and a fitting tribute to Sergeant Self. Our emotions had been stressed already today, but now it was time to stand tall and honor this Airman for his sacrifice on the battle field.

As the General and I made our way to the door, we

saw and felt the presence of the OSI agents in full measure. Every agent assigned to Balad was standing tall outside the Town Hall tent with the Defenders. "These guys are our brothers, so we stand with them today", said one of the agents. It was priceless to see them standing together as brothers in arms here in combat. Today they were here to honor Sergeant Self.

Another wonderfully orchestrated ceremony was pulled off by the 732d team. Chaplains, Honor Guard, singers and most notably, the other Airmen stood vigilant on the stage. But there were only three. This was what would become known as the Missing Man Fire Team. A fire team normally comprising a leader, gunner, assistant gunner and grenadier, this formation was clearly missing their leader. It was an amazingly fitting way to honor our Fallen Airman this day. Staff Sergeant John Self was a leader and he would be truly missed by everyone in the unit.

As the end of the ceremony neared, I reached into my pocket and pulled out the notebook. I stared at his name and committed it to memory. His name, his legacy would never be forgotten. Staff Sergeant John Self, killed in action, 14 May 2007.

General Rand, Colonel Jackson and Chief Dearduff join a
Detachment 7 team prior to their mission

Chief Dearduff discusses tactics, techniques and procedures with
Detachment 7 members

Staff Sergeant John T. Self, killed in action, 14 May 2007

Chief Dearduff and General Rand pay a final tribute to Sergeant Self

17
DAY IS DONE, GONE THE SUN

The stress of these memorials and losing Airmen was mounting on me like I would never have imagined. I was taking it all too personally, and it was eroding away at my physical health. The best plan would be to compartmentalize this pain and press on with the mission at hand, but it was not in my nature. These were all my Airmen and they meant something to me, whether or not I knew them personally. I had to go on with the mission, but I also had to find a way to deal with these losses.

Somehow I made it to combat without enough time on my enlistment to complete the tour and if I decided not to reenlist, I could pack up and go home early for retirement. Even on the toughest of days I was going to retire, and there was only one way I was going home early from this tour…and I had no plans on taking that path.

19 May 2007:

The General agreed to conduct the reenlistment ceremony and offered to make it a special moment as many others had done in the past. He asked me where I would like to hold the ceremony. He offered some pretty neat options, but I wanted this to be simple and private. I asked him if we could just meet late at night by the memorial and take care of business.

He smiled, we walked, and as we left the building, Major Kelly asked me if he could come and witness the ceremony. Although the intent had been just the two of us, I thought, this Exec is a great guy and I really like him; and besides, we should have somebody take a photo to send back to the family. I looked at him and said, "Sure, Major Pain, come on and bring the camera." His name was not Major Pain, but whenever I found a Major in the Executive Officer's seat who I liked, he got this nickname and it stuck. He was only the second one to get the name in many years.

We completed a short discussion about the day and my plan for this final reenlistment. The General looked at me and said, "What did you have in mind?" I told him I committed the Oath of Enlistment to memory, and did not need him to read it to me. From previous experience I knew it was legal for me to recite the oath, so all I needed was for him to say; "State your name, and state your Oath." I would simply recite the oath of enlistment, sign and be done.

His smile told me he was proud and he agreed with the plan. We snapped to attention and he said, "State your name and state your Oath." With exacting precision I stated, "I Scott H. Dearduff do solemnly swear that I will support and defend the constitution of the Unites States against all enemies, foreign and domestic. That I will bear true faith and allegiance to the same. That I will obey the orders of the President of the United States, and the officers appointed over me, according to regulations and the Uniform Code of Military Justice, so help me God." I dropped my hand, we shook, stepped back and exchanged salutes, and with that it was done, committed for four more years of service to my nation at all costs. Major Pain stood silent, waiting to take the photo for posterity. I was now committed to serve my nation for many more years with no regard to location or danger and it was time to get back to work.

I headed for the Balad hospital because I knew there was a planned medical evacuation mission tonight. Upon arrival they told me that Airman Brooks would be going home. Immediately I headed for the ICU to be a part of his departure. He was ready to go, so I followed him out to the bus and helped load him on. Jumping into my truck I headed straight for the flight line so I could see him start his journey. At the flight line there were several buses parked behind the C-17 and each one looked to be full. Once they started to file into the airplane, one of the Balad hospital staff members told me it was a full load tonight, but not all of them were injured. His comment got my attention because there were so many wounded in the hospital. Why would any of them not be on the plane? Then he said, "Chief, some of them are going home because of combat stress." Anger filled my chest. "Combat stress" I said? Who doesn't have combat stress? We all have combat stress and yet we were not loading onto a plane and heading to Germany. I controlled my thoughts so I did not say something out of line. Confusion and anger continued to fill me.

The last bus, the one with the wounded warriors arrived and it was time to load them. I asked the team of volunteers to allow me to load Airman Brooks when it was his turn. They were happy to oblige me and paired me up with a team of Airmen. When it was Josh's turn we received him from the back of the bus and started walking him up the ramp. We chatted as we loaded him into position and I noticed something on his arm on the opposite side. Once he was settled I reached over toward the item and asked him what it was. As he started to talk I was able to see it. He had taped Sergeant Self's memorial pamphlet to his arm. He said, I may not be with him, but he will always be with me. I was choked up and could only get the words, "I know he is" out before they told me it was time to step off the plan. Another sobering moment in a year full of moments.

21 May 2007:

Another long day of visiting Airmen around Balad took a toll on my energy level. Arriving at my office before heading to the quarters for the night, I decided to open my email. There was a message from Mags and it told me something was wrong. She needed me to call home immediately. Thoughts raced through my head about what could be wrong. I dialed quickly and even though it was still early morning there, she was already waiting for my call.

Answering the phone she sounded like something was truly wrong, so I asked, "What is it, darling?" Gathering herself, she said that she had just received a message from our friend Mo. She said her sister Francie called her after being notified that her son Bobby was killed in Baghdad today. I dropped the phone. Seconds later I gained enough composure to pick it up and finish hearing what she was saying. My heart ached for Francie and the family. Bobby Dembowski was a great young Soldier who wanted so much to serve his country honorably like his father had years before. Now Bobby was gone and I had never made contact with him. I felt like I failed in keeping my promise to Francie and now her son was gone.

We finished the conversation and I told her I would do what I could to help find where Bobby was being transported and if he came through Balad, I would see him during the dignified transfer. I thought about trying to become his escort home if it was possible. It was one of the hardest phone calls ever. I had to gather my thoughts and head to the hospital to see if they had any info on Bobby.

Walking into the patient tracking area, I asked for the Army casualty representative. A young staff sergeant came over and we discussed the situation. She informed me Bobby would be transported through Kuwait and he was not coming to Balad. She said it was normal procedure and there would be no changing it. I thanked her and left without another word. I needed to let Mags know I would not be able to see him. The only thing I could tell her was that Bobby was on his way through Kuwait for his journey home.

This night needed to end for me. Laying in the bed all I could think about was Memorial Day ceremony for the Fallen Airman that would take place in a few days. Now my heart was even heavier knowing that our good friends have lost their son. Their Memorial Day weekends would never be the same again.

22 May 2007:

There was always a need for a diversion from the horrors of combat, but we seldom took advantage of all that was offered. Our days were filled with constant demands and we rarely took any time for ourselves. After dealing with the emotional strain of the previous evening, I was hoping for something to take my mind off of all the tragedy for a short time. As I entered the office someone in the hallway said they had heard about some celebrities who were on base as part of a USO Tour. When I paused, they said, "It's Lt Dan and he is visiting with all of the forces in Iraq." Stopping in my tracks, a huge smile came across my face. Gary Sinise was a great American who has been traveling with the USO for several years and always brought a great morale boost to the crowds when he visited. We had previously met in 2005 and 2006 when he visited Luke Air Force Base when the Lt Dan Band performed for the troops. I looked forward to the opportunity to spend time with him at Balad. I stopped in to see the General, and we talked about seeing Gary. The General was excited to see Gary, as they were good friends.

The General informed me that Gary and his brother-in-law would be coming over to the headquarters after their USO duties were complete so we could take in the night from the TOD and catch up on all that he had been doing. We invited the wing and group leaders to hang out with him.

Arriving on the roof, Gary approached me and we exchanged a battle hug. This was an American patriot and we all appreciated what he did. He could not remember how many USO trips this made for him to visit the troops, or he was just being modest; but you could tell he was highly experienced at being in combat, and tonight he was ready to enjoy some time with the Tuskegee Airmen. After a couple of hours of light discussion, many of the chiefs and colonels wondered if Gary would mind taking a photo with them. Laughing, I told them he was always willing to oblige a photo for groups of warriors like them. We grabbed him and spent the next 30 minutes giving everyone a chance to get a shot with Gary – even I stepped in and had mine taken with this great American.

Staying long into the night until he could see that all were ready to hit the rack, Gary thanked everyone and excused himself for a few hours of sleep before he went off to the next location. We stood in admiration for this man who was so willing to sacrifice for our morale. The troops in Vietnam had Bob Hope, we had Gary Sinise in Iraq.

25 May 2007:

We needed to travel to Kirkuk Air Base in the north for a Change of Command ceremony for the last of our group commanders. As the trip planning took place, R2 mentioned to me that his sister was a Defender who was currently deployed at Kirkuk...I told him to prepare for the trip. When I first brought the idea to the executive officer, he told me this trip was full and there was no more room on the aircraft. After a few minutes of intense conversation, I convinced him to change his mind. Next I contacted Chief Lisa Kessinger at Kirkuk and asked if she could arrange for Senior Airman Cindy Rositas to be assigned to me for the day. I had a plan and needed the chief's support to make it all fall into place.

Our C-130 aircraft landed at Kirkuk and we were met by a large contingent of Airmen. I told R2 to walk behind me, as his sister had no idea that he was coming. She had been told by Chief Kessinger that she was going to be my escort for the day. Walking toward the line of Airmen, he remained behind me in his combat gear. As we finished greeting the leaders, Chief Kessinger took us over to meet Airman Rositas. I shook her hand and simply said, "Glad to meet you. I brought you something today." I moved aside and there stood her brother, smiling brightly.

Her reaction was classic. She jumped toward him, grabbing him in a tight hug. I think she began to cry, but I could not tell, and besides, Defenders are not allowed to cry. As we started to move out for the day, I told her she was really here to spend the day with her brother and she did not have to worry about me. She seemed happy to have this new mission and I knew that siblings spending time together in combat would keep them both motivated for a long time.

Our mission at Kirkuk was simple, and once the ceremony was complete, we boarded the plane and headed back to Balad. R2 was very thankful for the combat reunion opportunity. His motivation would move to an all-time high.

On my way into the building I stopped by the memorial and let my thoughts roam back to the home front. As I scanned across the names I wondered what those families were dealing with or how they were coping with life after loss. I shook my head as I walked away, not knowing what answers could ever be given to those families when I had the chance to meet them. I wondered how I would handle the task face to face versus on the phone or by email.

27 May 2007:

The sun was shining bright as I woke on the morning of the ceremony. There was a prediction of bad weather, maybe the last of it for the year. I was hopeful the sun would last, and we would not have people standing in formation for the ceremony outside in the rain as we had in January for the original dedication. Many hours of planning had gone into the details of the ceremony, and all we needed was for the weather to cooperate for a perfect day.

The General, Colonels Renfrow, Colonel Bradley and I arrived at the Town Hall tent for the beginning of the ceremony and went inside. The place was as full as it had been for many of the memorials held under this roof. The musical team was ready and the chaplains in place at the podium.

As things started and the crowd took in the enormity of the day, my fears about the weather began to be realized. I could hear the wind picking up over the music, and saw the top of the tent start to move...bad weather was on the way. I tried hard to focus on the details of the ceremony and about honoring those who had given the last full measure of service in the course of this war. At center stage we placed eight chairs, each one covered with cloth.

Following an invocation by the chaplain, it was time for General Rand to speak. I knew we were in for something special; he took the microphone and delivered a speech that will stick in my memory for my lifetime.

He talked about people from his 28 years of service who paid the ultimate price. A roommate from the Air Force Academy, the best man at his wedding, a student from the Air Force Weapons School while he was an instructor, and the eleven Airmen we lost while serving together at Luke AFB prior to this tour. He spoke about those who served and died during previous wars in many parts of the world. Then he focused on the Airmen who have made the ultimate sacrifice while serving here in Iraq. There were no dry eyes in the crowd by this point. Each person there knew someone from their life who had been killed while serving, and this speech brought all of the emotions to the forefront.

The General finished and departed the stage while the entire crowd remained motionless. The magnitude of this ceremony, being held in the center of the Iraq battlefield, on the same grounds where many of the Airmen we honored, had given their last full measure of effort. This was one of the most emotional events I had the honor of attending in all my years in the military.

As the ceremony progressed, several slide shows played on the large screens at either side of the stage. When they were complete, the narrator began to read the names of the Fallen Airmen from our unit during the year. As each name was read, a member of the Honor Guard would unveil the chair placed in his honor. On each was a large photo of the Airman, and on or in front of each one was something symbolic of their career field. Mostly they were helmets, which had lone significance to each one, separate and distinct. It was a hard moment, almost like we were seeing them each sitting there wanting to share lessons with the crowd so nobody else would have to perish. The room sat silent. In the background the song "Amazing Grace" played softly. I thought about each one, and then thought about Bobby, his family and how they must be grieving during this Memorial Day weekend.

Although it was not intended to be this way in the script, something hit the crowd and nearly simultaneously they all stood. It felt right and seemed to be the best gesture to pay honor to these Fallen Airmen. At the conclusion of the song, the narrator explained that we would all now depart the tent together and make our way to the headquarters building by marching, to close out the ceremony.

The General led us out, followed by the group commanders and their chiefs, then the rest of the crowd. Neither of us would take the time to look back as we marched to see the crowd forming behind us, but we could feel their energy. We looked skyward to see the darkness of the clouds closing in on us, and could feel the temperature dropping rapidly. Surely there was rain on the way and we could only hope to complete the ceremony before it happened.

We came to the headquarters building a minute later and found a large crowd had already gathered, mostly those who could not get into the tent for the beginning of the ceremony. There was also a formation standing prominently in front of the memorial. Only a few of us knew what they were for, and if it worked, it would be a touching moment for all who attended.

Once the entire line had arrived and taken their places around the memorial grounds, the narrator began. He thanked everyone for attending and completed a short speech about the meaning of Memorial Day, including some historical notes.

The narrator told the audience about the significance of laying a wreath at the foot of the memorial. As he was talking, General Rand, Colonel Jackson and myself made our way to the wreath and slowly walked it over to the memorial. We stopped in front of the memorial, knelt down together, and placed the wreath at the foot of the monument. We stepped back and saluted in unison.

Colonel Renfrow read a list of Fallen Airmen whose names appeared on the monument. Slowly, each name was read along with their career field, duty station, and the date of death. I had a lump in my throat from beginning to end.

Once the last name was called for the roll, the Honor Guard stepped forward to the edge of the headquarters building roof. MSgt Kelly Winston stood next to them, prepared to sing. The whole formation looked surreal, almost like they were in the sky, looking down upon us.

The NCO in charge of the Honor Guard called out to prepare them for a 21-gun salute. The crack of those seven rifles was in perfect harmony. Three times they fired, each one sounding like a single report from the distance. After the last shot was fired, they snapped to attention and the singer began.

What happened next was special. Sergeant Winston sang the words to Taps. It was like something out of a movie. Before today I could not have imagined something this beautiful, yet somehow we pulled it off perfectly. There were tears in the eyes of many, and there were few words shared between the crowd.

When she was done singing, the narrator thanked everyone for attending and invited all to come forward and view the memorial. He also told them it would be under the protection of the base Honor Guard for the next 24 hours as a symbol of our respect to the Fallen. R2 took the post as the first ceremonial guardsman and he looked magnificent standing there.

My heart was warm. The ceremony was a fitting tribute to those who had sacrificed. For the next hour I stood and talked with people after they were done paying their respect. I watched grown men and women walk up, salute, and then place their hands on some of the badges and name plates. There were many who had personal connections to the Fallen, and now they had a place to come and honor their friends and comrades. It was touching to watch these hardened combat warriors shed a tear or say a short prayer in front of the memorial. I knew we got this one right.

The rain never came. The day ended with a calm breeze gently flapping the flags in the direction of the memorial. The Fallen Airman Memorial stood as a place of honor. It provided solitude for those in pain, grieving lost friends. Long into the evening Airmen waited their turns to pay tribute. Honor Guard Airmen would stand guard at the memorial for the next 24 hours as a tribute to the Fallen. As I watched, calm came over me.

The words to Taps were stuck in my head and kept replaying.

Day is done. Gone the sun.

Chief Dearduff and Chief Halverson spending an evening with Mr. Gary Sinise on the TOD.

General Rand and Chief Dearduff lead a long line of Airmen from the Town Hall to the site of the Fallen Airman Memorial on 27 May 2007.

Master Sergeant Kelly Winston and members of the Balad Air Base
Honor Guard on the TOD during the singing of Taps on 27 May 2007.

Technical Sergeant Richard Rositas standing guard at the memorial.

18
FALLEN AGENTS

The month of May was gone and we only had a little over a month to complete this mission. The days were passing like hours, the hours like minutes. The end of our tour was looming, and I could not feel satisfied that we had done everything possible unless we were pressing right up until the end. My replacement was named and he was an old friend and fellow Defender. It gave me great peace of mind that what we had put in place would be carried on, but I did not want to leave any stones unturned. Setting up this foxhole so he could come in and make it even better was going to be my primary goal in the remaining 45 days.

2 June 2007:

I woke to the sound of the CRAM defensive guns firing and suspected this would be a long day. Landing on the floor of my quarters, I also realized I had neglected to clean my room well on the two previous Sundays. So while the attack went on, I did some extra cleaning of the floor. Once the all clear came in, I decided to call in and see what, if any damage occurred. The command post said the guns did their job perfectly and they had two direct hits, meaning nothing hit inside the wire and there were no injuries and no damage. It was a piece of good news I needed to hear, and one that would give me added strength to start going about the long day. Just a few hours later the base came under attack again. This time several rounds landed on the base. The tension was rising and people were showing obvious signs of stress. The General called his senior leaders together and explained the situation with indirect fire landing on the base, the persistence of the enemy, and the need to continue our flying operations. He shared that while he knew how important it was to push through and complete the mission, he was also concerned about the safety of our Airmen. He made the decision to place the wing in Uniform Posture 2, which required everyone to have their protective gear on while outside and with them at all times. Some in the room took deep breaths, thinking this would stress the force even more. I knew different and nearly jumped out of my chair with excitement.

Finally, I would be able to make everyone wear their gear and take these attacks as serious as they needed to be. The tone would be set for the remainder of our tour, and we would do everything we could to protect our Airmen from this unpredictable enemy.

Over the next 48 hours everyone moved with a purpose. Not once did an Airman complain about having to wear the gear, even when the heat was soaring over the 110 degree mark. They knew this measure was implemented for their protection and nobody wanted to tempt fate.

5 June 2007:

Airman Jones caught my attention when I entered the building. He seemed a little off his game which made me stop and hold a conversation with him rather than just passing by. We often had great conversations about life, the military, and the things I had seen in combat. He seemed to enjoy hearing about my travels around the country and I enjoyed hearing his perspective on things happening around the base. Something was unusual about Indiana on this day, his smile controlled and his motivation level way below the norm. I asked him what was wrong, and he asked, "Chief, I guess you have not heard the news that just came in?"

I could tell by the way he said it and by his non-verbal's, this was not good. Without saying a word, I turned and headed for Colonel Renfrow's office to get some details. Before I could reach his office the call came across the radio. "All Red Tails report..." I hate that sound and walked with purpose to the briefing to face the inevitable. Would this be another aviator, a Defender, or yet another EOD Airman taken far too early?

Inside the briefing room there was an all-too-familiar look around the room and on the face of the briefer. His words burned my ears; "Sir, we have two casualties to report from Kirkuk Air Base." As he went on, I opened my notebook preparing to write the names down as they were read. "Ryan Balmer and Matt Kuglics were killed today when their vehicle was struck by an IED." The names sounded familiar to me as they were mentioned, but I could not figure out why. Then the briefer said they were OSI agents. My emotions were uncontrollable and I said very loud, "No, it can't be."

Everyone in the room stared at me. The briefer went on. He provided details about the incident and everyone in the room remained silent. Most knew we were working the initiative to get our Defenders officially tasked to provide security support for those agents while they were outside the wire. My heart ached for this terrible loss of life. I could not help but feel we were losing the battle to gain support for these missions. There was no way I was giving up, and I knew that General Rand and General North would continue the fight.

Nobody knew what was wrong or why I left the room in frustration. They had no idea how I felt about these agents. They were my brothers in arms, and like all of the previous casualties, their loss would be very personal for me. Having spent time on missions with them brought me even closer. Their sacrifice as a career field was mounting as they continued to be on the front lines of this dangerous and unpredictable war.

Certainly there would be agents in the detachment here at Balad who knew these two agents personally. They would be suffering and mourning their loss. It was time to compartmentalize and go check on them.

The General also had a great relationship with the OSI and knew all of them well. His history with OSI went all the way through his career, during which he had formed a strong bond with them through many events and the way he treated them. To him they were unit members, and we had to take care of them, even though they reported through a separate chain of command by structure. We went to visit the local detachment and see how they were doing. As expected, when we arrived they were all standing tall ready to visit with us. The General put them at ease quickly and told them this was a personal visit to see how they were all doing. He also told them he wanted to know more about the two agents who were killed in action today. The General always made this a deep, personal discussion and his passion for the Airmen came through brilliantly.

The stories went on and on about Matt and Ryan. Agents from across the OSI community spoke about how terrific they were as agents and how loyal they were as friends. They talked about Matty being the happy single guy with a huge brain and the ability to figure out things when others could not. They told stories of Ryan, the family man, whose wife and kids were at the forefront of every conversation he had. Some of the agents in this detachment had been assigned with them and some had gone through training with them to become agents. This strong bond could not be broken; this loss would be especially hard.

The General was talking with Major Matt Modarelli, so I did my best to answer any and all concerns the agents had. I updated our effort to get a Defender support team for them and we would not give up until it was done. I assured them I was ready and willing to go out on a mission with them any time, which brought smiles to their faces. Airmen liked knowing leaders were willing to do what they did.

As we departed the facility, we were treated like part of the brotherhood. Battle hugs went all around and the hard looks on their faces seemed to soften for a moment. We all felt a little peace of mind at a terrible time. We had a brief discussion about travel to Kirkuk for the memorial, and the General assured them we would make it happen.

7 June 2007:

The look on my face must have said more than I knew. R2 seemed upset at my reaction to the radio call, and he was visibly moved with emotion. He asked if I thought it could possibly be another KIA. I told him that you can always tell by the voice of the controller if it's something serious or not, and that voice was serious. But I did not want to jump to conclusions, and I did not want to deal with another loss while still dealing with the horrible news about our OSI agents. We drove silently to the headquarters building. Upon arrival I told R2 to go and get something to eat, because this would probably be a long day. Inside I passed the entry control point without saying much to Senior Airman "JJ" Walker who was posted at the door. In the briefing room, I noticed the commander and chief from the civil engineering squadron in the room. Having seen them under these circumstances before, I could see the emotion on their faces. We had a casualty within EOD.

The room remained quiet and within seconds the General came in. I took out my notebook and prepared to write down the vital information from the briefer. General Rand took a deep breath, hesitated, then told everyone; "I need you all to pay particular attention and get every detail of this incident." His message was clear to me. He wanted this to sink in and he wanted everyone to know that even though we had been through this type of briefing many times before, he did not want this to become routine. This was about losing an Airman, and we needed every ounce of energy and focus we could muster to make sure we handled this to the best of our ability.

"Today we had an IED incident in which one EOD member was killed and another was injured…" said the briefer in a solemn tone. He began to describe the location and the scene of the incident but I could not hear him. My focus was on the faces around the room. I looked intently at each person, making sure they paid attention to the General's comment and making sure they all got it; we, the entire team, lost another Airman today. After several minutes of careful study of the room, I was convinced everyone took it in and were internalizing the event and the cost of human life.

I watched the EOD leadership as they held their emotions inside. They secretly wished this day would never come. It had been five months to the day since our last EOD Airmen were killed in action; and considering all the dangerous missions they were on daily, it was remarkable there were not more. That was no consolation to any of us, and everyone showed signs of stress.

When the briefing was complete and follow-up actions had been discussed, everyone was dismissed and started about their business. I watched as each person in the room walked over and shared their condolences with the EOD leadership. We had become one team in this fight against a determined enemy. Once everyone was done, I shared my own personal thoughts for this loss, and encouraged them to remain strong and steady. I reassured them the entire wing stood behind them.

When our conversation was over, I realized I had been so caught up in the moment that I never wrote down the name of the fallen warrior. Moving back to the conference table, I asked the briefer to bring the info slide back up so I could record the information. As I began to write down the name it dawned on me, I had eaten dinner with Senior Airman Will Newman recently during a visit from the Chief Master Sergeant of the Air Force.

I remembered Airman Newman specifically because he approached me at the end of the dinner and asked if he could have his photo taken with the Chief Master Sergeant of the Air Force. We walked over, and after a brief introduction of the Airman, the Chief said, "Come on over here so I can get my picture taken with a true hero." Little did he know those words would ring so true on this day as we began the process of honoring Airman Newman for his service and sacrifice. He was a hero who gave the last full measure of his being on the battlefield.

I became lost in those thoughts for a minute and failed to realize I was the only one left in the room. Quietly, I held my breath, wondering why. Why this Airman? What was the cost of his service? What would his young bride and parents do now to carry on with their lives? The pain I was now feeling inside began to burn and I could not shake it. I sat back in the chair and tried to catch my breath as I began to feel like the oxygen had gone out of the room. I felt a tear welling in my left eye and yet another lump in my throat. Feelings which had become too common in my life.

This Airman was a fellow service member; this was a brother. A loss so significant I could feel no other way than how anyone feels when losing a family member. It came to me again that I was not just serving with great Americans who risked their lives for the sake of some cause. I knew I was serving with and leading men and women like me, who were willing to serve their country, protect liberty and freedom and pay the ultimate price to defeat the enemy. They were my brothers and sisters in arms.

Stopping in the General's office I was told he was waiting on a call back from Hawaii and Airman Newman's family. The executive officer closed the General's door because he was relaying information about Airman Newman to General North. He asked me to stand by and be ready to talk with the family in case the General was not completed with his notifications. Seconds later the phone rang. The executive officer said quietly to the person on the other end, "The commander is unavailable right now, but I have the Command Chief here and he would like to talk with you."

As I reached for the phone I had no idea who was on the other end, I just assumed it was family. The executive officer whispered that it was a master sergeant who was with the family. That gave me some sense of what to say and how to start this hard phone conversation. Conversations like this were always easier in person.

The sergeant identified himself immediately and I asked if he was the Family Liaison Officer (my assumption at the time). He said he would probably handle those duties in the following days, but for now he was the cousin of Mrs. Newman. He explained to me that she was of Korean descent and her language skills in English were not that good. He feared she would not understand what was being said, and so he asked to speak for her.

We talked for a minute and I explained to him what I could reasonably tell him on the phone. He asked me if I knew Airman Newman before the incident. I offered the story about the dinner with the Chief Master Sergeant of the Air Force and told him I was very impressed with Airman Newman. I only wished I had spent more time with him. He asked if Airman Newman was doing a good job and seemed happy. I told him from all indications, he was doing a great job and all of his supervisors reported he was a highly motivated Airman. He seemed relieved and then asked me to hold on. Moments later he came back on and said that Mrs. Newman wanted to talk with me.

Not being sure what to say or what she would want to know, I braced myself for anything. The sergeant told me she was 19 years old. I thought to myself, this is such a young girl, and now she is a military widow…what do you say to provide any comfort to this young lady? She came on and I could hear her tears and the shortness of her breath. Then the only words I could find were the same ones I had become accustomed to using. "Ma'am, I am truly sorry for your loss." With that, I could hear her say "Thank you," in a very faint voice.

She handed the phone back to the sergeant and we talked some more. I asked him if he wanted to wait and talk with the commander who was still behind closed doors. He told me they needed to move along and go meet with the chaplain and it was best not to wait. I thanked him for his assistance, assured him we would hold a fitting memorial service, and shared the sentiments of General Rand and more than 8,000 fellow Tuskegee Airmen when I said, "We're all sorry for your loss." He could barely get the words out, but thanked me before hanging up. It was the hardest phone call I had ever experienced. This made it even more personal to me. I could not feel her pain nor take it away. I felt helpless but knew others would be with her in this most difficult time.

The General and I spoke shortly after and I shared the conversations we had. He planned to call the family soon, something he always did to let the family know how he felt. Our focus now turned to ensure EOD had everything they needed for Airmen Newman's memorial, in addition to providing updates on the other EOD warrior who was injured.

Major Robert Kelley performed his duties as the executive officer with exacting perfection. When he told me he needed something, I knew he was serious. He entered my office and I could see the look on his face. "Chief," he said, "The General wants you to join him over at the hospital because we have another injured Airman from the wing in Kuwait and we would be presenting him with a Purple Heart medal." The look on my face told him I was tired, but would absolutely make the trip and check on this wounded warrior. We departed immediately.

As we walked into the hospital we were briefed that this Airman was from the transportation unit at Barksdale AFB in Louisiana and he was performing convoy duties from Kuwait into Iraq when his truck was hit by an IED. This scenario sounded just like the very first Purple Heart General Rand presented to Airman First Class Joshua Collins back in August of 2006, shortly after our arrival.

We reached the area where Staff Sergeant Thomas Knudson was located for his recovery. He appeared to be banged up but was conscious and seemed to have high spirits. The General talked to him and found out his story. After he formally presented the medal, it was my turn to talk with the young sergeant. I moved in close to him so he did not have to talk loud. I thanked him for his service and asked if he was doing OK, all things considered. He assured me he was in pain, but he was receiving the best care and would come out of this just fine. I asked him what base he was from and he told me Barksdale. I laughed and asked him if he knew Airman Collins who was also from Barksdale and earned a purple heart back in 2006. He laughed and said, "Chief, I am his supervisor back at Barksdale." We laughed for a minute until we both started to cry.

Sergeant Knudson told us that Airman Collins was recovering well and he was expecting him to deploy again soon. At that moment I began to admire just how much courage and resilience these Airmen had. It was incredible how they could leave the battlefield injured and the first thing they think about is the next deployment. I thanked him again and wished him well on his journey. His courage gave me a boost of energy I needed to press through this most difficult week. I needed some rest.

8 June 2007:

There was no time to sit around feel sorry for ourselves as we dealt with the pain of losing three Airmen in one week. We had to compartmentalize our emotions and prepare for memorial services to honor our Fallen Agents, and then another for Airmen Newman. We headed for the flight line to board our C-130 transport with Major Modarelli and several OSI agents by our side.

Arriving at Kirkuk we were met by Colonel Doug Tucker. A tough commander with an extensive deployment background. A friend to the OSI, and he always cared for his agents at Kirkuk.

As we arrived to meet the agents from the Kirkuk detachment, we noticed there were leaders from U.S. Army units around Kirkuk, all standing tall and showing their support for the loss of these Airmen. I knew several of these senior leaders and we had spent time talking during some of my battlefield circulation. They were all hardened by tragedy just as we were, and they completely understood how it felt to lose a warrior. It was meaningful to every Airman in the room to see them with us.

The General was in a conversation over in the corner and I wanted to find out what was going on. It turned out the interpreter who was with Matt and Ryan when the incident happened was now here. He had been injured in the same incident, but left the hospital to come and attend the memorial.

He was an American citizen born of Iraqi descent. He came back to Iraq to perform duties as an interpreter in order to do his part to regain control of their country and make sure we kept the former regime out of control. He was on this mission for more than two years at the time and had been in several other incidents. As the conversation went on I heard him say this was the first time he lost anyone, making it sound like he felt responsible. I found out from the agents that he treated them all like his own sons, and he definitely felt responsible for them when they were out on missions.

The General reassured him it was not his fault and he should not blame himself. Several Iraqi military members entered the room where we were meeting. These particular Iraqi Air Force members were working closely with our forces and the relationships had progressed quite well. We exchanged greetings, and then it was time to go into the memorial service.

The entire gymnasium on this former Iraqi Air Base was full from side to side. It was not quite the same atmosphere as the tent back at Balad, but walking in you could feel the air was heavy and the mood was very blue. At

Kirkuk there were only 900 US Airmen, so many were familiar with these agents and the important things they had done for the security of the base.

The ceremony was solemn and the testimonials were spot on. This was a class act and would be locked into my memory bank as one of the best executed memorials we had attended. The General and I moved to the battlefield cross memorials for Matt and Ryan and rendered our final salutes. Slowly, in unison, we felt the pain deep inside as we lowered our right arms. Walking out of the building it appeared everyone remained in place, waiting their turn to pay their respects. It was an awesome sight and a fitting tribute.

At the conclusion of the service, we spent a few minutes consoling those unit members who stayed behind. The normal procession of coins being laid at the foot of the memorial went longer than normal. An hour after the ceremony ended, all of the OSI Agents remained standing at their chairs, waiting for everyone else to finish. Seeing them standing shoulder to shoulder was an unbelievable sight. They were a resilient group of warriors waiting to pay homage to their friends, their comrades, their brothers.

When everyone else was finally complete and the agents moved forward, we stepped out to ensure they could have their moment in private. This was a place for OSI Agents only.

We departed Kirkuk with heavy hearts and additional motivation to overcome hurdles in taking care of these agents. I planned to sleep on the plane so I would have some energy to attend the second memorial for the agents once we arrived back at Balad. Sitting back into the cargo netting of the C-130 seat, I opened my notebook and made sure I had the names of our 9th and 10th Airman lost on this mission properly annotated. Special Agent Matt Kuglics and Special Agent Ryan Balmer, killed in action, 5 June 2007. Those names would now be etched into my memory forever as I drifted off to sleep.

R2 picked me up he asked if I would like something to eat. I told him I really was not hungry and would rather just head straight for the Town Hall and the second of two memorial services for Ryan and Matt.

Entering the Town Hall felt calming. We had been through so many ceremonies in this location that whenever we walked in it just felt warm, like somewhere we wanted to be. I had personally been through so many emotions in this tent it became a solemn place for me. The ceremony was executed to perfection by the chapel team and OSI leadership. Teams of Defenders stood watch outside the Town Hall tent to ensure nothing interrupted this ceremony for their brothers.

At the conclusion of the ceremony the General and I were the first to depart the tent. He insisted we stay around and watch how the Airmen of the 332d Air Expeditionary Wing would react to this memorial. We watched from a distance as more than 250 filed out of the tent, each one stopping to shake hands with the OSI agents on hand. I doubt any of they knew the agents before this ceremony, but you could feel the brotherhood. It was touching to watch the show of appreciation for the OSI agents.

Once everyone departed, the General asked me to gather the OSI agents inside the tent. Inside, there was an incredible collection of coins and personal items laid at the foot of the battlefield cross. The agents gathered together near the front of the room and I stood to the side of the chairs, waiting to hear what the General had to say. For the next five minutes he told them how much he appreciated their efforts and that what they were doing was not being done in vain. He expressed his gratitude for the dangerous mission they undertook, and acknowledged the level of danger they faced each time they went outside the wire. His words were exactly what they needed to hear. They were encouraged by this show of support from the wing commander, and it brought obvious strength to these warriors so they could continue the mission. There were no dry eyes in the tent.

We walked out of the tent, having spoken with each agent individually over the past 15 minutes. As we got to the General's truck for our short ride back to the headquarters building I remembered something. I looked at the General and said, "Well sir, that's one hell of a way to spend your birthday huh?" He smiled, found it hard to say anything; we exchanged salutes and headed to the headquarters building.

The General asked what I was looking at inside my notebook. I showed him the list of Fallen Airmen that now filled two pages in my notebook. No words were necessary. Two more names had been added. Special Agents Ryan Balmer and Matt Kuglics, killed in action 5 June 2007.

OSI Special Agent Ryan Balmer, killed in action 5 June 2007.

OSI Special Agent Matt Kuglics, killed in action, 5 June 2007.

Senior Airman Will Newman, killed in action 7 June 2007.

Chief Dearduff meeting with Defenders on the Kirkuk Air Base flight line
following the memorial service for Agents Kuglics and Balmer.

19
HARD MOURNING

Arriving at my quarters inside Red Tail Village usually brought calm, like the day was over and I could start winding down. Tonight would be different, my mind would keep going, thinking about all the things that needed to be done. I realized there were now three names plates to be made for the memorial and time was limited. This is not a task I planned to leave for others to finish.

Four hours later I was back in uniform and moving out to get things done. Before stopping to get something to eat, I headed for the shop where they made the name plates. The lady working behind the counter looked at me and said, "Not another one?" She knew what we were going through, and I felt like she had internalized these losses much as I was doing. When I tried to tell her it was not one more, but three, the words would hardly come out. Turning away briefly I tried to compose myself. She understood and gave me a minute without speaking a word. Soon the plates were ordered and I thanked her for understanding.

The rest of the day was focused on projects. There were many positive things going on, and I did not want to overlook them as we dealt with the tragedies. The building was empty except for the door guard, the executive officer, command post controllers, the General and myself. We had been through a roller coaster of emotions in these past few days and we all needed time to clear our minds.

Once inside the office it was time to catch up on emails and paperwork, something I had neglected recently because of the casualties and all of the associated travel. Right away I notice an email from General North asking me where I wanted to go for my next assignment. Here I was one month from departing, and less than two months from being at my next assignment, and I did not know where I was going...hard on me, but it's really tough on the family. Knowing that you are going to move again, start over in a new school and make new friends was a routine. Not knowing where caused undue stress on the family members.

We never make it easy on the military families, but for mine it's been especially tough. Most of our moves have been done with less than 60 days of notice, and most of the assignments were not to places we would have chosen to live. Of course like all military families, we always make the best of it. I responded to General North that it did not matter as long as my family was with me we could go anywhere.

He came back right away, even though it was nearly 0100 in the morning. Nobody really ever knew where he was in the world. He traveled so much he could be on either continent and in any number of countries. This guy rarely slept, so his quick response was not surprising. He's also very blunt, so he said; "Chief, tell me where you want to go."

I did not want to sound like a hard head, but I really did not know where I wanted to go or even which units would be open. He said I would not be able to move to the numbered Air Force level at the time of my return because there were no openings, but if I was willing to serve at the wing level again, he would be sure and find me another opportunity to serve as a wing command chief.

All I cared about was leading Airmen, the location didn't matter. I did not want someone to make up a position for me. I finally said; "I know the Command Chief at Charleston AFB in South Carolina would be retiring soon and that would be a very appropriate place for me to go."

The General thanked me and said, "Shaw is close to Charleston, so let me get back to you." Finishing the discussion allowed me to get back to the mission at hand. Whatever happened, my family would be by my side and we could put up with just about anything.

Reviewing emails seemed an endless task, but provided valuable information on what was going on back home. The Air Force announced approval of a combat medal that would be awarded to Airmen who were engaged in direct combat action. It was called the Air Force Combat Action Medal and it came after a four year journey to approve a legitimate medal for ground combat action. Prior to this announcement, many Airmen were awarded the Army's Combat Action Badge (CAB) following direct enemy action. The Air Force never formally approved the wearing of the Army CAB, yet Airmen wore it as an unofficial badge of honor. It caused a dilemma when I saw it. I knew it was not authorized to be on their uniform, but I knew they earned it if it had been awarded by an Army unit.

This new medal created a huge workload to figure out which Airmen had earned one. There would be a ton of paperwork to review in order to get them well deserved recognition. There was a media release showing the first six Airmen who were awarded the medal back at the Pentagon. Each of them had clear reason for the award of the medal and that information helped formulate a sense of what it would take to meet the standard. The message also said General North would be the approving official, which meant we had to meet a high level of scrutiny from a leader with firsthand knowledge of combat actions. This was a much better situation than to have someone not associated with combat in Iraq trying to make determinations. The first medals needed to be awarded to those who were killed in action and I started on them right away.

Another situation caught my attention. There was official word that a mass reenlistment ceremony would take place in Baghdad at the Al Faw Palace on 4 July 2007.

General Petraeus and CSM Hill were the official hosts for the ceremony and they expected hundreds of warriors to attend and extend their commitments to serving the nation. Only those who were located in the Baghdad area could participate. This was done in anticipation of troops wanting to travel into Baghdad for the ceremony, putting themselves in harm's way and using military aircraft for non-mission essential reasons. I understood the reason for the decision, but knew it would not be easy for everyone to understand.

The very next email stopped me in my tracks. It was from Colonel Jackson and was a request for assistance in sending someone home early from their tour. I read on, and the more I found out, the more infuriated I was. After seeing all those "combat stressed" troops heading home on the C-17, this was something I was not ready to comprehend. Colonel Jackson wanted to send a senior NCO home because she was unfit to serve. He wanted me to notify the home station command chief and let the major command know what was going on. I picked up the phone because I needed to know more about the situation.

According to the chief on the other end of the line, this senior NCO was seen sitting at the gate shack near the entrance to the H-6 housing area. When the chief asked the Defenders who she was they said they were unsure, but she stopped there every day and sat for a while, then just got up and walked away. She rarely said anything. They only knew she walked to the building where the 732d Air Expeditionary Group worked. Once they had more time to look into the situation, it was determined she was walking from her quarters to the work center and had to carry her battle gear, as it was required to be with you at all times. Apparently, she became so tired from the walk, which was less than 500 meters total, she needed to sit down and rest.

I told the chief I needed to call her home station and find out what the whole story was in case there was some medical situation. But I would support Colonel Jackson's decision to send her home once we spoke. There was definitely no room for someone in combat wing that could not take care of herself. I picked up the phone and called her home station. After some quick pleasantries, I told the command chief what we were dealing with and passed the name to him. He immediately became defensive and told me she was the number 1 ranked senior NCO in their wing, and they sent her to combat specifically so she would get more experience, receive a combat decoration, and get promoted to chief. He must have thought the line went dead because I did not say a word. Had something come out, he would not have liked it at all. I was not sure we were talking about the same person. After a minute I told him the name again, and shared that her combat unit commander brought her in, asked about her most recent fitness test and had her height and weight checked. I told him she was 5'2" and weighed 224 pounds. I thought the phone went dead. He said nothing.

I told the command chief that we did not have room in combat for a senior NCO or anyone else who was significantly out of shape, she was a combat liability. He must have been looking at her fitness scores while I was talking to him because the next thing he said was, "Chief, I apologize, she scored a 28 (out of 100) on her fitness test just before leaving for Balad. Nothing else needed to be said. I told him we would have her on the next plane out and would appreciate if he generated a replacement from his unit. He agreed and we ended the call.

The stress of non-combat related situations was wearing me down and took my focus away from combat warriors who were performing at high levels. For the next two hours I compiled notes on everything I thought was important for my turnover to Chief Wheeler. It would come faster than I wanted it to, so time was of the essence. One thing I knew for sure, Chief Wheeler would not need advice from me on how to lead, I just want to give him information on things he should concentrate on. The first thing on the list was the Fallen Airman Memorial. I hoped he would maintain a high level of importance on the memorial after I left.

I sent Chief Wheeler an email detailing the living quarters he would inherit. He responded immediately and seemed to have the same thoughts I did back when I heard about it. Was this for real? Like me, Chief Wheeler's previous deployments in combat were spent in a large tent with many other warriors, no private bathroom, and certainly no TV. We shared a good moment through email exchange, and I was done for the night. Sleep would become critical for the remaining weeks and the night was passing by quickly. It seemed the insurgents were planning to leave us alone tonight or maybe they could hear the F-16s flying low overhead around the perimeter of the base, likely deterring their actions.

10 June 2007:

The morning of the memorial service was especially sunny and the sky was extremely blue. The wind was blowing and the summer heat was creeping up fast, so early morning was the best time for this type of large audience event. As we had become accustomed to, the EOD crew had put together a great memorial service complete with music and the proper testimonials. There were memories about times in technical training and time here on the mission in Iraq. There was talk about family and sacrifice, those things most fitting for this memorial. We had a chance to honor this Airman and his family for the great sacrifice he had made.

My heart was warmed by this tribute. I could not help but become attached to these Airmen I was serving with. Will Newman was no exception. Hearing his story and knowing how well he served made me feel like a proud uncle. For a moment I was at peace.

As we paid tribute, his EOD colleagues could feel the love and support from all those who came out to honor him and their career field. As always, the tent was full and there was standing room only, even with temperatures soaring over 100 degrees before most people had eaten breakfast. The ceremony was dignified and packed with emotion. As the ceremony came to a close, the crowd remained, so each person could pay their personal respect to the Fallen. These moments would always make me stop and reflect on how grateful I was to be a part of such a strong brotherhood. The General and I once again stood side by side to say our goodbye, render our final salute.

In the hours following the ceremony, I looked for positive things to do. There were good things going on all around the base. We flew successful combat missions resulting in the termination of insurgents on the battle field. Besides dropping bombs, there was also a large following developing for the unmanned aerial vehicles that made daily impact on the bad guys. Our wing was setting records for enemy killed in action, reduction of bombings on the roadside, and reductions in US casualties. And more important than setting records, we knew every C-130 mission meant dozens of troops were not put in harm's way to move cargo across the main supply routes of Iraq.

We were also making huge progress and direct impact on the less obvious battlefields of Iraq. Building schools, fixing utilities for cities, and other public functions did not make for exciting press back home, so few outside of the military really knew what we were doing to make it all better. The public knew about every IED that hit one of our patrols, or every firefight started by the insurgents, sometimes even without a known target. They knew about the strife in some areas and the constant battles between religious and political factions within the Iraqi society. Reporting about the good we were doing was scarce.

We decided to let people know about all those good things and the General decided to establish a campaign which described all those things for the public to hear. He called it the "Tell Your Story" campaign and challenged everyone to go home at the completion of their tour and tell their story to anyone who would listen. During one of the many meetings we had, he said "Share the lessons learned, share the challenges, go back and tell the Expeditionary

Airman story. Each of you needs to educate your contemporaries on what this means and what they can do." He then promised he would do this himself, and he would not stop until there was no longer a need. It caught on, and I was pumped to focus on his brilliant idea.

The phone in my office rang and R2 said my friend, the Command Chief in Kuwait was on the phone. I was really looking forward to hearing a friendly voice and hoping we would have time to catch up. As soon as I heard his voice, I knew something was wrong. I knew Chief Thomas Narofsky well enough from working together in a previous command before we both came to combat. I could tell he had some bad news and he wanted to share it.

I asked him what happened, and he took a second to gather himself. He said, "I lost one today." I knew what he was talking about, but hoped I was wrong. I said, "Thom, do you mean you lost an Airman today?" He confirmed that one of his convoys from Kuwait into Iraq was hit and one Senior Airman was killed by the IED and several were injured.

The only appropriate words at the moment came out; "Thom, I'm sorry for your loss. Is there anything we can do from here to help you and your unit?" He assured me that everything was being handled and he would be getting with me in the days that followed to have a memorial service in country with the convoy team as they stood down at their present location. I then offered him any assistance he may need with the memorial since this was the first for their unit and we were quite well versed. He thanked me and asked for any checklists and guidance I was willing to provide.

While we talked, I gathered some electronic files and sent them to his email so he could have quick access to them when time permitted. I could feel his pain and knew it would kick him in the gut like it always did to me. As we concluded our discussions, I assured Thom I would be available to him if he needed to vent following this loss. At the end of the conversation I shared with him the list of Fallen Airmen maintained in my notebook. I told him that even though his Airman was not a part of our wing, I wanted to add his name in my notebook. He agreed, and told me he appreciated the support. I also started telling him about the song, "I Can Only Imagine" that we always played at our memorials. I told him how important the song had become in my own dealing with the tragedies of our Fallen Airmen and encouraged him to use it when they conducted their memorial.

Opening the notebook to page 3 I wrote: "Airman First Class Eric Barnes, killed in action, 10 June 2007. Another great American tragically taken.

I glanced back at page two and reflected again as I read the last entry of 332d Air Expeditionary Wing Airmen, Senior Airman Will Newman, killed in action, 7 June 2007.

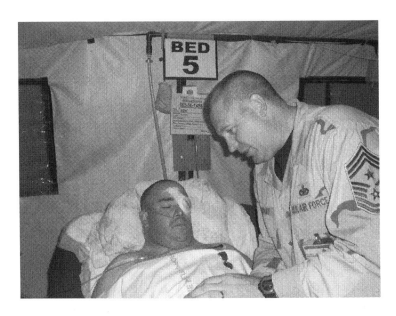

Staff Sergeant Thomas Knudson from Barksdale Air Force Base received the Purple Heart for injuries suffered while performing convoy operations in Iraq.

A typical day of flying at Balad Air Base included frequent de-confliction of aircraft from F-16 Fighters to C-130 Hercules transport planes.

The presence of the Unmanned Aerial Vehicle (UAV) brought a whole new perspective to the battle field. This asset had a huge impact on Operation Iraqi Freedom.

A USAF C-130 Hercules takes off at sunset to provide safe transport of troops and logistics around the battlefield.

20
PAINFUL WAKE UP CALL

The attack warning alarm sounded. "Incoming, Incoming, Incoming." Rolling off the bed and onto the floor, I thought to myself, I'm lying on the floor again as they have shot at us over 400 times in 11 months. This is getting old.

Then I remembered my last days in Baghdad back in 2003 and how I took the chance of walking around one night without my protective gear on to fit easier into the porta john outside of the Base Defense Operations Center. That night a rocket landed within 100 meters of me, knocking me into the door of the porta john and scaring the life right out of me. I swore I would never take any attacks lightly. But this night, lying on the floor, I was pissed off at the insurgents for ruining yet another night of what could have been restful sleep.

Out the door I went, heading first to the flight line for a quick check of the aircraft parking areas. On the way I was diverted by the sound of the Defenders who were already on scene near the back of our housing area. They located two points of impact and reported no casualties or major damage. They did locate some damaged windows on vehicles and the sand filled barriers were badly scarred.

As I arrived on scene, I noticed where I was. Just inside these barriers was Red Tail Village. If you could have paced it off, it probably came within 200 meters of where the General and the colonels were housed. From the line of where it likely came from to the point of impact, you could tell it was on target, just a little short.

Realizing it was too late to get back to sleep now, I headed off to the DFAC for a nice warm breakfast, without being rushed for once. I sat with some young Soldiers who were passing through from another FOB. We talked for a while about the differences between the Army and Air Force deployments. It was the first time any of them had been explained why the Air Force deployed differently than the Army units. They seemed to understand the reason it was different, but they still wanted me to understand their pain.

All of them had been in country for four months and had eight to go. I listened intently while they asked their questions about Air Force deployments. Once they were done venting, I told them about the need to rotate airplanes off the battlefield and bring new ones into the fight. I also explained how our aircraft provided overhead protection every time they went on missions outside the wire...I had their attention.

They asked how long I had been in country. At first I was hesitant to tell them, then I figured they could use a taste of reality. I told them, "This is my 12th month in country, on this tour." The table was silent for a minute. One of the young Soldiers asked, "How many other tours have you been on?" I laughed, and said to the young-faced American warrior, "I suppose my first one here was while you were in high school, the second while you were in boot camp, and this one started while you were learning to be a Soldier." We laughed, and the breakfast came to a close.

Departing, they stood up and shook my hand. One young Soldier said; "We're not sure what to call you because we have never seen an Air Force NCO with so many stripes." I briefly explained to them my responsibility level, and they all immediately snapped to the position of parade rest.

The leader of this group looked at me and said, "Sergeant Major, we are sorry we took such a casual approach to this conversation, that won't happen again." I shook his hand and assured him it was not a problem and I was honored to sit and talk with them. We are all Americans fighting here for the same reason. I thanked the group for their service and wished them well on the remainder of their tour. I walked away knowing the chances of all of them making it home at the end were slim, and a sharp pain hit my chest…I could hardly catch my breath thinking about those young Americans heading out on another mission.

Driving back to the office gave me time to contemplate the dedicated service from our young American men and women. I walked in past the memorial and decided to sit quietly in the office to catch up on all the administrative work when the phone rang. I answered in a low and quiet voice, hoping that it was not someone wanting to talk long time. I hate to be rude, but I had a ton of work to get done.

The caller said his name was Jim Post. When he said it, my mind started drifting; for some reason I knew it, but could not figure out why. Then it hit me, I had just read that name in the book I was given by CSM Mellinger back in May. There was a reference to Jim Post, an Air Force Academy Cadet who was interviewed by the author while he was doing research on Lance P. Sijan for the book. I'm not sure what he said for the next minute as I was figuring out who he was, but then I heard him say, "I'm the Wing Commander at Shaw AFB and I would like you to become my command chief." That caught my attention and without hesitation, I said, "Sir, it would be my honor."

He asked me if I had any questions, to which I said, "Yes, are you the same Jim Post who was an Academy cadet in 1983, and whose name appears in the book, *Into the Mouth of the Cat?*" He laughed and said he was, but wondered how I knew that. I told him about the book I received from Mellinger and he laughed. It seemed like fate, like we were supposed to work together.

After a short discussion about moving the family and needing some down time, we agreed upon a report day and said goodbye. It was the easiest job interview ever. Then I remembered my conversations with General North and put all things together. What did this mean for the future? I did not have time to worry about it now, I needed to get back to the mission at hand.

Later in the evening I decided it was a good time to call home and let them know about moving to South Carolina. Somehow I knew this would not go over very well, but news like this does not get better with time. Mags came on the phone and we chatted for a minute before she said, "OK, give me the news, you had to have received an assignment or you would not have called in the middle of the week like this." She was very perceptive and always knew when something was wrong, or if I had something to share.

I said, "Brace yourself..." and before I could finish, she said, "We better not be going back to North Dakota, because you will be going alone!" I laughed and said, "No, North Dakota is not in our future, so let me make you happy with some warm weather. How does South Carolina strike you?" She sounded excited and said, "I've always wanted to spend time in South Carolina so this should be a great assignment; but the only place I know about is Charleston. Is that where we are going?" I quickly told her; "Instead of Charleston, we are going to Shaw Air Force Base and it was located in Sumter, South Carolina."

When I explained to her it was home to the 20th Fighter Wing, 9th Air Force Headquarters and Air Forces Central Command (AFCENT), the phone immediately went quiet. After a minute she said, "What are the odds they are going to pull you to AFCENT headquarters?" I had no good answer. I told her we were going to the 20th Fighter Wing and I have no plans beyond that. She knew any move to the 9th Air Force Headquarters meant I would be deployed to combat again...she knew me all too well.

There was something special about being in the combat zone, on the mission day in and day out. It felt like something was missing when I was not there...like I was not making a difference. There was no adrenaline because the stakes were not as high. She knew it, I knew it; but neither of us had any control of the situation. We would go to Shaw and see what happened. Hanging up the phone, I drifted off into a deep sleep.

Throughout the past months we had the chance to host many senior leaders from all of the services. They visited our Airmen and gained a new appreciation for their contribution on the battlefield. Today's visit would be no different. CSM Hill brought the new Senior Enlisted Advisor for Central Command, U.S. Marine Sergeant Major Jeff Morin to Balad. He was a seasoned veteran and a hard core leader. We spent most of the day meeting Airmen who described how they contributed to the overall mission. It was a proud moment for me, seeing our Airmen talk with great pride about their work. At the end of the long day, Sergeant Major Morin shared how impressed he was with Tuskegee Airmen. Following his departure, I headed to the hospital to ensure I started saying goodbye to the Tuskegee Medics. To my surprise, Colonel Smith and the surgical team had decided to induct me into their unofficial BAADASS association. When I asked what it stood for, they said, it's the Balad Air Base Association of Doctors and Surgical Specialists. I was floored, and honored to be thought of in that light by this talented team of medical professionals. Shortly after my visit to the hospital I drifted off to sleep thinking about how lucky I was to be associated with so many great Airmen.

15 June 2007:

The ringing of the phone brought me awake from a haze; I jumped to my feet and tried to gather my bearings. I glanced at the clock and saw that it was 0315. Quickly I thought about when I went to bed, about 0300, so there would be no long night as I had hoped. Picking up the phone

I heard a bunch of noise in the background. Finally the person said, "Chief, this is the command post and we need you to report to the headquarters building ASAP!"

Not again, I thought, not again, and not today. This has to be something different, please let it be something different. In the back of my mind I knew, this was the call, the one we had gotten just eight days before and the one that had occurred so many times; there was no mistaking it by now. I jumped back into uniform, armed and headed out.

Arriving at the entry way, Airman "JJ" Walker knew I was exhausted so he did not try to make any small talk. He snapped to attention and said "They are waiting for you in the conference room, Chief." I greatly appreciated his method, as I probably would not have been much of a conversationalist at the time.

As I walked in, the briefing was already under way and I saw the bad news on the slide, another Airman had been killed in action. The briefer went on with details about an aircraft accident and the possible location, with rescue or recovery efforts underway. Glancing around the room I could see pain on the faces of the aviators. They thought about their own futures and how many more sorties they would complete before the end of their tours. Would something like this happen to them? Would they become another casualty and fail to complete their missions? It was a difficult moment for them. A difficult moment for all of us.

I caught up and found out we lost contact with one of the F-16s shortly after takeoff, and his wingman could not locate him or make radio contact. Someone reported seeing a flash from a loud explosion off the perimeter, so things were coming together. By now we had reports of other aircraft seeing the flash as well, so there was little hope that we could be mistaken and the lost aircraft found.

Details came in of the name and unit of the pilot. Major Kevin Sonnenberg. His name did not sound familiar to me at the moment. I would not expect to know them all since we had so many units, many from the Air National Guard, who rotated in and out so often it was hard enough to keep up with which units were on station. All of the pilots kept pretty low key when they were not flying, because they needed what rest they could get to be sharp for the five-hour sorties they flew.

An hour or so into the incident, footage from an unmanned aerial vehicle confirmed our aircraft crashed and the rescue teams were on scene. The effort began immediately to recover any human remains from the site. Our brave PJ teams would do what they could before sunrise at the risk of being exposed by the sunlight about to take over the skyline. They knew they needed to get the job done and return inside the perimeter soon.

It was an awful day for the wing, and everyone would soon know we had lost another Tuskegee Airman. I had a discussion with Colonel Spider Webb from the operations group who told me to expect some interesting dynamics with this Fallen Airman. Being from an Air National Guard unit, there was a real possibility there were some lifelong friendships and even family relationships within their unit. This one could hit the unit members harder because of those personal and family relationships.

I was glad he brought it to my attention and I began to prepare for the dynamics to follow. Shortly after our discussion, we received word that some remains were located and the PJs were on the way back to the base. After a short period of time at Balad, his remains would move on to Kuwait for further processing and the eventual ride back to Dover Air Force Base and the Air Force Port Mortuary.

Hours later a call came over the radio and we were told to report to the flight line for the dignified transfer of the remains. When we arrived, there were two lines of Airmen, one on each side facing in and leading off the back of the C-130 cargo ramp. The lines stretched for about 200 yards and they were shoulder to shoulder. What normally took place on dignified transfers was the commander, chief and chaplain were the last ones to enter the aircraft. Then following the chaplain's last words we would salute and depart the aircraft. On this day it only seemed right to allow his unit members to be have this honor. We knew there were family members and extremely close lifelong friends present. Saying goodbye to a fellow warrior who was a family member was even harder.

As the remains moved slowly to the ramp, both lines of Airmen snapped to attention and rendered a final salute. It was a long, slow procession, but there was no way anyone would drop their salute. Rendering honors for a brother who had made the ultimate sacrifice was a warrior's highest honor. The flag-draped casket passed slowly through the formation. It was a sobering moment.

I wished we would have been able to have a dignified transfer for each of the Fallen, but due to the locations where they were killed, it often happened at other FOBs or bases and we could have never been there in time to make the transfer. It seemed appropriate that we would have attended all of them, it was just not possible.

I also thought about the impact this moment would have on me and the others who stood beside me. We do so many things when we serve in combat, but few will compare to this. The feeling you get inside, the beating of your heart so strong you can hear it over the jet engine noise, the solemnity of the moment, and knowing you are paying tribute to a fellow American who will never see their family again, is overwhelming. This tragic event was yet another opportunity for our leadership team to exercise courageous leadership through tough times. The strong brotherhood amongst us could not be broken.

Major Sonnenberg was headed to Dover Air Force Base and we would begin to help the unit deal with this loss. As we dropped our salutes, I wondered if anyone ever got used to this part; and hoped nobody could. I never wanted this to become an acceptable part of our mission. It would never be easy. The pain inside was awful, but there was no way we would give up this fight.

Painstakingly, I opened my notebook one more time to write the name of another Fallen Airman. Major Kevin Sonnenberg, killed in action, 15 June 2007. I prayed this would be the last one.

Chief Dearduff, Chief Charlie (Cole 2nd from L) and Chief Rudy Lopez
(far right), discuss treatment of battlefield wounded inside the Balad
Hospital with US Marine Sergeant Major Jeff Morin.

Chief Dearduff is inducted into the Balad Air Base Association of
Doctors and Surgical Specialist (BAADASS) by Colonel Smith and two
young surgeons.

The Fallen Airman Memorial stands in front of the flags at the
headquarters building.

Major Kevin Sonnenberg, killed in action, 15 June 2007.

21
REWARDING EXCELLENCE

17 June 2007:

It was now Father's Day, another holiday away from the family, with thoughts wondering back home before I even rose from the bed. Rather than jump to my feet and move out as normal, I lay in bed and thought about things for a while. It was still early and there was time to get a long run on the treadmill.

I had time to think about my life, my commitments and the sacrifice of my family. It made me contemplate whether or not this had all been worth it. Back when the General was notified of his assignment to Iraq, should I have taken him up on his offer and stayed behind? What would my future have been, what would life have been like? Would the Air Force have given us some premium assignment or would we have stayed in Arizona until retirement? All of those thoughts went through my head and made me challenge my decisions.

The phone rang; I hesitated to answer. I did not want to hear the command post controller as I had on so many other Sundays, telling me it was time to report. Maybe if I let it ring the caller would go away and I would not have to deal with whatever was to come. It stopped ringing and I remained stuck on the bed, feeling paralyzed by my brain.

Minutes later the phone rang again and I knew it must be something important so I decided to reach over and answer. To my surprise it was Chief Jeff Rogers, one of my friends who simply wanted to know if I was going to breakfast on this Sunday morning. Initially I tried to decline and saying I had some things to do, but with his persistence I changed my mind and said I would meet him shortly, but that I was going to go in physical training uniform so I could easily transition to the gym shortly after. I also did not feel like getting into uniform today…only the third day in the last year I did not get into full uniform.

We grabbed chow and had a great conversation. Jeff shared how proud he was to be serving in combat. He also told me that his maintenance Airmen reported to him every time they saw me walking around the flight line with my gear on. Apparently they became worried that something had happened or was about to happen every time they saw me out there. We laughed. Jeff knew I was out there with his Airmen but I always had to be prepared for battle at the drop of a hat. Sitting with him on this holiday solidified an already strong relationship.

The rest of the day was uneventful and went by in a flash. The routine was done and there were many hours left before I could possibly fall to sleep. I called home to talk with the family and once again could feel their pain and genuine concern for this tour to be over. Our conversation was cut short by the operator for some reason so I called back. There was no way I could leave Mags hanging on the phone again with her not knowing what happened.

We talked for a short while, and she asked me to promise her that I would not go out on any more missions and try to talk the General into not flying any more missions. She told Kim I would keep him inside the wire. I laughed and told her that he was setting his own flying schedule and I doubt he would allow me to input. He had reached a personal goal of completing over 100 combat sorties, so I was doubtful he would fly too many more, we just needed him to fly the traditional "fini flight." Even though I knew he would not take my input, I told her I would try.

During these final conversations, I always listened carefully to the things she said because I wanted to grow our relationship even better once home from combat; and a good starting point would be listening better when we were talking on the phone. Before we hung up, she confirmed they would meet me in Philadelphia when we landed. It would be a great way for the General and I to arrive back home, with our families waiting for us together at the point of entry. I was real excited, it felt like a light at the end of the tunnel.

19 June 2007:

I knew this memorial service would be special. A way to honor an Airman, aviator, friend and brother. I had no idea what we were really in for. The tent was full as usual and the music team was ready for their part. The unit members filled the chairs close to the stage and others who came to pay their respects were sitting on the bleachers and standing in and around wherever they could find room. On the screen was a photo of the Fallen Airman, a humble man in his 40s, kind and gentle.

During most of the memorial ceremonies there were testimonials from members who had known the Fallen for the last year or two. Maybe they went to technical training or pre-deployment training together and had formed strong friendships. I knew this one would be different.

The first speaker came to the stage and with a tear in his eye, began by saying, "Kevin and I have known each other since the 2nd grade." Wow, I was floored; emotions flowed. I could not clear the lump in my throat. This Fallen Airman was being honored by his lifelong friend. A guy he went to school with, shared birthday parties with and likely played with in the back yard, dreaming of joining the military together, maybe even flying planes side by side one day. The pain level in this ceremony was indescribable.

Always before you could see and hear crying and heavy breathing in the background because we do care for each other and the loss of any Airman is like losing a family member. But now we were having a memorial with the family members, so the emotions were stronger than ever through the crowd. The next speaker talked about Kevin as a high school wrestler who led the others and brought great character to the team.

Reliability and many other accolades were used to describe this warrior whom we had lost. It was a fantastic ceremony to honor this hero, and I knew once it was over I needed to get his name posted on the memorial immediately so these other unit members could go there and pay their respects. The custom of honoring our Fallen Airmen with a final salute was completed by everyone in the crowd. It took more than an hour to complete, and stretched our emotions to their limits.

I decided to drive around the base to clear my thoughts and figure out how to get everything done before it was time to depart. I headed for the east side of the base and found myself passing the new building for Catfish Ops where we often went to fly out on helicopters. Catfish Ops, started by a Mississippi National Guard unit to maximize helicopter usage, was always a hotbed of movement, day or night. Helicopters landing, taking off, people waiting for movement, or coming to Balad from FOBs and other more distant locations.

By now it was easy to tell who was new in country and who had spent time on the battlefield...a quick glance at their uniform was a dead giveaway. You might think someone completing a tour at a FOB would want to clean up and come in wearing their best uniform. Truthfully, it was their best uniform, and it was as clean as they could get it.

The facilities at Balad were better than anyone could imagine and I liked to remind people how good we had it. Whenever someone lost focus on why we were here, I would find a Soldier or Airman coming in from one of the FOBs and have them sit down for a little perspective discussion. You don't know how good you have it if you have never been out where they have little or nothing. Some of our Airmen needed this, and I took pride in making them get it first hand from a battlefield warrior…it seemed effective.

Although I was not hungry, I decided to stop in at the DFAC on this side of the base because I had seldom been in it to eat and thought a change of pace would be good for my appetite. With all the tragedy in the past 11 months, I had lost most of my appetite and would often eat food as a chore and not for the nourishment or any type of enjoyment. I found the same food was on my plate day after day; most of the DFAC workers knew what I wanted. Food had lost its taste, and I stopped enjoying being in the DFAC, taking my food out on most days.

By the time I was done driving around the rest of the perimeter it was late afternoon. Heading back to the office I knew there was work to be done and the piles of military decorations needing coordination would be higher than I wanted. On the way into the headquarters building I made a stop at the memorial and looked over the names of the Fallen. As I stood there, the song "I Can Only Imagine" just stuck in my head. It would always come back to me as I stood at the memorial and would always be my way of remembering to stop and think about these warriors.

Time went by, and not knowing how long I had been there, I noticed some people were watching me from the door. They seemed hesitant about approaching me, thinking I wanted to be left alone. Finally one of the female Airmen who frequently worked the door came toward me with a worried look on her face. As she came closer I stepped back from the memorial and rendered my salute as I always did.

I turned toward her and asked if everything was ok. Airman Jasmine Winfield looked at me and said, "Chief, I did not want to bother you, but I wanted to ask if I could have my picture taken with you here in front of the memorial?" I was caught off guard, thinking something was wrong when in fact she wanted to honor me by having our picture taken. I flashed back to earlier in the year when this had haunted me after having my photo taken with three of the first four Fallen Airmen. But I had come to grips with this by now and figured her duties would not place her directly in harm's way very often and the chances of her getting killed inside the wire were slim. Our defensive systems were working very well now and it had been 18 months since an Airman was injured and longer since anyone was killed inside the wire.

I told her I would be honored to have my picture taken and here at the memorial would be a great place. The other Airman who was standing at the door ran out and grabbed her camera. We took a few photos and I presented her with a coin. She had been doing a highly professional job guarding our building, and I had often been so busy or concentrating on other matters when I went through that I failed to thank her and the others who were posted there. She smiled like she had just been given a winning lottery ticket. The impact of that presentation was a humbling moment.

I remembered back to a time in 2005 when the General and I took our wives with us to visit an injured Airman at the Brooke Army Medical Center in San Antonio, Texas. We were all there meeting with Kevin who had lost his left leg in a vehicle accident. He was upbeat and looking forward to getting his prosthetic leg, and we all got personal inspiration from his motivation. As the night went on, the General presented a coin to Kevin and then turned and presented one to his dad. While that was going on, Kevin watched the General with undivided attention. The General's actions would impact Kevin for a long time.

Later when they returned to their room, Kim spoke to him in a clear and concise manner. "Did you see the way Kevin was looking at you when you presented your coin to his dad?" The General had not really noticed because he was focusing on Kevin's dad at the time. She said, "He was looking at you like you were very important. It made me realize that you are a very important person, but I never want you to forget that it's because of the position you hold and not some other reason." The General looked at Kim and in his own funny way said, "Kim, I've been trying to tell you how important I was for many years." She laughed briefly, and then said, "Just remember how powerful you are because of the position, and don't ever screw it up."

That conversation was all I could think about at this moment. I knew as the Command Chief of the 332d Air Expeditionary Wing and the enlisted leader of the modern day Tuskegee Airmen, it was my honor to present coins to deserving Airmen. She told me she had received other coins during her tour but this one would be very meaningful to her because of the time she spent around me in combat.

She thanked me and the two of them walked away smiling and looking closely at the coin. Before today I had no idea how much impact those presentations could have, and now knew I owed many more and had few days to get caught up. To this point I had probably been way too stingy with my coins and there were so many more deserving warriors who would get a coin they earned before I left.

Inside the office, I was reminded of a ceremony coming up and it would take place on the TOD. R2 and the executive officer wanted to know if I had completed the script I was supposed to prepare for the presentation of awards. That caught me off guard and I needed to regroup. Knowing I had things to do was one thing, but remembering what those things were was quite another.

R2 gave me the material and informed me we were giving out Iraq Campaign Medals to the Wing Staff Airmen and the crowd would be huge. He also said we needed the citation to read and the ceremony was in less than two hours. We had a goal of presenting those medals to everyone before they left, erasing past precedence of most people going home without recognizing their service in combat.

Back in July of 2006 we decided that presenting the Iraq Campaign Medal and the Air Force Expeditionary Service Ribbon to each and every qualifying Airman was something we would do throughout the year. The General would specifically present them to the wing staff members along with the Chief of Staff. Since this was the end of the tour for the group commanders, he would also be making those presentations. Group and squadron commanders would then present medals to the Airmen in their units at appropriate ceremonies. It seemed like a small thing to some, but to receive a combat campaign medal from your commander, while still deployed to combat, was really a big deal. I knew this would be a great moment for these Airmen and from previous tours, there was sufficient feedback to confirm it meant something special.

Creating a proper citation to document all of the accomplishments by the team was an easy thing to do. This team was setting records with all they accomplished. The draft came together easily and within minutes I had a draft to the executive officer for his review. Before the end of the first hour we completed the citation and made copies, then prepared the medals for the ceremony.

A significant amount of Tuskegee Airmen were gathered in formation. This ceremony would take some time to accomplish and we were worried about having so many people exposed for a long period of time on the TOD. We would need to be efficient in our execution. General Rand would have much to say to this group. I also knew this would feel like the first real "going away" speech.

The formation was called to attention as General Rand came up the stairs to the TOD. As the General moved to his position, I could hear the sound of a C-17 cargo aircraft landing to the east directly behind me. There were helicopters landing at the hospital landing pad to the west of our location. In the far distance we could hear the roar of the mighty F-16 Viper drawing on full power to take off with the maximum load of weapons to take combat power to the enemy. The wind blew lightly, and sun was burning in the clear blue sky. I began to read the citation: "Attention to Orders."

"Members of the 332d Air Expeditionary Wing staff distinguished themselves in service to the United States Air Force while assigned in the country of Iraq for 120 consecutive days in support of Operation Iraqi Freedom. Displaying bravery and confidence in their collective effort to meet the United States government's mission of helping Iraq transition to democracy while under the regular threat from indirect fire attacks on the installation, members of the wing staff directly contributed to the successful accomplishment more than 8,200 combat sorties and the delivery of munitions during 137 kinetic strikes and over 16,000 rounds of ammunition fired.

"Staff members provided service and support during the establishment of a new Air Expeditionary Group with nine A-10 attack aircraft and over 400 personnel, the addition of an airborne surveillance platform that completed over 3000 hours of surveillance on dangerous roads, and further increased the largest combat search and rescue squadron assembled to include 10 rescue helicopters used in recovery and rescue operations.

"Wing staff members supported the efforts of more than 1,700 "in Lieu of" forces at 48 forward operating bases and over 4,000 combat support Airmen assigned to five major installations located throughout the country of Iraq. Working hand in hand with the US Army's 13th Sustainment Command (Expeditionary), members of the staff contributed to the sustainment of eight critical airfields, helped the Iraqi Air Force build its military flying squadron and mitigated more than 800 ground convoys through precision delivery of 23,000 passengers and 600,000 tons of critical combat cargo.

"Additionally, staff members provided direct combat support to hundreds of distinguished visitors including senior military and political leaders, each time contributing to creation of a positive image for the entire wing. The distinctive accomplishments of the members of the 332d Air Expeditionary Wing's staff brings great credit upon the United States Air Force and they are hereby awarded the Iraq Campaign Medal."

At the end of the reading the General moved to the first person in the formation and presented the medal, pinning it on their left breast pocket. He moved to each and every one, taking the time to personally thank them for their service and sacrifice. I could tell that each of them was genuinely moved by this act by a passionate commanding officer. After he presented the last one he came back to the front, thanked everyone again and then told me to disperse the flight to go and eat the BBQ prepared for them.

You would have thought most people would have headed to the BBQ line immediately and grabbed chow, but most of them wanted to thank the General and Colonel Renfrow. Then many of them came to me and asked for a copy of the citation. Obviously they enjoyed this ceremony and receiving their campaign medals before leaving was a highlight for many. The power of public recognition would go a long way on this day.

I thought back to the ceremonies we did for the previous rotations of Airmen on the wing staff. None of them seemed to be as meaningful to the people involved. I was not sure why this was the case, but thought that maybe it was a matter of my own perspective. I may have overlooked the emotion of the previous ones and now I was paying close attention. My emotions ran high.

The group commanders and group chiefs appeared to be touched by this presentation. They spent an entire year serving with us and suffering losses right by our side.

The rest of the day went by in a blur, and I never did find time for all those decorations needing coordination. I told R2 I would need to take them to my room and work on them through the night and get caught up. Knowing me well, he said there was a problem with some of them and there were only about 30 to review tonight. He was protecting me, knowing if I took all of them to my quarters I would spend the whole night reading and never get any sleep. He was right, so it was a good thing he was looking out for me.

Four hours of sleep, a hot shower, a quick breakfast and I was back in the office and ready to go for another fast paced day as we neared the end of our tour and got things ready for our replacement leadership team. I made a commitment that I would spend the whole day in my office to get everything done and nothing was going to stop me.

Sitting quietly catching up on the work piled high on my desk, the insurgents decided to have a say in my plan. "Incoming, Incoming, Incoming" came blaring over the loud speakers. Everyone in the building hit the floor and took cover. The first mortar round hit close to the headquarters building and people were worried. A second round landed even closer and our comfort level was shrinking. Was this going to be it, survive eleven months and then get hit by a stray mortar round that was not even aimed at me?

I felt the need to respond and check on people around the base as I always did. No matter how long I was there, and no matter how many insurgent attacks we saw, my Defender mentality kicked in and I had to go see what was going on. There were reports of problems at the pool over by the Base Exchange so I headed that way.

When I arrived I found one of the Defenders who was first on scene. He had just talked with one of the civilian employees who manages the pool. It seems she was quite shaken and was trying to gather her thoughts. I asked him if she had been injured and needed any assistance. He said she was not hurt, but was quite shaken. He told me she ate her lunch at her desk every day since her arrival six months ago. This day, for some unknown reason, she decided to go out and get some lunch and not sit at her desk. I looked at him and said, "OK, so what is the rest of the story?" He laughed shyly and said, "Chief, that rocket hit the building, went through the wall and exploded on her desk!"

I did not know what to say, or if anything needed to be said. Fate was a powerful thing, and we all took a moment to take in what just happened. She walked back into the pool office with us and showed us where she was sitting just before departing for lunch. I believe she would have been killed instantly had she remained in place. I leaned toward her and offered a hug, one she gladly accepted.

Back in the office I closed the door in order to get a few minutes to myself. I needed to soak in the moment. Notebook open, I reviewed the list which now contained twelve names of Fallen Airmen from the wing. Major Kevin Sonnenberg had to be the last one we would add to the list. It had to be.

Blackhawk helicopters from Catfish Ops preparing for another long day
of flying around Iraq.

Iraq Campaign Medals are prepared for presentation to the staff members
of the 332d Air Expeditionary Wing.

General Rand speaking to the wing staff members during a presentation of the Iraq Campaign Medal.

General Rand and Colonel Renfrow taking photos with wing staff members following an Iraq Campaign Medal presentation on the TOD.

22

BROTHERS IN BLOOD

Monday came and the final weeks of preparation were in full gear. The day started with a visit to the Defenders guardmount and some well-deserved recognition. I gave out some coins, thanked the entire team, and updated them on the current threats to the base and events from around the battlefield. I asked them to maintain their highest state of alert as the statistics showed that insurgent activity was at an all-time high for Operation Iraqi Freedom. I told them, "Your actions on post today could save the life of a fellow Airman, a Soldier or civilian, and I am counting on you to be ready and get the job done no matter how hard it is." They gave me a great "HOOAH" letting me know they understood and accepted the challenge.

Based on the limited time we had remaining, there would be limited travel outside the wire to the other FOBs and no more combat missions. It was truly time to knuckle down and get the administrative stuff done once and for all. I also knew we were planning to hold a going away event for the group commanders, Colonel Renfrow, General Rand and myself. It was planned for Saturday, 23 June, and would take place on the TOD complete with food.

The event was planned to be a simple celebration of Tuskegee Brothers who would be linked for their lives by the trials and tribulations of combat. Colonel Renfrow told me he would take on the duty of organizing since he would be the last one to leave, about a month after we did. He knew we were working other issues to get ready, and he would likely have more time to make it all work. I asked R2 and several NCOs from the front office to jump on board and help out. Finally, I could attend and enjoy an event without having to do any planning or coordination...something not often experienced. I headed back to the office and decided to close the door and take it easy for a little while.

"Incoming, Incoming, Incoming" came the alarm from the giant voice within minutes of the door closing. I knew the alarm was coming from our sector so I hit the floor as was required. I didn't want to. I didn't want to be constrained once more by the insurgents who were not courageous enough to stand toe to toe with us, but kept shooting from those far off distances hoping to hurt or kill Americans they did not even know or see. "Boom!" hit the first round and it was close. Moments later a second round, then a third. Being inside with the hard walls I could not tell where they had landed, but certainly they were inside the wire and maybe close to one of the housing areas, the flight line or even the hospital.

As I tried to leave the building the guards asked me not to. They said those rounds were close and there may be more coming. The radio traffic was chaotic and there were reports coming in from many locations. I stopped, thinking of my wife and kids and decided to go into the command post and check out the situation from there. Inside the team of controllers was hard at work pinning down three points of impact while taking calls from multiple parts of the base. They told me we had at least one round hit on or near the air traffic control tower and contact was cut off. While they continued to work I thought I could help by walking outside and looking at the tower which was about 200 meters away, almost directly in front of the building. If it had been hit and damaged or was on fire, I may be able to see it from there. Then I figured I would go on the TOD and observe, giving me a better vantage point.

Once on the TOD, everything appeared OK at the tower and the damage was minor to the structure. It may have hit their communications, or maybe they were just so busy trying to control aircraft they could not get back to the command post. I reported what I saw and shortly thereafter, they confirmed they had contact with the tower and they were all secure. Minor damage was caused to the lower level, some glass was broken out of the windows, but fortunately nobody was in the area when the rounds hit.

The controllers had taken cover on the floor but had jumped back up immediately as they had aircraft on final approach and others ready for takeoff. They had to get on the radio and do their job. They showed great courage standing there in front of those large windows as well-identified targets, and faced danger head on. By the end of the first hour after the attack, they were 100% operational and all controllers were hard at work cleaning up the mess. The Air Traffic Controllers used the same level of resiliency in handling the attack which enabled them to perform more than 640,000 air traffic movements during the past 12 months. An incredible operational tempo.

I remained on the TOD and watched the actions of the first responders for an hour. It brought a different perspective being able to watch from this view of the events as they transpired. Defenders, Firefighters, and many others responded to the scenes where these three rockets had landed, and all of them showed the true courage it takes to respond to the scene while others were running from it. Finally I headed back inside and planned to get back to work.

"Incoming, Incoming, Incoming" came the sound of the giant voice again. It seemed like we just had an attack, could this be happening again? By the time the attack was over seven more rounds made direct impact inside the wire at multiple points around the base. It was not the worst attack from the year, but it was close. I pondered why the attacks were growing in size and frequency and thought hard about wearing protective gear even inside the wire just so I could survive. I also knew there were many new Airmen and Soldiers around the base, and this large scale attack would shake their confidence early in the tour, so I had some confidence building to do.

After about two hours, all responders had cleared from their areas, and the post-attack teams were complete with cleanup actions where the rounds damaged buildings or roadways. Replacing the windows on the tower would take some time, but they placed plywood in the openings for a short-term fix. Finally, this attack was over and we could find some peace for a short while.

I thought back to the morning guardmount and what I had asked the Defenders, wishing I had done the same with the Firefighters and other first responders. I knew they stood tall in the face of danger today, and they more than met the challenge I had put in front of them. I was a proud Chief, walking tall with my tired shoulders back, knowing the enemy had a vote, but today their vote did not count.

The rest of this week was set aside to go around and thank all those agencies and organizations who provided support throughout the year. This would be a fun week, saying thanks to so many, handing out coins and letters, and giving lots of handshakes and battle hugs to so many deserving people. Somehow this felt therapeutic. Maybe I could not change the pain I was feeling, but I could bring some positive moments into my life in order to counter the negative. Knowing I would probably miss someone along the way, I dedicated myself to not passing by anyone without greeting them and telling them thanks. Even if they were brand new to the wing, I would thank them for being prepared and coming forward to serve in combat.

20 June 2007:

The Master Chief from the US Navy Customs detachment invited me to participate in a time-honored ceremony. The Master Chief said he would appreciate a visit to his team before I departed and he would share some key points about Navy tradition during the visit. The customs team had significantly improved everything from process times to customs and courtesies, and I wanted to thank them personally. I asked if I could hand out coins, and he agreed. He also explained the impact a formal letter from a general officer could have on a Sailor's promotion opportunity. He appreciated the gesture of my coins, but asked if the letters could be presented instead.

I explained the request to the General and he agreed. Arriving at the customs yard, I was greeted by the Master Chief Jeff Sergeant, who explained that I would be "whistled aboard the ship." Although there was no real ship, they had fashioned their entryway to resemble a Navy ship and they used it for Sailor entry only; it helped teach the young Sailors about Navy traditions. I was thrilled, but a little unsure about my role. He told me what I needed to do and we shoved off.

We started up the ramp and the whistle sounded to announce my arrival. I saluted as I walked and entered into the galley. It was a great feeling and seeing those Sailors standing in line formation was quite impressive. Moving to the front of the formation, I spoke to them for a minute and thanked them for the great work they had done to improve the customs process, impacting everyone who passed through Balad at the end of their combat tours. Then we walked the line and pass out letters.

For good measure, I also presented them one of my coins as my personal thanks for giving us their all. Pride was on all of their faces and some of them liked the coin better than the letter. As we finished and departed under formal procedures again, the Master Chief thanked me for spending time recognizing his team.

This ceremony made my day and brought a smile to my face that would be hard to displace. The rest of the day was spent visiting all types of organizations, Army, civilian and contractors. Similar feelings were gained from each experience, and it felt good to bring joy to others.

Departing the final engagement and heading back to the headquarters, I thought about what had just happened. We made great progress in forming the joint environment around the base and were doing more and more with the other services; sharing responsibilities, and attending each other's ceremonies. I wondered what it would be like in another year, maybe two. Maybe the base would be operated by a single command authority.

There were so many things changing and it was all happening fast. The Base Exchanges were selling flat screen TVs as large as 42 inches, the restaurants and coffee shops were selling products nobody ever expected to see in a combat zone; and the entertainment shows from the USO were filled with world-class entertainment. The last few rows of living tents were being taken down, all being replaced with trailers to improve the living conditions.

Driving back to the building I went past the area where a new Taco restaurant was being built right next to the Air Force Clinic. For me, any time I wanted to have tacos I could go to the DFAC, where they almost always had a full taco bar, and it was free as part of my combat benefits. For some reason the young crowd would take a day or two of their per diem and go buy tacos or pizza from the vendors. I never could understand it and never once partook; but on this day I was intrigued. Driving by that lot where there was a construction fence, a sign had been posted. It read, "Coming Soon! TGI Fridays!" Now that sounded great, but wait... this is the combat zone and we did not need sit-down restaurants for people to visit. There were plenty of food choices and this was going overboard. I planned to hit the office, call the AAFES Manager and find out what was going on.

Arriving at the door I asked if R2 was in the building, and they told me he was. I asked to have him come and see me right away. R2 arrived and I asked him to call AAFES and get me an appointment with the manager because I needed to know why we were getting so crazy that we needed to have full-fledged restaurants on this base.

He began to laugh and I wondered why. He had this big grin on his face and said, "Chief, did you see the sign for TGI Fridays?" I told him I was not happy about it. Again he laughed. So I asked what the deal was and why he was laughing. Having a hard time getting it out, he said it was a joke someone was playing and it really was not a construction zone for the restaurant, but simply a sitting area they were building for the taco restaurant. We laughed and I went on about my day. I needed that laugh, as my stress level was at an all-time high. R2 knew when I was stressed and always helped bring me back. Like Frankie and Michael before him, they were extremely important to me in getting through this year. I valued their support and loyalty.

The previous day behind me I felt like something special was going to happen today. Not being sure what it would be, I just went about things and kept my eyes wide open. Passing through entry control points, I took special notice of the smiles and professionalism of the Defenders. I watched as Airmen walked down the streets in their PT Uniforms, shoulders back, displaying pride in who they were and the organization they were a part of. By going around and spreading positive energy, I was getting it back in many more ways. Things were starting to go well.

On my way to the fire station to meet with the firefighters I was interrupted when the command post called me to return to the General's office and meet with him immediately. I knew he just completed a combat sortie and thought he might have something to share with me about the mission. Once inside his office I could tell from his expression it was not good, but somehow felt comforted that it was not a death. He told me that reports had just arrived about some mortar rounds landing inside the camp at our unit location on the Baghdad International Airport yesterday and there were some badly wounded Airmen being medically evacuated to the Balad hospital. We made plans to meet at the hospital again once word of their arrival came.

His red truck came around the corner near the emergency department where we always parked as I stood talking with Colonel Masterson and Chief Charley Cole the medical chief. They updated the General about the two Airmen being treated. While both were stable, they said the injuries were severe and we should prepare ourselves. Both had facial lacerations, and one had a sucking chest wound, one of the worst you could have on the combat battlefield. He said both of them were breathing through tubes, so it would be hard to communicate with them.

Although we planned to pin Purple Heart medals on them, Colonel Masterson informed said they may not even be conscious and aware of what was happening. General Rand would find a way to make the ceremony dignified and meaningful even under those circumstances. This time would be different, so we all walked quietly into the ICU with low expectations, other than awarding this medal to some badly wounded Americans.

At the ICU the charge nurse told us we had two NCOs who were in their 40s and both were from the same National Guard unit back home. They received shrapnel wounds from a mortar round that landed in their vehicle maintenance complex, and these were the worst two of several who were injured. She told us one of the NCOs, named Paddison, was still unconscious and his prognosis was not good, yet they were not giving up hope. The other NCO was doing better and was able to respond to their demands, making eye contact and breathing on his own. He was not able to talk, but he definitely knew what was going on around him in the hospital.

With that knowledge, the General took the lead and we went to Paddison first. As he always did, the General got down real close to this wounded Airman and whispered words only they could hear. After a short pause, which told me he was saying a quiet prayer, the General stood back up and placed the Purple Heart medal on the sheet near his heart. He pinned it on so it would not fall off, even though the medical staff would have to remove it later and place it with his other belongings before he was transported.

Shortly thereafter, we made our way over to the other wounded Airman and began the same ritual. As the General finished speaking to Sergeant Juliano and stepped back to place the medal on his bed sheet, the hardy NCO reached out his badly wounded arm with several tubes sticking out of it, and shook the General's hand, then attempted to salute him. We all got a little choked up when we saw what he was trying to do, and the General gently grabbed his hand and helped him before placing the wounded arm back by his side. Each of us in the room held our breath and knew we were witnessing a courageous warrior battle through tough pain and still have the resiliency to render a military salute to the General. It was awe-inspiring.

Each of us took turns speaking to Juliano and wishing him well for his recovery and the trip home. As the last man was done, we all stood back and gave him some breathing room until the General noticed something about him. It looked like he was waving his hand again and trying to get our attention. By now everyone else had moved on and it was just the General and I standing there. The General said, "Chief, I think he is trying to tell us something." And then it hit him, this warrior was signaling to us that he wanted to write something to us since he could not talk. He said, "Chief, get him something to write with."

Now there are plenty of things lying around in an ICU room, even this one made from tents and field-expedient furniture. But there were not a lot of pens and paper lying around for such an occasion. Then I noticed the chart hanging at the end of the bed and the pen attached by a string. I grabbed it, turned the chart over and handed the pen and clipboard to the General and said, "Here sir, have him write what he wants on here, it can't hurt anything."

The General placed the pen in his hand very gently and closed his fingers around it tight enough so he could hold on. Then he placed the clipboard so he could see what he was writing. It was turned away from us so we had no idea what he was writing. After a painful period that seemed like minutes, he laid the pen down and looked exhausted.

The General looked at the paper and held his breath; he turned it toward me and revealed the one word written on the paper. "Paddison?" All he wanted to know was the status of his buddy that he knew was with him when the attack happened. We were stunned, and I had a cold chill run through my body like none before. The General's voice rose to a level of excitement and he said, "Didn't they tell you? Paddison made it and is in the bed right across from you. He is doing OK and is expected to be alive and well when you both get home. In fact, you will both be going to Germany on the same medical evacuation flight."

I watched in near disbelief as our wounded warrior smiled through the tubes and wrappings then closed his eyes and passed out cold. I now knew why this day would be so special. My feelings were once again validated and I knew clearly why we served here. It's not about the mission of creating democracy for this country, and it's not about some noble cause like Duty, Honor and Country. It's really about the man next to you in the same foxhole. It's about the fellow Airman you serve with, their families and their futures. This was a special day.

Chief Dearduff meeting with a Defender while conducting post visits prior to a helicopter ride to Baghdad.

Chief Dearduff attending Security Forces Guardmount prior to the Defenders taking post for the evening to defend Bald Air Base.

Chief Dearduff and Command Sergeant Major Rob Hall, from Balad Air Base's own US Army Cavalry Unit.

One of several vehicles damaged inside the vehicle maintenance lot at Baghdad where Sergeants Paddison and Juliano were injured.

23
THE PERFECT AIRMAN

Friday morning, and the end of the week brought much concern about the time we had left to finish things up. With the Red Tail going away coming Saturday night, I wanted to get some things together to present to the commanders for their cooperation and support of the enlisted men and women of the wing. There was one thing I had that was unique and was deserving of giving out to the commanders as my way of saying thanks. My brother Jeff, who has been a great supporter of mine, my family, and the military in general is a part-time song writer who was dabbling in music and producing songs. He had worked up some songs and created a music CD that he sent me and there were enough copies. I could think of no better candidates to receive these than those in the Tuskegee Brotherhood. The commanders and chiefs I served with during this year.

Over the next week there would be promotion ceremonies, US Army Change of Command ceremonies, the opening of the trash incinerator and so many more things.

There was one thing I had been working on throughout the year and had tried to share with others. For each of my deployments in the past, we always did things as a unit to leave a legacy for those who followed. I called it, "Leave your name on the wall." Everyone understood it was intended to show you were there, improved the place in some way, and completed your mission. There were many ways it could happen and there were examples all over the base.

The Army was great at this, leaving their unit markings on the large concrete barriers located in front of their buildings and in their compounds. In the past two years the Air Force had caught on and that energy was spreading fast around the base, leaving a great impression of the pride in all of the units within the wing. I contemplated my legacy and what I would do to leave my name on the wall. There had been many hours of sleepless thought in my quarters wondering what would be right and how I would create it.

Maybe I should just let my legacy be whatever it was in the eyes of others. I did not need a visible or tangible item to leave behind my contribution to this wing and this war. It was by the grace of God my name was not on the memorial. Maybe this was better left alone. Sitting in my office, I opened an envelope which had been on my desk for several days. There were no markings on it, so I wondered if it was even for me. Inside I found an 8x10 photo of Major Kevin Sonnenberg. I knew then we needed to put the photos of our Fallen Airmen on the wall inside of the headquarters. Many months ago I had begun hanging photos of the wing's Fallen Airmen. The photo display needed work and time was running out to get it right.

I took down all the photos, found better frames and prepared them for remounting. But looking closely at the wall, I noticed the entire room needed paint; and we needed to improve the look of the room by adding the 332 AEW and AFCENT official symbols on the wall for video teleconferences. Now we could have an impressive background when talking with higher headquarters. This is how we would leave our name on the wall.

23 June 2007:

This should be an easy day with not much to accomplish and a small celebration to end the night. The weather was great for this part of the summer, not as hot as normal. It seemed like the perfect day. I departed the building to go around the base there were many people yet to see and thank. My excitement was soon interrupted. "All Red Tails report to the Command Post." No, it can't be, I thought. Not again, not today, and not so close to the end.

I grabbed my notebook and walked back in, slamming the door of my truck behind me. I got to the conference room before anyone else and decided to go into the command post and get the details now. I could not wait to hear about another lost Airman; I wanted to know now if something was wrong. I hoped I was.

Entering the command post I could tell it was not good as each of the controllers and even the officer in charge were busy taking calls and reporting information. As the next few minutes passed I pieced together the information I needed, and could not stand to have a conversation with anyone so I walked out.

Entering the conference room I moved to the wall and stared at the faces of the 12 Fallen Airmen and I briefly spoke to each one. Having committed their names and faces to memory, I often found myself talking to them as if they were in the room. Since there were now others in the room I kept my conversations inside and apologized to each of them for having to add another warrior to their wall.

Soon the briefing began and all the Red Tails were present. The briefer went through the information. Remembering what General Rand said to all of us following the last casualty notification, I paid close attention to everything going on in the room. The briefer stated we lost another Defender. Senior Airmen Jason Nathan from the Police Training Team in Tikrit. I was still so caught up in my anger that the name did not sink in right away. I was already dealing with pain and agony for his family, and the units he belonged to back home and deployed. Then Colonel Jackson stood up and brought clarity to the situation. He said, "General, this Airman was present during our last visit to Tikrit;" another kick in the gut. We took photos with most of the teams there, and he would certainly be in one of them.

The briefer went on about what a dependable Airman Nathan was and how all of his teammates and others from his home station considered him "The perfect Airman." This would be the 13th Airman lost under our leadership during this year and our fifth Airman lost in the month of June.

Anger crept into my heart. I had not felt this angry since we lost Major Gilbert. I wanted to mount up and head to Tikrit right away and find the bastards who took his life. I really wanted to leave right away…I was serious.

Before the briefer finished he said it was possible that Airman Nathan's remains would be coming to Balad tonight and we would have a dignified transfer event. Many in the room felt relief because we could exercise the honor of participating in this battlefield tribute. He was a great Airman and deserved our time and attention.

Someone interrupted and mentioned the going away for tonight and wanted to make sure the times were deconflicted. The General promptly said we would stop anything we were doing to participate in the dignified transfer detail, no matter what, and no matter the time. His tone was firm and there was no question when we all departed that this was the number one priority for the day or night, regardless of what we had planned.

The time had arrived for the going away and we all started to gather on the TOD. Major Kelly and others were preparing food for the event and it appeared everything was in order. The atmosphere was somber and it was easy to tell that all Red Tail commanders and chiefs in attendance had our minds on many other things, mostly Airman Nathan and the Defenders from his detachment.

Colonel Jackson was there, but it was obvious he was deeply affected and his mind was in another place. When the General went over to him and asked how he was doing, the Colonel told him, "We will survive and get through this. The unit is resilient." The General asked him if he needed to go and take care of anything else or go and be with the unit. Colonel Jackson said he had dispatched the squadron commander and the first sergeant to go to Tikrit tonight and they should be there anytime, having boarded a C-17 some time ago for the 45-minute flight. He wanted to be there for the transfer and then would head to visit the unit the next day. He told the General we should go on with the event and if the transfer came in he would tell us immediately.

Colonel Renfrow had the lead on this event and he did his best to sound excited, but he too was deeply affected by this loss. He was a tremendous warrior who knew the pain of loss. Over the years, working in special operations units he had lost many brothers and now he had been down this road with us. He was a man who took each loss to heart but continued to work his part with passion.

Sitting with Colonel Renfrow at a leadership luncheon earlier in the year, someone had asked him for his leadership philosophy. He could have taken that in many directions, but he chose wisely to talk about standards and how important they are in combat operations. He said, "You never know the value of a thing, no matter how small it starts out. The little things can make all the difference in the world." It was a simple philosophy, but made great sense in the business we are in.

He got us started and we began giving out some gifts. I could see some movement in the back, but did not know who it was. Colonel Renfrow went on and all of the presentations were made. He offered the microphone to me to say a few words. As I started, Colonel Jackson came back up with a strange look on his face. We could not tell if he was laughing or there was some other emotion in play. The General told me to hold on and asked, "Larry, what's the matter?"

He said "Sir, if I may, there is some good news and some bad news. First, the good news is we were informed that Airman Nathan had just been selected for early promotion to Senior Airman below the zone. The bad was just relayed to me from Major Kenneth Woodcock. Apparently, the commander and first sergeant did not arrive at Tikrit as planned. In fact, they got on a plane headed for Lakenheath, England, and are now in the final minutes of flight, preparing to land in England with their full combat load and all battle equipment."

Everyone looked around, nobody wanting to move or say a word. The General laughed and said, "You have got to be kidding me." He wanted to get to the bottom of what happened, but it was done and he had to start working to get two of his battle Airmen back from England right away. He also stated he would send Major Woodcock to be with the unit and every attempt would be made to make sure he got on the right aircraft. There was controlled laughter by most in attendance. We just could not believe what had taken place in the hours since finding out we lost another Airman. Frustration had set in and we all knew things were out of our control. Laughter turned to tears for me so I quickly walked off to a dark corner of the TOD to catch my breath.

Most of us skipped the food portion, not having much of an appetite on this day for any kind of food or celebration. I apologized to the team for having to make all that food, and told them to enjoy it themselves, or we could deliver it out to some of the folks on post or the flight line.

Sitting in my office looking at photos from the Tikrit visit, I found Airman Nathan. There he was, as described, the "perfect Airman." His gear was in order; he was standing tall, but standing in the back, not wanting the attention from the visiting commander and chief. He stood there proudly and the photo reflected a humble young man.

After losing yet another brother, I could not shake the feeling of losing a family member. My mind searched for ways I could have kept him out of harm's way, protected him from danger, but knew it was not possible, this was combat. Had I listened intently when they told me what they needed and how they were operating, or had I missed something along the way that I could have taken on and advocated for, leading to the successful mission completion and reduction of casualties? I wanted so badly for Jason to have one more chance, but I could not take it back.

The call came in about the dignified transfer, and all you could see were trucks driving as fast as we safely could to get there. The line at the end of the ramp was long in the dark warm night air, and nobody cared how hard we were sweating from the heat being produced by the C-130 engines still running during the transfer actions.

The flag draped casket was moved from the transport vehicle onto the plane with all of us standing at attention, saluting as it passed. Once the casket was inside, we invited everyone in the formation to enter the cargo bay. The chaplain conveyed his thoughts and asked us all to pray with him. He delivered words of prayer with perfect emphasis and ended with the Psalm that always grabbed my heart. "Yea though I walk through the valley of the shadow of death, I will fear no evil..." The 23rd Psalm had become way too familiar with each of us. We saluted and slowly departed. No more words were said.

As we drove away, the General came on the radio and told everyone the going away event was over and we would reassemble on another night with another plan. It brought great relief, nobody was in the mood to celebrate. We just lost one more Airman.

24 June 2007:

Word came across the radio for all Red Tails to gather at the Communications Squadron building tonight for the going away celebration. None of us were in the celebratory mood, but the General knew better and he always had things in the right perspective.

When we arrived at the building, we were directed to the roof where the Communications Airmen had arranged an outdoor theater for watching movies. There was a smell of popcorn in the air and some cold drinks in a cooler by a series of foldout chairs. Once everyone had arrived, the General announced that this was our farewell event. He went on to share how he felt about the Tuskegee Brothers in attendance. When he told us we were about to finish the event by watching the motion picture, *The Tuskegee Airmen*, a lump formed in my throat that would not clear. For a few moments, it all felt better and my pain seemed to subside.

Here we were gathered, all of the commanders and chiefs who had been through this entire year or represented those who had served and finished, celebrating our tours by solidifying the bond of this brotherhood. And what better way than to watch the movie that clearly depicted the reason we had such a great legacy to follow? I had not seen the movie before tonight, even though I had a copy and planned on many occasions to watch it...the enemy just never let it happen. I was happy to sit back, take it in, and just relax for a couple of hours.

As we sat for the start, something hit me. It was not just the movie or the gathering of brothers on this roof. It was a whole scene, an entire complex mix of sights, sounds and emotions brought together with the smell of combat all around. As we sat preparing to watch the movie, two F-16 fighters pushed the throttle forward and screamed down the runway with a full load of combat munitions, rising into the night's dark sky with full afterburners, lighting a streak of fire across the sky. On the far runway we could hear a C-17 cargo jet landing with enough force to indicate it was full of critical supplies or vehicles for some far off mission. And overhead, we could hear the thump of rotors from two HH-60 rescue helicopters heading into the hospital to deliver patients from the battlefield. This was a movie scene in and of itself, one even the greatest of movie producers could not replicate, and one only a few in this world will ever get to experience. No words were said, but I could tell we were all experiencing this glorious moment. This was surreal and I cried as my heart ached and my mind raced.

For the next two hours we sat quietly, taking in the legacy being played out on the screen and each to ourselves pondering what we had been through together, and certainly wondering what we could have done better to ensure those 13 Airmen had made it home. Our brotherhood was solidified on this night, something to cherish for many years. We made a pact that someday we would meet again and have an experience like this.

Walking back to my truck, the gravity of the moment stopped me in my tracks. From previous combat tours there were bonds and friendships that would carry on forever, but nothing to this depth. It felt good to be a part of this brotherhood. It would impact the rest of my life.

26 June 2007:

Another long day of completing administrative work, visits to work centers and reviews of combat decoration packages was done. Colonel Renfrow and I grabbed a cup of coffee and sat down so we could talk about our Tuskegee Airmen and how impressed we were by all they were doing in the face of danger. The General entered the building after flying a combat mission, so we went to see how he was doing. I walked in first and he said, "Chief, do you know what I just did?"

"Yes sir, you just flew a great combat sortie for your nation and brought airpower to bear on the enemy."

He laughed and said, "Yes I did. But more importantly, I just flew my final combat sortie."

I stopped in my tracks and said, "Sir, your final sortie? Isn't it supposed to be some big to-do with photos and all the commanders and chiefs around to help you celebrate?"

He laughed again and said, "Well, I pulled one over on everybody, because that was my last one and there is no celebration, just one old fighter pilot walking away after his last time in the skies over combat."

I said to him, "Boss that is perfect. To walk off into the sunset with no fanfare, no public affairs and not taking time away from anyone. His actions showed everyone how serious he was about this mission right up to the very end and never once did we make this about you or me, or anything other than the mission and those Airmen who perform the critical pieces each and every day."

His humility made a huge statement, a lesson that he often taught by his own actions with few words. In the privacy of his office, I grabbed my General in a combat hug and thanked him for all that he had done to lead our wing.

29 June 2007:

Once again the Tuskegee Airmen gathered in the Town Hall to honor an Airman for service and sacrifice. This memorial was supported like all the others, and the crowd exceeded capacity. Defenders stood tall in formation outside the building, posted on all corners and in vehicles with heavy machine guns mounted as a tribute to their fallen brother. OSI agents were out in full support and so many others who neither knew Jason nor had any other connection with Defenders, all came out to show their love and support.

The service went exactly as planned with personal and touching testimonials from his detachment commander and superintendent. They continued telling the same stories about the "Perfect Airman" we heard from his fellow Defenders. Tears were flowing freely among the crowd and the visible absence of the fourth member on stage in the Missing Man Fire Team punctuated a touching ceremony.

In 22 years as a Security Force Member, I never lost a fellow Defender in the line of duty. During previous combat tours with Airmen in harm's way, I never lost a Defender. This year we lost three of them in combat and the reality of that thought was a pain I could not make go away. Others took notice and asked me how I was doing. There was no good answer to share with them, so I just thanked them and moved on. Most would think I was crazy, but holding it in made me feel better somehow, and I had to figure out how to deal with this on my own. It went beyond the pain of loss as a leader, because all of the Airmen held a place in my heart, not just the Defenders.

When the ceremony was done, we took our place at the front of the line and stood tall in front of the battlefield cross built for Airman Nathan, saluted and approached to place our coins. The General and I stood side by side as we had so many times before. Without uttering a word, we both rose to our feet and rendered one final slow salute before facing to the right and making our exit.

Anything that happened in the final two weeks of this combat tour would pale in comparison to saying goodbye to a warrior, a fellow Defender. It hurt knowing his family would be without him for the remainder of their days. Knowing his unit would not have him around to be a part of the things they did also hurt. The pain of knowing this was the third Defender lost this year was more than I wanted to grasp. It brought yet another layer of pain to my agony.

I opened my notebook and scanned down the list. There was one more name to add. My hand was shaking, it was hard to hold the pen. Slowly I wrote; Senior Airman Jason Nathan, killed in action, 23 June 2007.

Brigadier General Robin Rand preparing for his first of 104 combat missions in the F-16 while serving as the Commander of the 332d Air Expeditionary Wing.

Senior Airman "Indiana" Jones with Chief Dearduff inside the 332d Wing Headquarters standing by the Air Force Creed poster. Airman Jones was the first person in the wing to memorize and recite the new creed.

Chief Dearduff and Colonel Renfrow spending time on the Balad Air
Base flight line.

Senior Airman Jason Nathan, killed in action 23 June 2007.

24
FINISH STRONG

Another morning started like so many others had at the hospital to see how the medics were doing and to spend a little time with any wounded warriors. On this morning I noticed something for the first time. To me the hospital would always be the formation of 28 tents strung together. It was the low hanging plenums inside the hallways, the sandbags at the floor to keep the rain out, and the plywood walls lining the walkways between tents. My hospital was the one with the famous emergency room where many trauma situations came through and many miracles began. It contained the operating rooms where we witnessed surgical procedures only possible in combat where the patients have burn wounds to go along with their puncture wounds. These injuries were unlike anything you see in a hospital trauma room back at home. There was so much character in the old place. The new place was starting to look like any other hospital. I knew we would continue to provide the same level of service, but there was just something about the old one.

I stopped and talked with Chief Cole and he informed me the new hospital building would officially open before we departed. The opening ceremony was planned and I could not change it, nor would I want to since the bottom line was to provide the best facility for the patients and the caregivers and certainly that was the case with the new facility.

There was a plan to begin operations in the new place so they could begin to tear down the old hospital. Somehow I hoped the tear down would start after we left, as this would feel like another loss to me...I did not want to see it taken down. Some would call me crazy, but unless you have walked in those hallways and witnessed the great things that took place in there, the spirit of those Army and Air Force doctors, nurses and medics, it's hard to relate.

Time was not on my side. I planned to finish driving around the base, thanking everyone I came in contact with as I had started to do the previous week. But it would not happen, as there were meetings, ceremonies and so many more things to do, and time was flying by. We knew General North and his staff would be arriving on July 3rd and the change of command would take place on July 4th. Before that we had a promotion ceremony to hold, one last chance to share our thanks with the larger audience of the wing here at Balad and hand out some well-deserved promotions.

The reality of our tour coming to an end included the need to pack my personal gear and get stuff sent to the next base. Thankfully it was all arranged by R2 and I just needed to figure out what to ship and have it in the office at the right time. It brought me to the realization that my tour of duty was significantly enhanced by having a personal assistant who handled all of the administrative push and went way above and beyond to make sure I was where I needed to be and had what I needed for each meeting or mission. I had been blessed with three highly talented NCOs who each knew their job and took it very seriously. Reflecting back on the previous 12 months, I knew each of them had given their all to make sure I completed my mission in combat. There was no way to properly thank them or reward their service.

30 June 2007:

More than 500 Tuskegee Airmen were gathered inside the Town Hall for the celebration of those being promoted and who garnered personal recognition. Standing in the front with the Honor Guard presenting the colors for the last time in this manner, many memories came to me and it seemed to last much longer than it really did.

I thought back to the first ceremony we had and how it felt to hear the National Anthem being sung inside the combat zone with a full house of warrior Airmen. I thought about standing in front of audiences preparing to speak, only to take cover because of the sirens going off or indirect fire hitting in the vicinity. I thought long and hard about the memorial services and hearing the words to "I Can Only Imagine" being performed in honor of the Fallen. Finally, I could hear the words and sense the feeling each time the entire crowd would join in the singing of the Air Force song. It was always loud and always brought a chill. No matter how many times I would hear it in the years to come, it would always bring me back to the Town Hall.

The ceremony went along smoothly and was about to finish when General Rand took the microphone and said he was about to break with tradition and do something special. He called Colonel Renfrow up to the stage, and then looked at me and motioned me over. As I walked toward the center of the stage, a weird feeling came over me. I wanted to walk off the other end of the stage and just keep walking, pretending nothing happened.

As I went by Colonel Renfrow, he grabbed me and told me to stand fast. Respecting his wishes I came to attention at his left and faced a crowd of proud Airmen and even a few Soldiers and Sailors. The emcee began with "Attention to Orders…" and then went on to read a citation for Colonel Renfrow in honor of his receipt of the Bronze Star Medal. I knew he had earned much more, and was proud to be standing beside him while he received his award.

Suddenly the emcee read; "Attention to orders, Citation to Accompany the Award of the Bronze Star Medal, first Oak Leaf Cluster..." I was shocked. I had no expectation of receiving another medal from this tour. I had already earned the Bronze Star Medal from my previous combat tour in Iraq. My only rewards for this tour would be getting home to my family and getting him home to Kim.

When the emcee was done I realized my mind had drifted during the reading and I never heard a word of what was read. I stared into the crowd to study the faces of the commanders and chiefs in the front row. I found faces in the crowd of the many Airmen encountered during long days and nights out walking miles in their work areas. I was in a far off place wishing my family could be here in the audience hearing these words.

Before I knew it, the General was standing beside me placing the medal on my uniform, and shaking my hand. It felt great to turn to him and render this salute, proudly in front of the gracious audience. For a brief moment it felt like the end was near.

Both of us departed the stage and General Rand thanked the audience for their dedicated service to the wing. Since there were so many newly arrived Airmen in the audience, he encouraged them to continue this pace and the great work they were doing when the new leadership team arrived, as that would be important for them to get off to the right start. We ended as we always did, with the singing of the Air Force song. It felt great, and brought a tear to my eye, as I figured this would be the last time I heard it in the Town Hall and this kind of setting.

2 July 2007:

Brigadier General Burt Field, the incoming Red Tail Commander and Chief Master Sergeant Paul Wheeler, the new Red Tail Chief, arrived at Balad. Chief Wheeler and I were already acquainted, so it was great to see him. General Field and I had never formally met, but he immediately gave me the impression he would proudly carry on the legend of the Tuskegee Airmen. They were excited to be at Balad and talked about the challenges in front of them. We were tired, but fed off their excitement and knew we could push through the final 48 hours. Chief Wheeler looked at me and told me that I looked tired. I would have liked to argue with him, but knew there were clear signs on my face of my fatigue level. I was tired.

3 July 2007:

The final 24 hours of duty would be packed with transitioning the new leadership team into our operations. I knew we could not complete everything we wanted to do, so I sat and reflected before starting the day. I began to wonder what had taken place in the last twelve months. One year of service, lots of sacrifice and many memories created; some better than others, but memories nonetheless.

General North and his team arrived and he immediately met with Chief Wheeler and me, along with the chiefs and first sergeants from around the wing. He commented about how impressed he was with the accomplishments of the wing. He ended a long discussion by saying "You are one fired up wing." Knowing he visited every combat wing in the Central Command Area of Responsibility, this was a huge complement. If General North did not feel that way, he would not have made the statement. It felt great to hear his level of confidence.

I was pleased to have Chief Wheeler, a very capable and likeable leader who would pour his heart and soul into the wing and carry on the established traditions. In our early hours of driving around, I asked Chief Wheeler to take one thing on for me. I asked him to keep the memorial alive and well, updating it as needed and making sure it was cleaned and serviced for longevity. He assured me he would carry it on just as I had and it warmed my heart knowing he would.

We planned a dinner for the senior leaders to spend time with General North so he could share some thoughts. Nothing formal, but a nice setting with all of the appropriate people, and some time for casual conversation. As we were about done eating and getting ready to retire for the night and prepare for the actions of the next day, I could see the staff moving around and they were up to something. I had no idea what was going on, so I continued my conversation with Chief Small about the things our wing had done and how great it was to have Chief Wheeler here to take over this post.

About that time General Rand stood up and spoke to the Airmen in the room. It would likely be his last chance to speak with most of them. After a few minutes, he introduced General North to everyone in attendance. General North looked at me and said, "Chief, get up here. I have something for you." I looked at him with hesitation, thinking he must be talking to someone else. I hesitated, then made my way toward the front of the room and stood next to the imposing figure wearing three stars and smiling like someone who had just got away with stealing cookies from his mom's kitchen. He looked at me and said, "Well Chief, this one is about you, no matter whether you want it to be or not, so suck it up and stand there."

The emcee read, "Attention to orders..." I was thinking this was a mistake and I wanted to break ranks and stop them. Then he said, "Award of the Air Force Combat Action Medal..." I stood speechless. Thinking back to the email I received about the new combat action medal, I had no idea General Rand submitted me for this recognition based on my actions during a previous combat deployment where I had several direct enemy engagements.

The emcee went on to describe one of those engagements from 2003 and for a minute I was back at that place, thinking about all those Airmen to my left and my right who were not standing next to me receiving this same award. When the emcee was done, and General North looked at me and grinned. I could not say anything but "Thanks." He placed a makeshift medal on my pocket. The actual medal was so new that we had not received any in the combat zone. This one would do fine for the moment, and it was the generosity of General's Rand and North that made this possible.

Once the presentation was complete and people started filing out of the DFAC, we sat down for a few minutes with General North and Chief Small. Among the many things they talked about, one thing caught my attention more than others. General North said that progress had been made on the Security Force support of the OSI mission. He felt like we had won the battle and the ball was rolling. Back at the Pentagon there was movement toward approval and soon we would see Defenders being selected for training. There was an agreement between OSI and Security Forces to begin joint training to add increased cohesiveness on the mission. I sat back in my chair and took a huge breath. It seemed like the right thing was done and this was a victory.

I wanted the night to be over and move on to the change of command ceremony the next day so we could prepare for departure. Chief Wheeler and I spent the next several hours driving, walking, talking and sharing thoughts. We laughed, we shared stories, and we headed for the quarters. My things were already out and he was settled into the permanent quarters. That was our policy and I was going to follow it to a tee. It's what I expected from every Airman when they got ready to leave, and so it was appropriate.

Chief Wheeler settled in and I headed to the office for one last check of the email system and any administrative actions I needed to take care of. As I sat quietly in the office, Major Kelly came by for one last visit. He noticed a stack of

Iraq Campaign Medals sitting on my desk and told me how much he appreciated the actions we took to make sure everyone got theirs presented before departing.

Major Kelly said he did not remember me or the General receiving our medals. I told him we had a plan to have one presented to General Rand so that would be taken care of. And then I asked him if he would do the honor of presenting one to me right here in my office.

He looked puzzled at my request. It was late at night and we were alone in the office. And we both knew that as the executive officer he spent most of his time in the background, always making sure things were done right, but he was never the guy out front making presentations.

Major Kelly stood up and said, "Chief, I would be honored." He came up with some formal words on the spot and pinned the medal on my left breast pocket. We shook hands and I rendered him a crisp salute. I thanked him and told him how much I appreciated his service and his loyalty to the wing and General Rand. We talked for a few minutes then decided it was time to get some rest. Walking out of the office for the last time I took one last look around, and one last deep breath. I reached for the light switch and flipped it to the off position. Leaving the building there was one more thing to do. I stopped at the Fallen Airman Memorial one last time. I paid my last respect to the Fallen. I allowed my tears to fall and I stood silently mourning these great Americans.

4 July 2007:

I hit the bed around 0130, knowing breakfast was at 0630. Sleep was not restful, my brain would not shut down. I was preparing to leave, but my mind pondered the past 12 months and how our lives were changed here in combat. We saw action against the enemy and fought like champions. We tended to the wounded and tried to save every life we could. We brought comfort to those whose injuries were the most extreme. I thought about the friendships formed and the strength of those bonds. I thought about the families back home whose hearts were broken.

I thought about the chiefs and first sergeants who came to me in tough times and shared their pain and agony. And I thought about those 100 trips across the battlefield to be with our Airmen. There was so much to remember, and my brain tried to replay it all.

There was one last mission to accomplish and with the help of General North's staff we would easily pull this off. A continental breakfast was planned in the conference room at the headquarters building at 0630 and both Generals would be here along with Brigadier General Burt Field, the new commanding general. It was the perfect place to present the Iraq Campaign Medal to General Robin Rand and General North was the perfect person to present it.

Once the brief ceremony was done he politely said thanks and that he was glad everyone had now received their ICM during this tour. It was my last opportunity to have something presented to him and I was grateful to General North for doing the honors.

We headed to the change of command ceremony shortly after, and the end was near. I asked Chief Wheeler to join us on the stage for an appropriate passing of the wing flag. It seemed most appropriate to have me hand off the flag to General Rand and have General Field hand it off to Chief Wheeler once he had accepted it.

The ceremony was over in a flash and it would soon be time for us to depart with General North and his team to Kuwait via C-130. It was the way I first came into Iraq in 2003 and it should be the way I went home. Quietly, I hoped this would be my last time in Iraq, having finally felt convinced I had given all I had.

I took in every sight, every sound, and every smell of Balad Air Base in those last two hours. Heading to the flight line to board the plane we passed buildings that prompted memories. We passed Airmen walking down the street who made us think about the many who had served by our sides. General Rand looked out the passenger side window as I looked out the other. We both knew we had done what we could with this mission for 12 months and our time as modern day Tuskegee Airmen was over. It was time to let go. This foxhole was no longer ours.

We said goodbye to the new leadership team and never looked back. We walked into the C-130 at high noon and took our seats. Before takeoff, General North came and got both of us. He said we should ride up front in the cockpit with the crew, the most fitting way to leave combat.

The propellers cranked at full strength and we lifted off, heading south. Our first stop would be at Baghdad International Airport. My final flight out of Iraq would mirror my first flight into this country in 2003. After a brief stay on the ground, we re-boarded the plane, leaving Iraq together, the way we had arrived. I was about to complete my personal mission to Kim Rand and bring her husband home safely. I looked forward to seeing the look in her eyes and feeling the hug she would give me for this important piece of my journey. Kim was special to me, and it was going to be great to keep my promise.

As the crew pulled back on the stick and pushed the throttle forward, I reached into my pocket and pulled out my notebook. There on the first page was the beginning of the list that contained the names of the Fallen Airmen. I read each name slowly, letting the cost of combat sink in. I turned the page and continued reading the remaining names. I knew there was no cost higher in combat than that made by the 13 Fallen Airmen on this list. I wanted the names of these Airmen to be burnt into my memory forever.

Ascending into the clear blue sky on the fourth of July seemed like a great relief. We made a quick turn in Kuwait before the final flight home to our families. We sat next to each other even though there were plenty of empty seats on the plane. After all we had been through together, there was no way we could be separated on this final leg of the journey.

My brain would not shut down on the entire trip. I thought about the many friends I'd made during the year and the times we had been through. I thought once more about the Fallen and the wounded, all of whom would stay with me forever. And I thought about so many moments from the year past that would be etched into my mind with no chance of being erased. It was time to let go and get back home to the family.

I pulled my notebook from my bag and wrote this final entry: "I don't believe I can adequately describe the feeling I am having right now, but I know that I am excited to be going home to Mags and the kids. Here we go. I am coming home from Iraq to stay! Love Scott"

Kim Rand (2nd from left) greets General Rand and Mags Dearduff (far right) greets Chief Dearduff at the airport. Sean Dearduff looks on.

EPILOGUE

As you can only imagine, the trip did not end there on the plane. In fact, we liked to say that your tour was not over until you were safely on American soil, standing with your family and friends. Then, and only then, could I let my guard down and begin the transition to normal life.

This journey ended for General Rand and I when we arrived together in Philadelphia, Pennsylvania at the International Airport. After a struggle to get through U.S. Customs, we finally reached the area where our families would meet us. There was no media. There were no crowds and no parades. Just two men coming home from war and landing safely in the arms of their wives who waited so lovingly to receive us home. My son Sean and other family members were also there.

The first few minutes of holding on to my wife brought an incredible feeling of relief, likely for both of us. After getting hugs from everyone else who was there, we simply headed off to the baggage claim area where soon we would depart. A General and his Chief. After having served 3 years together, side by side, through thick and thin, this is where it would end. In an airport terminal at baggage claim. It seemed like there should have been something more. Both of us were OK with this path and we knew, in fact we vowed, that we would remain in close contact and would find ways to take care of some unfinished business from the battlefield in the months to follow.

Shortly the baggage arrived and we gathered for departure. General Rand presented Sean with a flag he flew on one of his many combat missions. It was a thoughtful and touching moment for all of us. Then the goodbyes started. My last goodbye was with Kim Rand. She grabbed me in a hug that I will always remember. She whispered into my ear, "Chief, Thanks for keeping your promise and bringing Robin home."

My eyes welled up and a large lump formed in my throat. I tried to say something, but nothing really came out. It felt good to know she felt strongly that I had something to do with his success on this mission and maybe I contributed to his survival. Although I knew I did not deserve the credit; the fact was he was protected by God's own hands on many occasion throughout the year, it felt good to know that my promise was kept. I felt like we were really home.

In the days and weeks that followed, Mags and I spent time with family in Philadelphia before heading back to our current home in St. Louis. Reuniting with the other kids was fantastic, and knowing that we were once again together in a safe area was reassuring to everyone. Time was of the essence. We needed to process out of Luke AFB and pack the house in St Louis in order to be in South Carolina by the end of the month. There was much to do and the days were flying by so fast I could not keep up. It was strange going from 20 hour duty days to having no schedule, but somehow each day was filled with enough business to make me exhausted by the end of the night.

The Rand's met with us for a short retreat in Scottsdale, Arizona after we completed our processing. It was great to spend time with them in a relaxing environment and talk about the future for all of us…time went too fast and before we knew it the loading truck was packing our stuff for the road ahead.

When we arrived at Shaw Air Force Base in South Carolina, we were greeted with true southern hospitality. We immediately felt welcome and tried to fit in with the new unit. What we did not know was that Mags' worst fear was just 6 months from coming true. In February 2008, I was selected to become the Command Chief Master Sergeant for the 9th Air Force and Air Forces Central Command, (AFCENT) working directly for General North. I was back in the combat theater of operations in Central Command by early March and once again in Iraq within days. It felt good to be back. It hurt to leave the family one more time. I spent all of 2008 and 2009 traveling into the combat theater every month with some short breaks to attend conferences back in Washington D.C, Langley Virginia, and a few other places around the country. In all my total deployed days topped 1200 days since 9-11. In all, 31 more Airmen died in Central Command during those two years, bringing the total of Airmen lost under my leadership to 44 in a three year period. This pain was absorbed, burned deep, and will never go away. I could not shake the feeling of responsibility for each and every American Airman who served under our watch.

During the months between Balad and the new position, I had many thoughts about all that took place behind the scenes while I was gone. I began to realize just how lucky I was to have such a great family to support me. There were so many people to thank, and there was no way I could find the time or the right words to get it all done.

I reflected on Jim Nolan my father-in-law, who has always had a special bond with his daughter, my wife Mags. Once again while I was deployed, he flew out to the house and spent time with my family took care of things that I couldn't. He provided comfort and entertainment for them while I was gone. Margaret Nolan, my mother-in-law, was so gracious to allow him to take breaks from Philadelphia so he could come and help out, and she herself came out when she could during some deployments. They were fantastic.

Many of my family provided relief as well. Phone calls at unexpected times made a huge impact on Mags and brought a smile to my face. They were always there, always available, and always willing to check in, and that made a huge difference as she told me so often.

We had many friends, who took the time to check in, helped take Sean to games and stopped by when they were in town, and just provided comfort or lent Mags a shoulder or allowed her to vent. People stepped up and always contributed to Mag's projects for the Airmen deployed with us and for the wounded military members in the hospitals.

349

During Holidays they were overly generous with their support for Christmas stockings and cookie drives both Mags and Kim worked on. Their support for "Operation Linus," a blanket program for the wounded, was out of this world. The Backpack project and the closet at the AF Theatre Hospital that was always in need of items for our troops. Our son-in-law Matt Trout, not only took care of our daughter Amber, but was around on a regular basis to help Sean through some of the tough moments of being a pre-teen whose father was deployed. He was a huge influence on Sean and helped Mags on many occasions when a mom just did not have all the answers. Amber and Matt were huge in their support of Mags during the tragedy of losing Major Gilbert and PFC Robert Dembowski. They took care of Sean and the house while she attended memorials in my place. Words cannot express how much it meant to us that they were available and helped out.

There is another group of people who deserve special recognition for the support they provide to all combat forces. The family members of our combat veterans are never thanked enough. Yes, they keep the home fires burning while we are off serving in forward areas, but they do so much more. They are both mother and father; have to make the hard calls that are not always popular with the children... They teach our kids how to ride bikes, drive cars, throw a curve ball, play catch, and shoot hoops. They complete homework they really don't understand themselves because that is dad's area. They even search the computer to find out how to properly shoot a jump shot so they can teach a teenage boy how it's done and help him try to make his school team. They are yelled at for throwing "...like a girl", they take the brunt of anger when dad is not around to help yet they get up each and every day and try the best they can to be everything to everyone! Yes, they do so much, ask for so little, and seldom receive anything for their effort.

The Fallen:

The families of the fallen are a unique group. During the years after serving my tour at Balad, I have had the honor of meeting with several of the families of the fallen as detailed in this story. I've been blessed to continue a relationship with several of them and I know General Rand maintains contact with even more. We've watched their families struggle, and we've watched them grow. We've met at their homes and we've even run into them at odd places where you would never expect an encounter. The struggle for the families of the fallen will never go away, they just find ways to deal with their loss.

February 2009

There may never be a more emotion packed encounter with a family of the fallen that what took place in February 2009. It was another long journey that started when General Rand informed me that Ginger Gilbert had still not received the final personal effects from the accident scene of Major Gilbert's fatal day. Those items remained at Balad and were in the custody of the legal office. He gave me yet another mission, to recover those items and get them to Ginger.

The details of how I took possession of Major Gilbert's possessions is better left unwritten, let's just say that I was able to get them back home. Over the next month, General and Mrs. Rand had a box made to hold the items so that we could present them in an honorable fashion. The box was simple but elegant. It was hand crafted of wood and contained a simple cross on the top of the box. It seemed perfect for the intent, and truly reflected Troy Gilbert.

General Rand and I met in San Antonio to present the items to Ginger. Kim and Mags wanted to join us, but decided that this was something that needed to be done by the commander and the chief alone. Private, honorable, and very personal. Ginger invited us to spend time over the weekend with her and the family. This would not be as simple as dropping off the box and leaving, this was far too important. We met on a Friday evening and enjoyed a wonderful dinner and conversation with Ginger and her new husband, Jim Ravella. We also had the chance to sit and catch up with Boston and Greyson. The following morning we planned to golf with Ginger's father so we met at the house. It was our first chance to see the girls and spend some time with them while everyone had breakfast.

Following dinner with Ginger and Jim, we returned to the house where the General said that we were going to hand Ginger the box and politely depart so that she could go through the items in her own time and in complete privacy. However, Ginger wanted us there when she opened the box and went through the items. With Jim sitting by her side, and having full understanding of what loss feels like (Jim's wife Andrea passed away from cancer the previous year), they expressed to us that it was important that we stay and join them. Over the next hour we sat quietly as Ginger meticulously went through each item in the box. She read the letters inside. She examined each item as it appeared inside of a plastic bag. Jim provided support for her and explained why certain things were presented as they were. As Ginger opened the bags and handled each of the items, the emotions in the room rose to a level that I have never before witnessed. Somehow it felt like we could share in her pain. It felt like we brought her some bit of relief, even as she went on this highly emotional journey once again.

When Ginger was done she eloquently thanked us for making this night a reality. She told us how much she appreciated the effort we made, and that she would need more time to come to grips with the reality of having these items which were with Troy when he died. Both of us stood silent, not needing to say much. She hugged the General and thanked him. Then, Ginger hugged me and whispered to me how much she appreciated my being with her on this night. The hug felt different than any I had ever experienced. It's a moment in my life that I will cherish forever.

Looking back I made many friends who would not only be combat brothers for life, but would become true friends that I could count on. That list is too long, but each of them know who they are. For during that year, as I remained closed in and to myself, I finally realized that life had more to offer when you opened yourself up to friendship. The true value of that lesson was not learned until I had time to spend with Chief Lefford Fate at Shaw AFB. Chief Fate helped me understand what friends I had and how much they meant to me, a lesson I gained while in Iraq, just never knew how to take it in. As of September 2017, the Tuskegee Leadership team from Balad had met for two reunions, maintaining our vow to remain in touch.

December 2013

In December 2013, seven years after the original internment of Major Troy Gilbert at Arlington National Cemetery, we all gathered with his family and re-interned some additional remains that were turned over by the Iraqi government. Although it was not the resolution we all hoped for it did provide some relief. We knew that our nation would never stop looking.

October 2016

Caller ID showed it was General Rand. He said, "Chief, sit down, I have something to tell you." My mind raced, wondering if he was sick, if Kim was sick, or if there was some news about his career that he wanted to share. Once I was sitting on a chair inside the foyer of the local gym in Tallahassee, Florida where I was working out with Sean and my brother Rob, the General continued. He said these words that I longed to hear; "Chief, we have Troy." My mind went blank, eyes welled, throat locked up, and my body was locked to the point that I could not get up from the chair. Rob came over and asked what happened, but I could not get the words out. He listened in and figured out what we must be talking about once I finally regained my ability to talk. I asked the General some questions about Ginger and the kids and whether they were headed to Dover Air Force Base and the port mortuary. As we completed the call I was overwhelmed with joy and knew that I needed to share this news with Mags. When I called her I locked down again and could not get the words out. Finally I mustered "We got Troy" and she knew immediately what I was talking about.

December 2016

After visiting the Gilbert family in San Antonio in November, Ginger asked me to be the official escort of Troy's remains from the Air Force Port Mortuary to Arlington National Cemetery for the final internment. Sitting in the office at my house, I looked at the wall and stared at the photo of Major Gilbert and I that was taken 7 days before he was killed. My heart grew warm and my mind went blank. Although there have been many things that made me proud throughout my military career, this would be the single highest honor I have ever been given in service to my country. Ginger explained there were some complications that she was working through with the Air Force Chief of Staff, but it was not likely to happen. Apparently, the escort for remains must be an active duty Airman in uniform. We talked about getting a waiver to allow a retired Airman in uniform, but I asked her to give me 24 hours to think about it. The next day I proposed a better plan, and offered to Ginger that since General Rand was an active duty Airman, we should give him this honor of being Troy's escort since he was his commanding general and close friend. Ginger agreed with the plan which included the idea of me becoming the convoy commander, taking Kim and Mags with me in our vehicle just behind the transport vehicle with Troy and the General. General Rand agreed to the plan and it was locked into place.

19 December 2016

Arriving at the port mortuary on Monday morning, 19 December 2016, it was 23 degrees outside, but the sun was bright and the roads were clear. The rain and ice of the previous days was gone and we would have safe passage for this final leg of the journey. We were immediately blown away by the amazing number of people who were present at the port mortuary. The Dover base honor guard, Airmen, and law enforcement officers who awaited our arrival.

Things moved fast inside the facility. Colonel Dawn Lancaster and the entire staff of the mortuary were present, including Airmen who were previously stationed with us. Introductions took place and soon we were asked to join in on the official briefing for the movement. A Maryland State Trooper, a retired U.S. Army First Sergeant, briefed everyone in attendance, including a dozen officers who came in on their day off to pay respects, on all aspects of the movement. The briefing was conducted very similar to the format we used in Iraq before completing a ground convoy outside the wire. We were all impressed by the amount of support provided by these law enforcement officers who showed great pride in this mission to bring Troy home.

General Rand and Colonel Lancaster each shared a few words with those assembled. Departure time came, and I locked into focus on the responsibility in front of us. Under the blanket of protection provided by everyone involved, I felt comfortable and knew this day would help us all heal.

General Rand and Colonel Lancaster preparing to address
the law enforcement officers before the movement.

Base Honor Guard members displayed flags as we
departed the mortuary.

Airmen stood along the road leading off base, saluting to
pay respects to Major Gilbert.

Local American citizens displayed pride in their
nation just outside the gate.

     The convoy was led by three units from the Delaware
State Police, included Troy's transport vehicle, our vehicle,
two support vehicles from the port mortuary, and four
vehicles from the Maryland State Police. There were other
vehicles in line, but it went back so far that I could not get a
firm count. I knew that we would be secured during this
convoy, on the roads and in the air, as they even arranged air
support from other agencies. For a brief moment, I was back
in Iraq, but this time I felt more secure, and had my wife by
my side.

     Over the next two hours our police escorts moved
swiftly to ensure our path was clear of threats. This allowed
me to remain focused on the speech that repeated in my mind
over and over. The emotions of the day and this convoy was
felt deeply by Mags and Kim who rode in the back of the
vehicle, but took photos of the great support we witnessed at
every turn. They smiled with joy and shed a tear of emotion
at the support we observed continuously throughout the
route.

Throughout small towns of Delaware and Maryland we moved under the watchful eyes of school children who stood on the side of the street with signs and flags.

There were families standing in the back of their pickup trucks showing their national pride.

Firefighters from departments along the route, along with ambulance crews and military veterans paid respects.

As we crossed the border between Delaware and Maryland, the troopers traded places, but the support remained the same.

Police units ensured there were no obstructions on the roadway and nothing that could interrupt our travels. At every overpass on the highway we saw local fire departments posted with flags in full gear paying their respects, bringing additional comfort to the feelings we held.

During that entire time my mind raced between the tremendous support for the task at hand, and the task I would complete at Troy's graveside later in the day. I repeated my thoughts over and over to ensure that I could meet the objective and stay within the five minute time limit given by the Air Force Chaplain.

Arriving at the Maryland and Virginia border, we took a break for the transition of authority between police agencies. Maryland and Delaware troopers would end the mission here and turn us over to the Arlington County Police Department for the final leg into Washington, D.C. We thanked the troopers and loaded up for the next phase, falling in line behind the 26 motorcycle units who would lead us home. Entering "Beltway" it seemed eerie that we were the only traffic on the road...it also felt appropriate that traffic was cleared to ensure that Troy would come home safe.

Arriving at Fort Meyer next to Arlington National Cemetery, we were rushed inside as the ceremony was about to start. Walking inside the chapel we met with Ron and Kay Gilbert, Troy's parents, and his sister Rhonda and her family. It was great to see them again. Around the corner we found Ginger, Jim, Ginger's dad Jay, and the kids waiting for us.

Walking into the chapel we noted that every seat was full. I looked around and saw many familiar faces in the crowd. Shortly the family entered and the chaplain began. The Air Force Honor Guard brought Troy into the chapel and placed him front and center. Expecting to be overcome with emotions, I was surprised at the feeling of warmth that hit me. Looking in his direction, I could not stop smiling as the family, each kid having grown so much over the past ten years, and the rest of the family, were about to get the closure they deserved. Among the many proud moments of the day was to see the kids stand at the podium as Boston read a passage from scripture that meant so much to him and the others. Ginger and General Rand each took the time to share some thoughts, followed by two songs performed by friends of the family. As that concluded, Troy was moved outside by the honor guard and placed on the horse drawn carriage.

The chapel emptied and more than 300 people formed a line behind the casket for the mile long walk to Section 60 of Arlington National Cemetery. It was cold outside, but I was warm inside.

The walk took longer than expected because of the crowd size. Once everyone was in place, Troy was moved to the grave site and the chaplain began. He asked everyone to stand ready to view the flyover before we started because they were already airborne. Moments later, four members of the 309th Fighter Squadron, one of Troy's former units, flew F-16s in a missing man formation, hitting their marks with exacting perfection just over our heads. It was a fitting tribute to the Air Force aviator we were honoring on this day.

The chaplain talked for two minutes, then introduced me. Once again expecting to be nervous and always on alert for becoming overwhelmed with emotion, I looked at the casket, then back at the family, and felt a great sense of warmth and strength come over me. I felt like Troy was standing behind me telling me that everything would be fine. Over the next five minutes I shared the words that I planned to share with the audience in honoring my friend, Major Troy Gilbert. I shared the story of my last conversation with Troy some 30 hours before he was killed in action. Looking around, I saw the emotion of that moment on the face of those close to me in the audience. I turned away sharply to avoid choking up myself and found comfort as I made eye contact with Troy's children. There were many ways that a speech like this could end, and many things that could be shared. This is how it ended;

Now that Troy is home, I have come to grips with a struggle that has haunted me since I first returned from combat. Each time I read, said, or heard the Airman's creed, I choked on the line, "I will never leave an Airman behind." I struggled because I did leave an Airman behind and until today, that has haunted me. Today, I rejoice in knowing that Troy Gilbert is home, we are here with him, and he is receiving the full honors that he deserves. Finally, all of my Airmen are home. Today, my war, Troy's war, is finally over.

Everyone stood silent through the remainder of the ceremony. My mission complete, it was time to look around and take in the moment. The Air Force Honor Guard was out in force, along with the Air Force band which I later realized was marching in front of us during our walk. There was a team of eight honor guardsman who stood during the entire ceremony holding a flag above Troy's casket, and my leadership brain kicked in, wondering how they could do this and not be cold while standing at attention on this frozen tundra. Words were shared and flags were presented to the family before the most emotional moment of any military funeral...the 21-gun salute and playing of TAPS. As we turned to witness this honor, once again I felt a warmth come over me.

For the first time in memory, I had no lump in my throat, nor tears in my eyes during TAPS. The sense of pride inside of me was driven by knowing that I served a country that kept its promise of never forgetting our service members, and always continuing the search for those we left behind. Closure if the word most often used, but this felt more like "mission complete" and a final chapter in a long and difficult story.

Following completion of the formal portion of the ceremony, people gathered around the family and shared their thoughts. We stayed back and watched with a great deal of comfort. I found Mags in the audience and we embraced. She knew better than anyone how important this day was to me. We knew that it was all about the family and their ability to start the next chapter of their lives, but we felt the same in our own way. Without sharing the words, we both knew that I would be a different person now that my war was finally over. We left the ceremony quietly, walking hand in hand.

Ultimately, the time spent serving in a combat unit is something that cannot be adequately described in the pages of a book. I hope that I have been able to provide some look into my life as I walked a long and difficult mile in service to my nation. I gave everything my heart and soul could muster on that field of battle. My war is finally over.

AFTERWARD

By Mags Dearduff

I have been asked by Scott many times to write my thoughts down regarding this book and my perspective from the year and I have always resisted. I am not 100% sure why. Don't get me wrong I had no problem giving inputs, opinions or making sure that things would be perceived correctly, I just never gave a lot of thought to actually writing my thoughts down for people to understand. It has finally become apparent to me that maybe I should do just that as I have had many people over the past few years who have asked me how I handled the repeated deployments and the reintegration process between Scott and the family. The perception of many people about military life and how they thought I felt was nothing like how I actually did. Maybe this explanation will help clarify how it really is. Good, bad or ugly I always tried to be honest about this life we lived and loved so much even in the worst of times. One thing I cannot do however is speak for other military spouses because they and their families (be it Active Duty, Guard or Reserve) had their own journey and walked a mile I may not understand. They have my utmost respect for what they had to endure. We each have our own way of looking at and accepting things, so for what it is worth here are my thoughts:

Scott told you a little about me in the book. What he did not tell you was the close relationship that I have always had with my dad, his huge influence on my life and how his story shaped my life. He left Ireland as a young teen came to America and joined the US Navy and served this country. I snuck out of bed many nights to stay up with him watching military shows and police dramas. Having learned all that he and my mother went thru in their lives and their need to give back to others is so ingrained into my DNA that I have no doubt it played a big part in my personal desire to serve our country. I'm grateful to my dad for helping me understand what service and sacrifice are all about. Additionally, my older brother Jimmy provided motivation for my need to serve, as I went thru JROTC with him and then watched with pride as he joined the United States Marine Corps directly after high school. His willingness to serve the nation at a time when it was not so popular gave me additional courage to take on this hard life.

Following my five years on active duty as a Law Enforcement Airman, I worked a variety of jobs until I landed in my true calling, that of 911 call taker and police dispatcher. For most of the next 15 years I worked in local departments as we moved from state to state as Scott was assigned new jobs and responsibility.

Prior to the terrorist attacks of September 11, 2001, our life was filled with temporary duty assignments and short training deployments to overseas locations. But nothing can prepare a military family for what happened to us over the next nine years. Month long training deployments became pre-deployment training, followed by six month or year-long deployments into a combat zone. Although he had served a year-long remote tour before, while the kids and I stayed behind, there was not as much fear of his demise because he was not facing an enemy on a daily basis. It would be different after 9-11. Reintegration from short deployments and temporary duty was awkward at times and we had some definite readjustment issues that always came up, but for the most part life just got back to normal for us and the kids relatively easy.

I remember 9-11 like most people in the world and where they were and the horror of the situation and how it impacted our lives; but for military families, our lives changed almost immediately and would never be the same again. I felt it in my bones and down to my soul that life as we knew it was never going to be the same. I remember thinking to myself that this is going to be a whole different chapter in our lives. Little did I know that a few hours later that my fears would come to light as Scott was on an aircraft (one of the only planes in the sky) heading to Tampa to work on some national security issues. He wouldn't stop combat deploying after 9-11, until late December 2009.

This journey taught me; "Life is not about me; it's about those around me." It's about taking care of my family first and foremost, and then it became about taking care of our military families and giving them a voice when they would not have otherwise been heard. My heart was filled with a need to do something more to help in this cause, I wanted to help them stand on their own two feet and handle situations with confidence and it would test everything I believed, all that I held dear. I knew that I would be challenged to step out of my comfort zone and face my fear of speaking in front of people and audiences, but I also knew it would make me a better person. For those that know me and are laughing at my last statement, so let me clarify; I can talk to anyone, anytime and anyplace. However I was terrified of standing up in front of a room full of people or a large audience. I wanted to contribute something meaningful back to the families as a way of honoring my husband's service as well and hoped to help others deal with the same things I was dealing with as a military spouse.

Through my experience I would come to realize the strength of the human spirit defies description and each and every person and story is different but no less remarkable. I would come to learn, understand and flat out respect how our wounded warriors, who suffered unimaginable horrors, pain and agony with their injuries and sometimes loss of limbs, wanted nothing more than to get back into the fight. How they longed to get back to their wingman, battle buddy, K9 partner, Band of Brothers & Sisters or their unit. I learned about selfless love and dedication thru the eyes and the actions of the military spouses, children, mothers, fathers, sisters and brothers who had to go on after the loss of those who gave the ultimate sacrifice and left it on the battlefield. I learned to stare it dead in the eye and conquer my own fears for Scott's safety and put one foot in front of the other as sometimes crippling fear and anxiety of "What if..." would not leave my heart and mind. I chose instead to jump in head first and to fully immerse myself in everything and anything that came with this military life. This meant that I had to learn the hard lessons like so many amazing women had done before me, of what it meant to be a wife and mother during a war halfway around the world. Being mom and dad to three children, holding them as they sobbed their hearts out and trying to offer some comfort each time their dad left without giving in to my own fear and pain was brutal; but necessary. Helping them to live as normal as possible during those months to be confident and independent knowing their dad was in harm's way on a daily basis was a challenge!

After Scott came home in 2004 from a very intense and stressful Security Forces combat deployment to Iraq he was approached and asked to put his name in the hat to be a command chief. I don't think either one of us had any idea what that meant but we both thought it would be an adventure, so why not. I'll be honest I thought it meant he wouldn't deploy for a while so I was willing to agree to anything that made that happen. One day he comes home and talks to me about a Brigadier General select Rand who reached out to him about being his Command Chief in Arizona. Frankly, I didn't know anything about the Southwest except that it was hot and dry and that sounded very appealing to me. Little did I know how much I would grow to respect General Rand and his wife Kim, people we spent the next three years with, and whom we shared so many laughs, tears of joy and tears of sorrow. The Rands made it easy for me to be me, and allowed, even supported me in being up front and direct in all of my dealings with deployed families. They also encouraged me to be totally hands on in all my dealings with the military spouses assigned to our units. Kim was my mentor; wingman, sounding board and she taught me so very much about friendship through the toughest of times. She was my saving grace and the most amazing genuine friend I could have ever asked for. Through this year that the men were in Balad, we cemented forever our "Band of Sisterhood" and helped each other thru some incredibly rough moments!

I made Scott promise me a few things before he headed into this year of combat. First I begged him to always wear every piece of combat protective gear he owned every day. Second I knew that I would not get much time on a phone with him and I understood that but by God he better find a way to email me every single day that he was OK. Considering the time difference, which meant when I woke up the first thing I did every day, was check to make sure he sent me something so I knew he was alive and breathing. When I went to bed it was the same drill. It's all we had and it's all that kept me sane, the computer and the TV was my lifeline and my world revolved around both. We did not have social media web sites and he only called a few times a month. Those were usually 15 minute calls split between 3 people. Life was difficult not having that constant communication but we made it work and we mailed actual letters to each other.

October in our family is always busy and full of birthdays so there was plenty to do. Every day I watched the news for anything on Iraq and at this time in the war, it appeared things were heating up. From the little operational news Scott could share, I also knew that many more Airmen were working outside the wire in dangerous missions that could mean more casualties. I could hear the stress in his voice as the months went by and he shared what he could, without trying to put any additional burdens on me. When he first shared the news about an Explosive Ordnance Disposal Airman and then a Security Forces Airmen being killed in combat, I could tell he was becoming different, even more determined to try and protect everyone in the wing, even though we both knew that would be impossible. As the months wore on and more Airmen were injured and killed in action, the toll on him was becoming more and more evident. I remember suppressing my own feelings while talking with him on the phone so that I could help him stay focused on his mission. Inside I was terrified and wanted to do more to help, but at those moments, I knew that listening and refocusing him was the best thing I could do.

As the 332 AEW Command Chief I knew he felt responsible for all of the losses and that they would hit him hard. What I wasn't prepared for was how hard it hit us as family members seeing those losses as well. Nothing can prepare you for hearing about a combat casualty, and certainly nothing can ease the pain of hearing the news about someone you personally know in that situation. In November 2006 our worst fears were realized when we heard the news about Major Troy Gilbert being killed in action. In the days following that tragic news, as Kim and I travelled together to Arizona to attend his memorial service, those were some of the lowest of lows for me. I knew that Scott, General Rand and the other Airmen in the wing were hurting, but as families we were also dealing with fear, loss, anxiety and pain. We did our part to help where we could, but it always felt like nothing we said or did would possibly take away the pain from the family. That was a sobering reminder to us all who attended and who still had our loved ones in Iraq.

I was aware that an F-16 had crashed and assumed it was from their unit. I also feared that it could somehow be General Rand. When Scott was finally able to call and talk about the situation, I asked him to tell me that it was not General Rand who was killed. Although he could barely get the words out, he said, "No, it's Trojan." My ears started to roar, the hallway started to spin and I remember sliding down the wall to the floor just as a co-worker came around the corner and saw me there with tears running down my face phone still in my hand but on the floor next to me. Scott was calling my name so I talked to him again asked him some questions he didn't have answers to yet so instead I asked if I could call Kim? He told me she should be notified by now and I was clear to call her. As always, Kim Rand provided comfort and understanding for me and others while we were all hurting. It was not an easy road, but with Kim on my side I felt like I was not alone and I knew that we would get thru the rest of this tour somehow.

The emotional drain of a memorial service following

the loss of a friend, knowing that your husband is still serving in harm's way, and knowing that you cannot be there to help protect him, causes an incredible strain on you personally. I can honestly say I was never more stressed in my life than during that time. When Scott came home on his 6 month R&R I knew he was worse off than he let on. He was so edgy and jumpy driving in the car, always looking at people on corners, trash blowing down the highway...he was always intense. I tried to prepare him for being back in the states and talked to Sean extensively about how different Dad would be when he got home and that he needed to relax and just let him unwind.

The first few days were brutal as Scott was not adjusted to the different sounds in the neighborhood. I told him over and over that our neighbor fixed cars in his garage there were a lot of backfires hoping he would not become alarmed at the sound. Even with the effort I made to prepare him, he proved that he was not ready as I found out about 0030 one night. A car in the neighborhood backfired and I found myself on the ground covered by Scott and a ton of pillows. "Well that was fun" I remember saying while we remained on the floor. I was trying to stay super calm so he would relax but seriously he gave me heart failure with the speed of that maneuver. That was just one of a few times he would show me how much stress he was under.

He also would never totally let go and relax he was always very short in his response to anything, tried to take over all the stuff he usually did and was barking orders left and right instead of speaking normally to us. I finally had to have a "chat" with him about this and his options were simple. Be present here and now in O'Fallon IL for the rest of the days you had left and enjoy your family or go back to Balad where your mind is anyway. Harsh maybe, but it was the reality check he needed to snap him out of it and he did relax somewhat for the rest of the R&R days. I knew the coming months were only going to be worse.

The next few months continued to take their toll on

Scott and I can honestly say that my stress level was thru the roof on a daily basis. Waking up at night when a car slowed near our home became commonplace for me; I would hold my breath, hoping and praying the doorbell didn't ring with bad news. It was something I couldn't stop or control it just became my new norm. Living thru the news & internet also was normal, not healthy to some people's way of thinking maybe, but a way I had to stay connected. I needed to know what was happening in Iraq. I tended to know things before Scott told me which was crazy because the internet is a powerful tool.

We were starting to see light at the end of this long deployment by the end of May and I was getting hopeful that maybe things were going to get back to normal soon and we could actually start to count it down. A phone call from my best friend changed that for me and brought reality crashing back in once again. Her nephew Private First Class Robert Dembowski was killed in Iraq 24 May 2007, Memorial Day weekend. I totally lost it at this news because I had let my guard down I had allowed myself to assume that death wouldn't touch us anymore this year, I was sadly mistaken.

I was devastated for her family, his mom, dad, brothers, sisters, and cousins … it all seemed so unfair and I was so far away from them in Pennsylvania. Luckily there were some things Scott could do over in Balad to help them with some answers on logistics and try and help ease some of the unknown questions hanging over them. Several more deaths occurred in June within the 332 AEW and I just didn't know how much more they could take as a leadership team and both Kim and I just counted the seconds until they safely touched down at the Philadelphia Airport. When I saw Scott coming thru those doors I thought my legs were going to give out the relief that washed over me was immense. I remember holding onto him and sobbing and not wanting to let him go because I knew but by the grace of God he walked through those doors back to me!

We packed up and headed to South Carolina and just

settled into the 20th FW at Shaw AFB when Scott came home with the "look" 6 months into our tour there. I was in the kitchen and I remember looking at him long and hard and said "So you're going to AFCENT/9th Air Force aren't you?" He got that sheepish look I knew so well and said "Well we should talk about that." I mean who was he kidding? At this point in our lives I knew that this was who he was and I knew he would do amazing things for our Airmen and I couldn't even be mad. So I hugged him told him I was proud of him. I also told him that he should do whatever he could for those Airmen on the battlefield so that one day he could walk thru the door and tell me "I'm done and I'm home for good."

He did not make that statement for three more years. Even after all that, I have to be honest--in retrospect; I wouldn't have changed a thing. The things we went thru, the people we met, the friends we made and the amazing spouses and families I had the privilege to be a part of, was the most amazing life changing experience of my life. No regrets!!

ABOUT THE AUTHOR

Scott H. Dearduff retired from the United States Air Force in January 2011 following more than 29 years of active duty service. At the culmination of his career he served as the Command Chief Master Sergeant for Ninth Air Force and United States Air Forces Central Command. He amassed more than 1200 days deployed to combat operations in the Central Command Area of Operations. Prior to his combat deployments in Iraq and Afghanistan, he served in more than 20 countries around the world and has traveled to more than 50 foreign countries worldwide. His leadership skills were honed under fire during nuclear security operations, Presidential security, disaster relief operations, humanitarian relief, aircraft accidents and an active shooter response with mass casualties. Along the way he obtained a Bachelor's Degree in Management and a double minor in Criminal Justice and Business Management. His military decorations include the Legion of Merit, 3 Bronze Star Medals, Afghanistan and Iraq Campaign Medals with multiple service stars, and the Air Force Combat Action Medal among more than 27 total decorations.

Chief Dearduff is also the author of the inspirational leadership book series called; *A Cup of My Coffee* and as of this edition, has published five versions.

You may contact the Chief at dearduffconsulting@gmail.com